Lucretius
De Rerum Natura V

Edited by
C.D.N.Costa

LUCRETIUS

DE RERUM NATURA V

LUCRETIUS

DE RERUM NATURA V

EDITED WITH INTRODUCTION
AND COMMENTARY
BY
C.D.N. COSTA

Senior Lecturer in Classics
University of Birmingham

CLARENDON PRESS · OXFORD
1984

Oxford University Press, Walton Street, Oxford OX2 6DP

London New York Toronto
Delhi Bombay Calcutta Madras Karachi
Kuala Lumpur Singapore Hong Kong Tokyo
Nairobi Dar es Salaam Cape Town
Melbourne Auckland

and associated companies in
Beirut Berlin Ibadan Mexico City Nicosia

Oxford is a trade mark of Oxford University Press

Published in the United States
by Oxford University Press, New York

British Library Cataloguing in Publication Data

Lucretius Carus, Titus
De rerum natura V.
I. Title   II. Costa, C.D.N.
871'.01   PA6482.A65
ISBN 0-19-814457-1

Library of Congress Cataloguing in Publication Data

Lucretius Carus, Titus.
De rerum natura V.

Bibliography: p.
Includes index.
I. Costa, Charles Desmond Nuttall.   II. Title.
PA6482.A65 1984   871'01   84-4334
ISBN 0-19-814457-1 (U.S.)

Typeset by Hope Services, Abingdon
and printed in Great Britain
at the Alden Press, Oxford

PREFACE

It is generally agreed that of all the books in Lucretius'
poem Book 5 offers the widest range of interest to the modern
reader — technical atomism, insights into ancient astronomy,
the famous survey of the development of human society. But
this very diversity of subject-matter seems to have deterred
commentators, and the only widely used separate edition of
the book has been J. D. Duff's of 1889. My aim therefore is to
offer an edition which might encourage the reading and study
of an unusually interesting text, and be of use to scholars,
undergraduates, and sixth-formers. Aiming at this range of
readership has brought its own problems in deciding what to
include in the commentary. Limits of space dictated that I
should concentrate on analysis of argument and discussion of
the scientific and philosophical background to Lucretius'
thinking; but I have tried also to remember that more element-
ary help with translation and syntax is increasingly necessary
in schools and universities. In this connection it should be
made clear that although a good deal of Greek material is
quoted by way of philosophical background and literary
parallel, this is translated wherever it is essential to the explanation, so that Greekless readers may be reassured that they
are missing nothing essential when they come to any untrans-
lated Greek.

My debts to earlier scholars will be clear from the commentary. Every editor of Lucretius recognizes that he follows
more or less closely where Lambinus pointed the way, and I
found myself constantly returning to his great edition. Among
more recent editors Munro and Bailey in their different ways
remain fundamental, and apart from them I have derived most
help from Ernout-Robin and Merrill. More personal obligations
are gladly acknowledged. Many friends and colleagues discussed
points with me and answered my questions, and I am particularly grateful to Professor A. E. Douglas, Emeritus Professor

E. J. Kenney, Professor R. G. M. Nisbet, and Mr. D. A. Russell, all of whom read the whole commentary in draft, making many acute suggestions and frequently saving me from myself. The errors and misjudgements that remain are mine. Finally, I offer my thanks to the staff of the Oxford University Press for their unfailing courtesy and help to me.

Birmingham   C.D.N.C.
May 1984

CONTENTS

INTRODUCTION   ix

SELECT BIBLIOGRAPHY   xxii

SIGLA   xxvi

DE RERUM NATURA V   1

COMMENTARY   49

INDEX   155

INTRODUCTION

1. *Lucretius*

The life of Lucretius is an almost total blank to us, and even the dates of his birth and death are uncertain. St Jerome, supplementing Eusebius' Chronicle under the year 94 BC (the usually accepted year, but the manuscripts vary), has the brief and sensational statement: 'Titus Lucretius poeta nascitur, qui postea amatorio poculo in furorem versus, cum aliquot libros per intervalla insaniae conscripsisset quos postea Cicero emendavit, propria se manu interfecit anno aetatis XLIIII.' Donatus in his *Life of Virgil* 6 tells us that Lucretius died on Virgil's seventeenth birthday (53 BC). A well-known remark of Cicero in a letter to his brother of February 54 ('Lucreti poemata, ut scribis, ita sunt, multis luminibus ingeni, multae tamen artis', *Q. fr.* 1.10(9).3) suggests that Lucretius was dead by then, since he almost certainly died before the poem was published. Out of this jumble of conflicting evidence the only safe inference is that he was born in the 90s and died in the 50s BC. (A sceptical question mark must be left hanging over Jerome's story of the love-potion, the madness, and the suicide: yet more discussion seems pointless in view of the total lack of independent supporting evidence either in the poem or from outside sources.) Furthermore it is a strange fact that Lucretius is almost entirely ignored by his contemporaries: the letter of Cicero just quoted is the only significant allusion to him. Why, for instance, he and Catullus never mention each other is a fascinating, though fruitless, speculation. Lucretius may have been a recluse; his poetry may have been too obscure for a wide readership, and his doctrines too austere even for contemporary Epicureans: we can only guess. There are of course many later references. Statius with perceptive terseness highlights the poet's most notable qualities: 'et docti furor arduus Lucreti' (*Silvae* 2.7.76); and Quintilian (10.1.87) refers to him respectfully, but warns that he is 'difficilis'. (For other references see Martin's Teubner edition, xiii ff.)

Although facts are lacking it is a reasonable assumption from the poem itself that Lucretius was of good birth. He writes as one familiar with the life-style of the well-to-do; he was clearly a man of wide literary culture; and he addresses Memmius without subservience. This Memmius, to whom the poem is dedicated, is generally agreed to be the Gaius Memmius who was the son-in-law of Sulla and praetor in 58, a minor poet as well as a politician, and the patron also of Catullus. Memmius is addressed sporadically in the poem (but only in Books 1, 2, and 5), and seems to fill the combined roles of literary patron, philosophical acolyte, and stand-in for the general reader. We cannot get very far in trying to distinguish the relative importance of these roles, and asking, for example, to what extent Lucretius really regarded Memmius as a suitable target for Epicurean evangelism. It seems, however a safe assumption that the *DRN* owes little of its original stimulus to his presence in it.

2. *Epicureanism*

Lucretius was a fervent disciple of Epicurus and believed that the ultimate aim of Epicureanism, freedom from mental disturbance (ἀταραξία), was the surest salvation for mankind. Living amid the turmoil of the late Republic, he might well have felt that man needed rescuing from the dangerous agitation of power politics and wars, and guidance towards a stable contentment. This tranquil happiness could be achieved only by ridding men of their two most dominant anxieties, fear of the gods and fear of death; and the fundamental purpose of the *DRN* is to do this by showing that (*a*) the gods, though they exist, have no interest in the world or in mankind, and (*b*) there is no after-life to be afraid of. This aim is kept in view throughout the whole poem, with its detailed account of the physical nature of the world underpinning the ethical lessons: Lucretius was convinced that a clear understanding through reason, *ratio*, of the material structure of things would banish needless anxieties and so produce in any rational person the desired attitude of mind.

Epicurus (341–270 BC) took over from Leucippus and Democritus (fifth century BC) the atomist theory of the structure of the universe, and using this as a basis for his ethical doctrines he gave to the world of antiquity one of its most dominant and enduring philosophies. A brief review of his system will indicate the background to Lucretius' assumptions and purposes.

This system had three divisions: Canonic, Physics, and Ethics. (*a*) The Canonic (κανών, 'rule' or 'standard') was what we should call epistemology or the theory of knowledge, and operated with three criteria of truth, sense-perception, preconceptions, and feelings. Sense-perception (αἴσθησις, *sensus*) supplies the basic standard of truth: our sensations of the world are never wrong, and error only arises from a wrong interpretation by our mind or reason of the evidence supplied by the senses. A preconception (πρόληψις, *notities*) is a general idea of any given thing which is gradually built up in the mind by repeated sense-impressions of that thing and to which new impressions supplied by the senses are referred, as it were, for identification. Sense-perception is activated by means of fine atomic effluences or films (εἴδωλα, *simulacra*) discharged from the objects of perception, and retaining their shape, which impinge on our sense-organs (thus creating vision, hearing, etc.) or on our mind (thus creating thought). Feelings (πάθη) arise from sensations and so form a bridge between them (and therefore the physical world) and ethics. All feelings can be categorized as either pleasure or pain; it is axiomatic that all creatures choose what is pleasurable and avoid what is painful; and so for men the moral choices underlying our behaviour and conduct in life are based on the test of pleasure or pain.

(*b*) According to the Atomists the physical structure of the universe is basically simple. There are only two realities, matter and void. Matter consists ultimately of an infinite number of tiny, indivisible, and indestructible particles, the atoms (ἄτομοι, *primordia rerum, corpora prima*). The atoms are all of similar substance, but vary in size, shape, and weight; and moving at random through the void they interlock and fuse together in different combinations to produce the constituents of the world which we know. This creative fusion of the atoms happens entirely by chance and is in no way controlled by the gods. Since the void too is infinite in extent, it follows that the universe is infinite, and the number of worlds in it is also infinite. 'World' (*mundus*) here means a complex system composed, like ours, of earth, surrounding air, sun, and other heavenly bodies (see introductory note to 509-770): there are innumerable other such systems throughout the universe.

(*c*) Epicurean ethics were based, as noted above, on pleasure and pain as guides to morality and conduct. This notion that pleasure is an ethical ideal naturally invited – and received – much derision and contempt from ancient opponents of Epicureanism; but Epicurus defined pleasure very carefully, and his view of it is by no means to be confused with hedonism. He explicitly disclaimed the pleasures of luxury and sensuality (*Ep. Men.* 131), and limited true pleasure to the satisfaction of natural desires and the removal of the pain arising from want. This state of being is a positive condition giving the highest form of bodily pleasure, and this pleasure once achieved can be varied but not increased. (See note on 1432-3.) The highest form of mental pleasure (which is superior to bodily pleasure) is the state of tranquillity (ἀταραξία) achieved by a clear understanding of the laws of the physical world.

Most of Epicurus' many writings are lost, but we have three letters addressed to his disciples, Herodotus, Menoeceus, and Pythocles (the authorship of this one has been questioned, but its content is clearly Epicurean), and two collections of maxims, the Κύριαι Δόξαι, 'Chief Doctrines', and the *Sententiae Vaticanae*, 'Vatican Sayings'. Fragments survive of his most important work, περὶ φύσεως, 'On Nature', from which Lucretius may have derived his own title. Epicurus was no literary artist, and his extant works are not easy reading, but he must take the credit for directly inspiring one of the greatest and most original of Latin poets to pass on his message.

3. The Poem

Ancient critics had no separate formal category or genre for
didactic poetry but linked it stylistically with epic. Thus the
De Rerum Natura is naturally described as a didactic epic, an
instructive poem written in the 'high' style of epic. In writing
such a poem Lucretius followed a tradition going back to
Hesiod's *Works and Days* (c. 700 BC); and in expounding more
strictly philosophical or scientific doctrines in elevated verse
he followed the tradition of scientific poets like Empedocles
(fifth century BC) and Aratus (third century BC). These two
poets are of particular importance in assessing the influence of
earlier writers on Lucretius. He had a strong veneration for
Empedocles, referring to him in glowing terms at 1.716-33,
and the title of Empedocles' poem περὶ φύσεως may, like Epicurus' similar one, have influenced Lucretius' title. The importance of Aratus can be seen indirectly through Cicero's verse
translation of his astronomical poem, *Phaenomena*; there is
clear evidence that Lucretius knew and used this work, which
in spite of Cicero's pedestrian rendering must have been of
considerable technical interest and assistance to him. Poetically,
one other major influence was Ennius, even in Lucretius' day
the grand old man of Latin poetry: Lucretius was clearly
steeped in his works and there are many Ennian echoes throughout the *DRN*.

It is often pointed out that in writing a poem about Epicureanism Lucretius was deliberately flouting a tradition that
Epicurus himself distrusted poetry and advocated the use of
plain language (Diogenes Laertius 10.13 and 121, Cicero *Fin*.
1.72). However, we should not make too much of this. Not all
later Epicureans regarded Epicurus' alleged views as binding on
them (Lucretius' contemporary Philodemus, for example, was
a poet); poetry in general has great mnemonic advantages in
persuasion compared with prose; and Lucretius himself was a
supreme poetic genius who could not otherwise naturally
express his inspiration than in poetry.[1] Let us now briefly
consider the poem as a whole.

[1] E. J. Kenney, *G & R Survey*, 10-12.

Though there is some internal evidence to suggest that the books were not written in the order in which they now stand,[2] the structure has a clearly defined logical plan:

The atoms	1	Atoms and void
	2	The characteristics of atoms and their combinations
The soul	3	The mortality of the soul
	4	Thought and sensation
The world	5	The history of the world and its mortality
	6	Celestial and terrestrial phenomena

In this design the outer pairs of books deal with the physical structure of the world, framing a central pair which discuss the nature of man and the physical mechanism by which he is aware of his surroundings. That is one symmetry, and it is combined with a linear development in the over-all argument, by which we start with the basic components of the universe, and as the books progress we gradually widen our view until it takes in the furthest and grandest possible objects of our comprehension. In any case the first two books are an essential preliminary exposition of the atomic structure of matter, on which all the subsequent arguments rest, and throughout the whole poem runs Lucretius' basic aim of proving that the nature of all things — even the human soul — is material and thus mortal, and that the creation of all things was due to chance and not to supernatural agency.

The *DRN* was clearly left incomplete at Lucretius' death, and though it is unlikely that he would have added substantially to the text we have, much internal tidying up remained to be done. (Jerome's statement (p. ix) — even if true — that Cicero 'emendavit' the poem probably referred only to the mechanical correction of scribal errors: Cicero was not likely to be interested enough to do more.) There are two important pieces of evidence for incompleteness. (1) An extended passage occasionally appears in two parts of the poem: the most notable instance is

---

[2] Bailey, i, 32–7; G. B. Townend, *CQ* 29 (1979), 101–11.

1.926-50 = 4.1-25, which cannot have been meant to stand in both places in the revised poem. It is harder to be sure about shorter repetitions, and several passages (and of course a great many single lines) which are applicable to two contexts could well have been intended to stand in both places. (See notes on 128-41, 351-63, 416-508.)[3] (2) At 5.155 Lucretius promises to deal with the nature of the gods 'largo sermone', but the poem contains no such discussion. The reader must also be prepared to note the occasional obscurity or inconsistency in an argument, and the (to many readers) unsatisfactory end of Book 6 as a finale to the poem, and console himself with the thought that the poet's final touch is surely lacking.

The DRN shows a great poet tackling a profound philosophical theme. This leads to a consideration of a notable feature of the poem, the contrast throughout between two stylistic levels — passages of technical exposition and argument, and passages on a much higher emotional level and written with greater poetic intensity. The former embody the bulk of the scientific reasoning and the careful articulation of premiss and inference; the latter register in a higher key the implications of the triumphant conclusions the poet reveals to us, and the same highly wrought stylistic level is the vehicle for many of the great illustrations and similes which light up the path of what might otherwise be an arid sequence of arguments. Thus we can explain and appreciate in their contexts the intensely written account of the sacrifice of Iphigeneia (1.80-101); the cow searching for her dead calf (2.352-66); the great personification of Nature (3.931-51); the lovely dawn simile (5.460-6); the procession of the seasons (5.737-47). We rightly remember these virtuoso passages for their own poetic sake, but part of their Lucretian *ars* is the subtlety with which they also give buoyancy to the arguments from which they arise. This alternation of technical and non-technical passages is a deliberate and controlled poetic technique, and is not a case of either 'Lucretius the poet' or 'Lucretius the philosopher' happening from time to time to be in control.

[3] Bailey, i, 161-5; Kenney, *G & R Survey*, 9-10.

A similar point can be made about the so-called 'digressions' in the *DRN*, passages of varying length in which the poet seems to get side-tracked into interrupting the course of his exposition: e.g. 2.600–60 (the account of Cybele), 5.110–34 (an attack on the theological view of the world). Such passages should be seen not as excursuses that have got out of control, but as deliberately leisurely decoration of a point which allows the reader to absorb its importance. This technique is related to what has been called Lucretius' 'suspension of thought', a mannerism by which he likes to revert, after an intervening lapse, to a topic previously under discussion.[4] In general he shows himself by all these means constantly concerned to avoid the occupational hazard of philosophical exposition, boredom for the reader. Poetic artistry of another kind is seen in the frequent use of alliteration and assonance throughout the poem, a feature particularly appreciated by people who were accustomed to read their poetry aloud. The more obvious examples are noted in the commentary, and it will be seen that in a significant number of these Lucretius uses emphatic alliteration in order to round off an argument and a section with a flourish.

Epicurus taught the Atomists' physical theories in order to expound an ethical idea. Lucretius on the other hand concentrates on physics and says very little about Epicurean ethics (for a rare exception see 5.1117–35). We cannot be certain of his reasons, but one likely explanation is his view that it was absolutely essential to explain in full detail the physical basis on which the ethical teaching was built. The moral ideas of the Epicureans — the value they placed on friendship, their contented quietism, even their unusual definition of pleasure as the standard of conduct — could probably be grasped in essence by the serious inquirer. But Atomist physics were technically difficult to the point of obscurity; they needed skilful, patient exposition; they were a real challenge to a poet; and success in

---

[4] Bailey, *AJP* 61 (1940), 278–91; M. F. Smith, *Hermathena* 102 (1966), 73–83.

explaining them should lead logically to an acceptance of Epicurus' moral teaching. Lucretius constantly points out how obviously an attitude of mind should follow from the conclusion of a piece of scientific logic; but it is the science which takes time and relentless *ratio* to put across, and this must account for the poem's almost exclusive concentration on physical theory.

In urging so fervently the Atomists' world-picture Lucretius must inevitably have been attacking other views of the cosmos, and it is often said that his target was mainly the Stoics. But while it is obvious that the Stoics were strongly opposed to the Epicureans, for example on the ethical side in their ideal of public service contrasted with the political quietism of the Epicureans, the main opponents of Atomistic physics were the Aristotelians, with their strongly teleological view of a finite and divinely controlled universe (all ideas directly contrary to Atomist/Epicurean beliefs). Occasionally Lucretius seems to take a sideswipe at Stoic beliefs (as perhaps at 5.140-3), but in more extended polemical passages (like 2.167 ff., 5.110 ff.) he is likely to be hitting out chiefly at the Aristotelians.[5]

4. *Book 5*

Book 5 is by far the longest, the most diversified, and the most interesting book in the *DRN*. In the intellectual grasp of the range of material covered it is Lucretius' crowning achievement, and with its exposition of the creation of the world by a chain of chance-causation, and of the development of civilization unaided by the gods, it occupies a climactic place in the scheme of the whole poem. A vital point was established in Book 3 that the soul of man is mortal; but apart from that, all we have learnt in earlier books about the atomic structure of matter and the mechanism of our sensations has been preliminary to the account here given of the origin of the world, terrestrial and celestial elements alike, and the history of man gradually

[5] D. J. Furley, *BICS* 13 (1966), 13-33

emerging from a brutish existence — and owing nothing to the gods for his advancement. The plan of the book is as follows:

1- 90   Introduction: eulogy of Epicurus and outline sylla-
         bus of the book
91- 508 The world (i.e. earth, sky, and heavenly bodies):
         (a) being mortal it will one day perish (91-415)
         (b) it was created by the haphazard union of
              atoms (416-508)
509- 770 Astronomical phenomena: movements and sizes of
         the heavenly bodies, sunlight, moonlight, day
         and night, eclipses
772-1457 The earth: (a) origins of life on earth (772-924)
                     (b) living conditions of primitive man
                          (925-1010)
                     (c) origins and growth of civilization
                          (1011-1457).

After the introduction the development of the argument is both logical (the world as a whole; then the celestial components of it; then the remaining component, the earth) and chronological (creation down to the emergence of civilization). Within this grand design Lucretius has grappled with the most profound issues of cosmology and anthropology; he looks outward and backward from man's present position on earth in order to explain how both his environment and man himself come to be as they now exist. Inevitably there is some unevenness in his treatment of the many topics covered. Selecting and organizing his material must have been a greater problem in this than in any other book, especially for the history of human culture, and in some places the order of topics discussed seems somewhat random and illogical (see introductory note to 1011-1457). Part of the reason must be that the extent of Lucretius' own knowledge naturally varied with different aspects of primitive beliefs and technology, according to the sources available to him and the degree to which he could argue backwards by analogy or conjecture. We must also allow for the obvious fact that Lucretius would have been more interested in some features of early man's developing culture and technology than in others. In the commentary the introductory notes to major sections suggest the sources apparently used by Lucretius, and other extant authorities which reflect the traditions he followed. Only exceptionally does he himself allude to his source-material (e.g. the star-maps at 694–5), but he was undoubtedly an omnivorous student of earlier Greek cosmologists and writers on astronomy, natural science, and biology. As we might expect, he tends to follow Atomist/Epicurean accounts and speculations where we have independent knowledge of these, and it is a reasonable guess that he also does so where we cannot confirm his statements. Among other accounts special mention should be made of the work of Diodorus Siculus, a younger contemporary of Lucretius, which incorporates a cosmogony and zoogony reflecting ideas going back to the fifth century, and provides us with useful parallels and background material to many of Lucretius' statements (see introductory note to 925–87).

Any analysis of Lucretius' account of primitive man involves a discussion of 'evolutionary' as opposed to 'golden age' theories, the view which sees man as emerging from bestiality into civilization contrasted with that which suggests that man has degenerated from a state of primeval purity and innocence (see note to 925–87). This in turn prompts the question of Lucretius' own attitude to mankind's cultural history, and there has been much debate on whether he thought mankind had improved overall or degenerated. But to ask whether Lucretius was a 'primitivist' or a 'progressive', whether he was 'pessimistic' or not in his view of man's development, is not to focus sharply on the implications of his account. In view of the harsh and grim details he gives of early man's brutish existence, and the distinct note of achievement sounded in the account of technological and other advances, there can be no doubt that we are to see man's physical condition as vastly improved. Morally, however, there are reservations, as in the reflections on the vanity of modern man's longing for possessions (1430–5). But even here the trouble lies not in material advances themselves but in the fact that man has not yet grasped the Epicurean truth about the limits of pleasure. If everyone adopted Epicurus' creed the outlook would be wholly bright and salvation assured: as most people have not done so the implication is that their philosophical and moral progress has not kept pace with their physical and technical advances. We should see Lucretius primarily as a dispassionate recorder of man's past history and a realistic commentator on his present values.[6] About the future he must himself have had mixed feelings, and his uncertainty is, after all, still with us.

5. *The Text*

The most important manuscripts for the text of Lucretius are O (Oblongus) and Q (Quadratus), so named from their shapes. They were both written in Carolingian minuscules in the ninth century, and both are now in the University Library at Leiden. They derive through an uncertain number of intermediate copies from an original written in capitals probably in the fourth or fifth century. There are also fragments of two other ninth-century manuscripts, G-V (separate parts of the same manuscripts) and U, both related to Q. (G is in Copenhagen, U and V in Vienna.) The other surviving manuscripts are all copies made in Italy during the fifteenth century and later (hence collectively called 'Itali'), deriving from a now lost manuscript [P] which was discovered in 1418 by the humanist scholar Poggio Bracciolini. He had a copy of it made which is also lost, but a copy of that copy, L, survives in the Laurentian Library in Florence. It is not yet certain what relationship [P] had to O Q G-V U. The usual view used to be that it was derived from the archetype independently of O and Q, but K. Müller (following Diels) has argued persuasively[7] that it was a copy of O (and that consequently the Itali have no independent

---

[6] D. J. Furley, *Entret. Fond. Hardt* xxiv (1977), 1 ff.
[7] See *Mus. Helv.* 30 (1973), 166–78, and M. D. Reeve in *Italia Medioevale e Umanistica* 23 (1980), 27–48.

authority). In fact the solution to this problem is not often of crucial importance in constituting the text of the *DRN*.

For reasons of economy the text printed for this edition is Bailey's Oxford Classical Text (second edition 1922), though I have occasionally recorded disagreement with a reading. I have also made some minor alterations of punctuation in the text, corrected some errors in the apparatus, and extended the list of sigla to include some manuscripts not cited by Bailey but referred to in the commentary.

SELECT BIBLIOGRAPHY

Editions (those with a commentary are marked *)

Editio Brixiensis (editio princeps) Brescia, *c.* 1473.
Editio Aldina (Avancius, H.) Venice, 1500.
*Pius, J. B., Bologna, 1511.
Editio Juntina (Candidus, P.), Florence, 1512–13.
Naugerius, A. (*ed. Aldina* 2) Venice, 1515.
*Lambinus, D., Paris, 1563–4.
Gifanius, O., Antwerp, 1565–6.
*Faber, T., Saumur, 1662.
*Creech, T., Oxford, 1695.
*Havercamp, S. (variorum), Leiden, 1725.
*Wakefield, G., London, 1796–7.
*Lachmann, K., Berlin, 1850.
*Munro, H. A. J., Cambridge, 1864, 1893[4].
*Guissani, C., Torino, 1896–8.
Bailey, C., Oxford (OCT), 1900, 1922.
*Merrill, W. A., New York/Cincinnati/Chicago, 1907.
Ernout, A., Paris, 1920.
Diels, H., Berlin, 1923–4.
*Ernout, A. and Robin, L. (commentary only), Paris, 1925–8.
Martin, J., Leipzig (Teubner), 1934, 1963[5].
*Leonard, W. E. and Smith, S. B., Madison, 1942.
*Bailey, C., Oxford, 1947.
Büchner, K., Wiesbaden, 1966.
Müller, K., Zürich, 1975.

Commentaries on Book 5

Benoist, E. et Lantoine, H. Paris, 1884.
Duff, J. D., Cambridge, 1889.
Lowe, W. D., Oxford, 1907/1910.
Lightfoot, G. C., London, 1934.

Translations

Munro, H. A. J., Cambridge, 1864.
Bailey, C., Oxford, 1910.
Latham, R. E., Harmondsworth, 1951.
Smith, M. F., Cambridge, Mass. and London, 1975 (revision of W. H. D. Rouse's Loeb translation).

General

(Square brackets indicate the form in which the work is referred to in the commentary)

Amory, A., '*Obscura de re lucida carmina*: Science and poetry in *De Rerum Natura*', *YCS* 21 (1969), 145–68.
Arrighetti, G., *Epicuro, Opere*, Torino, 1973².
Axelson, B., *Unpoetische Wörter*, Lund, 1945.
Bailey, C., *Epicurus: the extant remains*, Oxford, 1926.
—— *The Greek Atomists and Epicurus*, Oxford, 1928.
Boyancé, P., *Lucrèce et l'épicurisme*, Paris, 1963.
Chilton, C. W., *Diogenis Oenoandensis Fragmenta*, Leipzig, 1967.
Classen, C. J., 'Poetry and rhetoric in Lucretius', *TAPA* 99 (1968), 77–118.
Davies, H. Sykes, 'Notes on Lucretius', *The Criterion* 11 (1931–2), 25–42.
Diels, H. and Kranz, W., *Die Fragmente der Vorsokratiker*, Berlin, 1954⁷ [D-K]
Dudley, D. R. (ed.), *Lucretius*, London, 1965. [Dudley]
Edelstein, L., *The Idea of Progress in Classical Antiquity*, Baltimore, 1967.
Ernout, A. and Meillet, A., *Dictionnaire étymologique de la langue latine*, Paris 1959⁴. [Ernout–Meillet]
Farrington, B., *The Faith of Epicurus*, London, 1967.
Festugière, A. J., *Epicurus and his Gods* (tr. C. W. Chilton), Oxford, 1955.
Friedländer, P., 'Pattern of sound and atomistic theory in Lucretius', *AJP* 62 (1941), 16–34.
Furley, D. J., 'Lucretius the Epicurean. On the History of Man', *Entretiens Fondation Hardt*, xxiv (1977), 1–27.
Giussani, C., *Studi Lucreziani* (= Vol. i of his edition: see above).

Gordon, C. A., *A Bibliography of Lucretius*, London, 1962.
Guthrie, W. K. C., *A History of Greek Philosophy*, Vols. i–iii, Cambridge, 1962–9. [Guthrie]
— *In the Beginning*, London, 1957.
Hadzsits, G. D., *Lucretius and his Influence*, New York, 1935.
Hofmann, J. B. and Szantyr, A., *Lateinische Syntax und Stilistik*, Munich, 1965. [Hofmann–Szantyr]
Kenney, E. J., *Lucretius De Rerum Natura Book III*, Cambridge, 1971.
— 'Doctus Lucretius', *Mnemosyne* 4, 23 (1970), 366–92.
— 'The historical imagination of Lucretius', *G & R* 19 (1972), 12–24.
— *Lucretius, Greece & Rome New Surveys in the Classics* No. 11, Oxford, 1977.
Kühner, R. and Stegmann, C., *Ausführliche Grammatik der lateinischen Sprache*, Munich, 1962[4]. [K–S]
Liddell–Scott–Jones, *A Greek-English Lexicon*, Oxford, 1940–68 [LSJ]
Lloyd, G. E. R., *Early Greek Science: Thales to Aristotle*, London, 1970.
Lovejoy, A. O. and Boas, G., *Primitivism and Related Ideas in Antiquity*, Baltimore, 1935.
Manuwald, B., *Der Aufbau der lukrezischen Kulturentstehungslehre*, Mainz/Wiesbaden, 1980.
Martha, C., *Le Poème de Lucrèce*, Paris, 1867.
Merlan, P., 'Lucretius – Primitivist or Progressivist? *Journal of the History of Ideas* 11 (1950), 364–8.
Neugebauer, O., *A History of Ancient Mathematical Astronomy*, Berlin/Heidelberg/New York, 1975.
Nichols, J. H., *Epicurean Political Philosophy: The DRN of Lucretius*, Cornell, 1972.
Otto, A., *Die Sprichwörter und sprichwörtlichen Redensarten der Römer*, Leipzig, 1890.
Oxford Latin Dictionary, Oxford, 1968–82. [OLD]
Paratore, E., *Lucreti De Rerum Natura locos praecipue notabiles collegit et illustravit*. Commentariolo instruxit U. Pizzani, Rome, 1960.
Regenbogen, O., *Lukrez, seine Gestalt in seinem Gedicht* (Neue Wege zur Antike II.1), Leipzig/Berlin, 1932.
Rist, J. M., *Epicurus: An Introduction*, Cambridge, 1972.

Roberts, L., *A Concordance of Lucretius*, Berkeley, 1968.

Robin, L., 'Sur la conception épicurienne du progrès', *Revue de Métaphysique et de Morale* 23 (1916), 697–719.

Santayana, G., *Three Philosophical Poets: Lucretius, Dante, and Goethe*, Cambridge, Mass., 1910.

Schrijvers, P. H., *Horror ac divina voluptas. Études sur la poétique et la poésie de Lucrèce*, Amsterdam, 1970.

Sikes, E. E., *Lucretius: Poet and Philosopher*, Cambridge, 1936.

Singer, C., Holmyard, E. J., Hall, A. R. (edd.), *A History of Technology*, Oxford, Vol. i, 1954, Vol. ii, 1956.

Sinker, A. P., *Introduction to Lucretius*, Cambridge, 1937.

Soubiran, J., *L'élision dans la poésie latine*, Paris, 1966. [Soubiran]

Thesaurus linguae Latinae, Leipzig, 1900– . [TLL]

Usener, H., *Epicurea*, Leipzig, 1887. [Usener]

West, D. A., *The Imagery and Poetry of Lucretius*, Edinburgh, 1969. [West]

Abbreviated references to ancient works generally follow the conventions of *OLD* and *LSJ*. Epicurus' Letters to Herodotus, Pythocles, and Menoeceus appear as *Ep. Hdt.*, *Ep. Pyth.*, *Ep. Men.*

SIGLA

O = Codex Leidensis 30 (Oblongus)
Q = Codex Leidensis 94 (Quadratus)
L = Codex Laurentianus xxxv.30 (Niccolianus)
131 = Codex Laurentianus xxxv.31
C = Codex Cantabrigiensis
Vat. 640, 3276 = Codices Vaticani 640, 3276
Mon = Codex Monacensis
G = Schedae Gottorpienses
V = Schedae Vindobonenses priores
U = Schedae Vindobonenses posteriores
P = Poggianus deperditus
Ital. = codices Itali saeculi xv vel xvi
] = lectio Leidensium in textu conservata

T. LVCRETI CARI

DE RERVM NATVRA

LIBER QVINTVS

Qvis potis est dignum pollenti pectore carmen
condere pro rerum maiestate hisque repertis?
quisve valet verbis tantum qui fingere laudes
pro meritis eius possit qui talia nobis
pectore parta suo quaesita⟨que⟩ praemia liquit?   5
nemo, ut opinor, erit mortali corpore cretus.
nam si, ut ipsa petit maiestas cognita rerum,
dicendum est, deus ille fuit, deus, inclute Memmi,
qui princeps vitae rationem invenit eam quae
nunc appellatur sapientia, quique per artem   10
fluctibus e tantis vitam tantisque tenebris
in tam tranquillo et tam clara luce locavit.
confer enim divina aliorum antiqua reperta.
namque Ceres fertur fruges Liberque liquoris
vitigeni laticem mortalibus instituisse;   15
cum tamen his posset sine rebus vita manere,
ut fama est aliquas etiam nunc vivere gentis.
at bene non poterat sine puro pectore vivi;
quo magis hic merito nobis deus esse videtur,
ex quo nunc etiam per magnas didita gentis   20
dulcia permulcent animos solacia vitae.

2 maiestate hisque *Lambinus* : maiestatis atque *OQ*   5 que *add.*
O corr.   12 locavit *L* : uocauit *OQ*   14 Ceres *Ital.* : geres *OQ*

Herculis antistare autem si facta putabis,
longius a vera multo ratione ferere.
quid Nemeaeus enim nobis nunc magnus hiatus
ille leonis obesset et horrens Arcadius sus?   25
denique quid Cretae taurus Lernaeaque pestis
hydra venenatis posset vallata colubris?
quidve tripectora tergemini vis Geryonai

                        *

tanto opere officerent nobis Stymphala colentes,   [30]
et Diomedis equi spirantes naribus ignem   30 [29]
Thracis Bistoniasque plagas atque Ismara propter?
aureaque Hesperidum servans fulgentia mala,
asper, acerba tuens, immani corpore serpens
arboris amplexus stirpem quid denique obesset
propter Atlanteum litus pelagique severa,   35
quo neque noster adit quisquam nec barbarus audet?
cetera de genere hoc quae sunt portenta perempta,
si non victa forent, quid tandem viva nocerent?
nil, ut opinor: ita ad satiatem terra ferarum
nunc etiam scatit et trepido terrore repleta est   40
per nemora ac montis magnos silvasque profundas;
quae loca vitandi plerumque est nostra potestas.
at nisi purgatumst pectus, quae proelia nobis
atque pericula tumst ingratis insinuandum!
quantae tum scindunt hominem cuppedinis acres   45
sollicitum curae quantique perinde timores!
quidve superbia spurcitia ac petulantia? quantas
efficiunt clades! quid luxus desidiaeque?
haec igitur qui cuncta subegerit ex animoque
expulerit dictis, non armis, nonne decebit   50
hunc hominem numero divum dignarier esse?

28 * 29 *lacunam indicavit Munro*   29 [30] *hic locavit Munro, post*
31 *Lachmann*   nobis] et aves *Lachmann*   31 Thracis *Munro*:
Thracia *OQ* : Thracem *Lachmann*   35 Atlanteum *Gifanius*: Atia-
neum *O*: Atianeam *Q*   pelagique] pelageque *Lambinus*   severa]
sonora *L*   38 si *L*: sed *OQ*   victa *Ital.*: uincta *OQ*   44 tumst
Lachmann: sunt *OQ*

cum bene praesertim multa ac divinitus ipsis
immortalibu' de divis dare dicta suerit
atque omnem rerum naturam pandere dictis.
  Cuius ego ingressus vestigia dum rationes   55
persequor ac doceo dictis, quo quaeque creata
foedere sint, in eo quam sit durare necessum
nec validas valeant aevi rescindere leges,
quo genere in primis animi natura reperta est
nativo primum consistere corpore creta   60
nec posse incolumis magnum durare per aevum,
sed simulacra solere in somnis fallere mentem,
cernere cum videamur eum quem vita reliquit,
quod superest, nunc huc rationis detulit ordo,
ut mihi mortali consistere corpore mundum   65
nativumque simul ratio reddunda sit esse;
et quibus ille modis congressus materiai
fundarit terram caelum mare sidera solem
lunaique globum; tum quae tellure animantes
exstiterint, et quae nullo sint tempore natae;   70
quove modo genus humanum variante loquela
coeperit inter se vesci per nomina rerum;
et quibus ille modis divum metus insinuarit
pectora, terrarum qui in orbi sancta tuetur
fana lacus lucos aras simulacraque divum.   75
praeterea solis cursus lunaeque meatus
expediam qua vi flectat natura gubernans;
ne forte haec inter caelum terramque reamur
libera sponte sua cursus lustrare perennis
morigera ad fruges augendas atque animantis,   80
neve aliqua divum volvi ratione putemus.
nam bene qui didicere deos securum agere aevum,
si tamen interea mirantur qua ratione

53 de *Lambinus* : e *OQ*   61 incolumis *Marullus* : incolumen *O* :
vinculum est *Q*   64 me *ante* huc *add. Merrill*   70 nullo sint
Q corr. : nullos in *OQ*

quaeque geri possint, praesertim rebus in illis
quae supera caput aetheriis cernuntur in oris,   85
rursus in antiquas referuntur religiones
et dominos acris adsciscunt, omnia posse
quos miseri credunt, ignari quid queat esse,
quid nequeat, finita potestas denique cuique
quanam sit ratione atque alte terminus haerens.   90

    Quod superest, ne te in promissis plura moremur,
principio maria ac terras caelumque tuere;
quorum naturam triplicem, tria corpora, Memmi,
tris species tam dissimilis, tria talia texta,
una dies dabit exitio, multosque per annos   95
sustentata ruet moles et machina mundi.
nec me animi fallit quam res nova miraque menti
accidat exitium caeli terraeque futurum,
et quam difficile id mihi sit pervincere dictis;
ut fit ubi insolitam rem apportes auribus ante   100
nec tamen hanc possis oculorum subdere visu
nec iacere indu manus, via qua munita fidei
proxima fert humanum in pectus templaque mentis.
sed tamen effabor. dictis dabit ipsa fidem res
forsitan et graviter terrarum motibus ortis   105
omnia conquassari in parvo tempore cernes.
quod procul a nobis flectat fortuna gubernans,
et ratio potius quam res persuadeat ipsa
succidere horrisono posse omnia victa fragore.

    Qua prius aggrediar quam de re fundere fata   110
sanctius et multo certa ratione magis quam
Pythia quae tripode a Phoebi lauroque profatur,
multa tibi expediam doctis solacia dictis;
religione refrenatus ne forte rearis
terras et solem et caelum, mare sidera lunam,   115
corpore divino debere aeterna manere,

---

85 aethereis *Q corr.*: aetheris *OQ*   100 insolitam *Q corr.*: in-
solitum *OQ*   116 manere *editio Juntina*: meare *OQ*

proptereaque putes ritu par esse Gigantum
pendere eos poenas immani pro scelere omnis
qui ratione sua disturbent moenia mundi
praeclarumque velint caeli restinguere solem   120
immortalia mortali sermone notantes;
quae procul usque adeo divino a numine distent,
inque deum numero quae sint indigna videri,
notitiam potius praebere ut posse putentur
quid sit vitali motu sensuque remotum.   125
quippe etenim non est, cum quovis corpore ut esse
posse animi natura putetur consiliumque;
sicut in aethere non arbor, non aequore salso
nubes esse queunt neque pisces vivere in arvis
nec cruor in lignis neque saxis sucus inesse.   130
certum ac dispositumst ubi quicquid crescat et insit.
sic animi natura nequit sine corpore oriri
sola neque a nervis et sanguine longius esse.
quod si posset enim, multo prius ipsa animi vis
in capite aut umeris aut imis calcibus esse   135
posset et innasci quavis in parte soleret,
tandem in eodem homine atque in eodem vase manere.
quod quoniam nostro quoque constat corpore certum
dispositumque videtur ubi esse et crescere possit
sorsum anima atque animus, tanto magis infitiandum   140
totum posse extra corpus formamque animalem
putribus in glebis terrarum aut solis ⟨in⟩ igni
aut in aqua durare aut altis aetheris oris.
haud igitur constant divino praedita sensu,
quandoquidem nequeunt vitaliter esse animata.   145
    Illud item non est ut possis credere, sedis
esse deum sanctas in mundi partibus ullis.
tenvis enim natura deum longeque remota

117 par *Marullus*: pars *OQ*   122 a numine distent *131*: animin-
bistent *OQ*: a numine distant *Madvig*   123 videri] videntur
Madvig   131 crescat (*cf.* iii. 787): crescet *OQ*   133 a nervis (*cf.*
iii. 789): aruis *OQ*   longius] longiter *Lachmann*   142 glebis *Ital.*:
glebris *OQ*   in *add. Ital.*

sensibus ab nostris animi vix mente videtur ;
quae quoniam manuum tactum suffugit et ictum,   150
tactile nil nobis quod sit contingere debet.
tangere enim non quit quod tangi non licet ipsum.
quare etiam sedes quoque nostris sedibus esse
dissimiles debent, tenues de corpore eorum ;
quae tibi posterius largo sermone probabo.   155
dicere porro hominum causa voluisse parare
praeclaram mundi naturam proptereaque
allaudabile opus divum laudare decere
aeternumque putare atque immortale futurum
nec fas esse, deum quod sit ratione vetusta   160
gentibus humanis fundatum perpetuo aevo,
sollicitare suis ulla vi ex sedibus umquam
nec verbis vexare et ab imo evertere summa,
cetera de genere hoc adfingere et addere, Memmi,
desiperest. quid enim immortalibus atque beatis   165
gratia nostra queat largirier emolumenti,
ut nostra quicquam causa gerere aggrediantur ?
quidve novi potuit tanto post ante quietos
inlicere ut cuperent vitam mutare priorem ?
nam gaudere novis rebus debere videtur   170
cui veteres obsunt ; sed cui nil accidit aegri
tempore in anteacto, cum pulchre degeret aevum,
quid potuit novitatis amorem accendere tali ?
quidve mali fuerat nobis non esse creatis ?
an, credo, in tenebris vita ac maerore iacebat,   175
donec diluxit rerum genitalis origo ?
natus enim debet quicumque est velle manere
in vita, donec retinebit blanda voluptas.
qui numquam vero vitae gustavit amorem
nec fuit in numero, quid obest non esse creatum ?   180

152 quod *Marullus* : quod si *OQ*   154 de] pro *Lambinus* : ut
corpora *coni. Merrill*   175, 176 *post* 169 *collocavit Lachmann, ante* 174
Lambinus   175 an *O* : anc *Q* : at *Lachmann*   credo] caeca
Bergk : crepera *Munro*

exemplum porro gignundis rebus et ipsa
notities divis hominum unde est insita primum,
quid vellent facere ut scirent animoque viderent,
quove modost umquam vis cognita principiorum
quidque inter sese permutato ordine possent,   185
si non ipsa dedit specimen natura creandi ?
namque ita multa modis multis primordia rerum
ex infinito iam tempore percita plagis
ponderibusque suis consuerunt concita ferri
omnimodisque coire atque omnia pertemptare,   190
quaecumque inter se possent congressa creare,
ut non sit mirum si in talis disposituras
deciderunt quoque et in talis venere meatus,
qualibus haec rerum geritur nunc summa novando.

Quod ⟨si⟩ iam rerum ignorem primordia quae sint,   195
hoc tamen ex ipsis caeli rationibus ausim
confirmare aliisque ex rebus reddere multis,
nequaquam nobis divinitus esse paratam
naturam rerum : tanta stat praedita culpa.
principio quantum caeli tegit impetus ingens,   200
inde avide partem montes silvaeque ferarum
possedere, tenent rupes vastaeque paludes
et mare quod late terrarum distinet oras.
inde duas porro prope partis fervidus ardor
assiduusque geli casus mortalibus aufert.   205
quod superest arvi, tamen id natura sua vi
sentibus obducat, ni vis humana resistat
vitai causa valido consueta bidenti
ingemere et terram pressis proscindere aratris.
si non fecundas vertentes vomere glebas   210
terraique solum subigentes cimus ad ortus,

182 divis hominum *Munro* : hominum diuis *OQ* : hominum dis
Wakefield   185 sese *ed. Brixiensis* : se *OQ*   186 specimen
Pius : speciem *OQ*   187 multa modis *Lambinus* : multimodis *OQ*
191 possent *Lachmann* (*cf.* 426) : possint *OQ*   193 meatus *l 31* :
maestus *OQ*   195 si *add. Marullus*   201 avide *Bernays* : auidam
OQ : avidei *Munro*   208 bidenti *Ital.* : dibenti *OQ*   209 aratris
O corr. : atris *O* : *versum om. Q*

sponte sua nequeant liquidas exsistere in auras;
et tamen interdum magno quaesita labore
cum iam per terras frondent atque omnia florent,
aut nimiis torret fervoribus aetherius sol   215
aut subiti perimunt imbres gelidaeque pruinae,
flabraque ventorum violento turbine vexant.
praeterea genus horriferum natura ferarum
humanae genti infestum terraque marique
cur alit atque auget? cur anni tempora morbos   220
apportant? quare mors immatura vagatur?
tum porro puer, ut saevis proiectus ab undis
navita, nudus humi iacet, infans, indigus omni
vitali auxilio, cum primum in luminis oras
nixibus ex alvo matris natura profudit,   225
vagituque locum lugubri complet, ut aequumst
cui tantum in vita restet transire malorum.
at variae crescunt pecudes armenta feraeque
nec crepitacillis opus est nec cuiquam adhibendast
almae nutricis blanda atque infracta loquela   230
nec varias quaerunt vestis pro tempore caeli,
denique non armis opus est, non moenibus altis,
qui sua tutentur, quando omnibus omnia large
tellus ipsa parit naturaque daedala rerum.

Principio quoniam terrai corpus et umor   235
aurarumque leves animae calidique vapores,
e quibus haec rerum consistere summa videtur,
omnia nativo ac mortali corpore constant,
debet eodem omnis mundi natura putari.
quippe etenim quorum partis et membra videmus   240
corpore nativo ac mortalibus esse figuris,
haec eadem ferme mortalia cernimus esse

---

223 indigus *O corr.* : indignus *OQ*   227 restet transire *L* : re et
transirest *O* (transire est *Q*)   230 alme *Q corr.* : arme *OQ*   233
qui] quis *Christ*   239 eodem *Pius* : eadem *O* : edem *Q*   241 nativo
ac *Lachmann* : natiuom *O* : natiuum *Q*

et nativa simul. quapropter maxima mundi
cum videam membra ac partis consumpta regigni,
scire licet caeli quoque item terraeque fuisse   245
principiale aliquod tempus clademque futuram.
  Illud in his rebus ne corripuisse rearis
me mihi, quod terram atque ignem mortalia sumpsi
esse neque umorem dubitavi aurasque perire
atque eadem gigni rursusque augescere dixi,   250
principio pars terrai nonnulla, perusta
solibus assiduis, multa pulsata pedum vi,
pulveris exhalat nebulam nubisque volantis
quas validi toto dispergunt aere venti.
pars etiam glebarum ad diluviem revocatur   255
imbribus et ripas radentia flumina rodunt.
praeterea pro parte sua, quodcumque alit auget,
redditur ; et quoniam dubio procul esse videtur
omniparens eadem rerum commune sepulcrum,
ergo terra tibi libatur et aucta recrescit.   260
  Quod superest, umore novo mare flumina fontis
semper abundare et latices manare perennis
nil opus est verbis : magnus decursus aquarum
undique declarat. sed primum quicquid aquai
tollitur in summaque fit ut nil umor abundet,   265
partim quod validi verrentes aequora venti
diminuunt radiisque retexens aetherius sol,
partim quod subter per terras diditur omnis.
percolatur enim virus retroque remanat
materies umoris et ad caput amnibus omnis   270
convenit, inde super terras fluit agmine dulci
qua via secta semel liquido pede detulit undas.
  Aera nunc igitur dicam qui corpore toto
innumerabiliter privas mutatur in horas.

245 item *Bentley* : idem *OQ*   248 me mihi *Q* : memini *O*
251 nonnulla *L* : non ulla *OQ*   257 alit] alid *Lambinus*   258
redditur] roditur *Marullus*   272 secta semel *Q corr.* : semel secta
semel *OQ*   274 oras *OQ*

semper enim, quodcumque fluit de rebus, id omne   275
aeris in magnum fertur mare ; qui nisi contra
corpora retribuat rebus recreetque fluentis,
omnia iam resoluta forent et in aera versa.
haud igitur cessat gigni de rebus et in res
reccidere, assidue quoniam fluere omnia constat.   280
    Largus item liquidi fons luminis, aetherius sol,
irrigat assidue caelum candore recenti
suppeditatque novo confestim lumine lumen.
nam primum quicquid fulgoris disperit ei,
quocumque accidit. id licet hinc cognoscere possis,   285
quod simul ac primum nubes succedere soli
coepere et radios inter quasi rumpere lucis,
extemplo inferior pars horum disperit omnis
terraque inumbratur qua nimbi cumque feruntur ;
ut noscas splendore novo res semper egere   290
et primum iactum fulgoris quemque perire
nec ratione alia res posse in sole videri,
perpetuo ni suppeditet lucis caput ipsum.
quin etiam nocturna tibi, terrestria quae sunt,
lumina, pendentes lychni claraeque coruscis   295
fulguribus pingues multa caligine taedae
consimili properant ratione, ardore ministro,
suppeditare novum lumen, tremere ignibus instant,
instant, nec loca lux inter quasi rupta relinquit.
usque adeo properanter ab omnibus ignibus ei   300
exitium celeri celatur origine flammae.
sic igitur solem lunam stellasque putandumst
ex alio atque alio lucem iactare subortu
et primum quicquid flammarum perdere semper ;
inviolabilia haec ne credas forte vigere.   305
    Denique non lapides quoque vinci cernis ab aevo,

    282 recenti *Q corr.* : regenti *OQ*   288 disperit *Q corr.* : disperis *OQ*
291 et *Marullus* : ut *OQ*   295 lychni *O corr.* : lyclini *OQ*   296
caligine] fuligine *Bentley*   297 properant *Marullus* : proferant *OQ*
300 ab omnibus] obortis *Bruno*   301 celatur *Marullus* : celeratur
OQ   302 putandumst *Lachmann* : putandum *OQ*

non altas turris ruere et putrescere saxa,
non delubra deum simulacraque fessa fatisci,
nec sanctum numen fati protollere finis
posse neque adversus naturae foedera niti?   310
denique non monumenta virum dilapsa videmus,
†quaerere proporro sibi cumque senescere credas†
non ruere avulsos silices a montibus altis
nec validas aevi viris perferre patique
finiti? neque enim caderent avulsa repente,   315
ex infinito quae tempore pertolerassent
omnia tormenta aetatis privata fragore.

Denique iam tuere hoc, circum supraque quod omnem
continet amplexu terram: si procreat ex se
omnia, quod quidam memorant, recipitque perempta,   320
totum nativo ac mortali corpore constat.
nam quodcumque alias ex se res auget alitque,
deminui debet, recreari, cum recipit res.

Praeterea si nulla fuit genitalis origo
terrarum et caeli semperque aeterna fuere,   325
cur supera bellum Thebanum et funera Troiae
non alias alii quoque res cecinere poetae?
quo tot facta virum totiens cecidere neque usquam
aeternis famae monumentis insita florent?
verum, ut opinor, habet novitatem summa recensque   330
naturast mundi neque pridem exordia cepit.
quare etiam quaedam nunc artes expoliuntur,
nunc etiam augescunt; nunc addita navigiis sunt
multa, modo organici melicos peperere sonores.
denique natura haec rerum ratioque repertast   335

310 foedera *O corr.* : foederant *OQ*   312 quaerere proporro
sibi cumque senescere credas *OQ*: quaerere proporro sibi sene
senescere credas *Munro*: quae fore proporro vetitumque senescere
credas *Lachmann* : aeraque proporro silicumque senescere petras
Ellis: *alii alia*   318 omnem *Marullus*: omne *OQ*   321 nativo
ac *Bernays*: natiuum *OQ*   327 alii *Ital.* : ali *OQ*   331 natura
est mundi *Marullus*: natura mundist *OQ*

nuper, et hanc primus cum primis ipse repertus
nunc ego sum in patrias qui possim vertere voces.
quod si forte fuisse antehac eadem omnia credis,
sed periisse hominum torrenti saecla vapore,
aut cecidisse urbis magno vexamine mundi,   340
aut ex imbribus assiduis exisse rapaces
per terras amnis atque oppida coperuisse,
tanto quique magis victus fateare necessest
exitium quoque terrarum caelique futurum.
nam cum res tantis morbis tantisque periclis   345
temptarentur, ibi si tristior incubuisset
causa, darent late cladem magnasque ruinas.
nec ratione alia mortales esse videmur,
inter nos nisi quod morbis aegrescimus isdem
atque illi quos a vita natura removit.   350
    Praeterea quaecumque manent aeterna necessust
aut, quia sunt solido cum corpore, respuere ictus
nec penetrare pati sibi quicquam quod queat artas
dissociare intus partis, ut materiai
corpora sunt quorum naturam ostendimus ante,   355
aut ideo durare aetatem posse per omnem,
plagarum quia sunt expertia, sicut inane est
quod manet intactum neque ab ictu fungitur hilum,
aut etiam quia nulla loci fit copia circum,
quo quasi res possint discedere dissoluique,   360
sicut summarum summa est aeterna, neque extra
qui locus est quo dissiliant neque corpora sunt quae
possint incidere et valida dissolvere plaga.
at neque, uti docui, solido cum corpore mundi
naturast, quoniam admixtumst in rebus inane,   365
nec tamen est ut inane, neque autem corpora desunt,
ex infinito quae possint forte coorta

339 periisse *l 31* : perisse *OQ*   342 atque *l 31* : at *OQ*   349
isdem *Pius* : idem *OQ*   359 fit *Lachmann* : sit *OQ*   367 coorta
Marullus : coperta *OQ*

corruere hanc rerum violento turbine summam
aut aliam quamvis cladem importare pericli,
nec porro natura loci spatiumque profundi   370
deficit, exspergi quo possint moenia mundi,
aut alia quavis possunt vi pulsa perire.
haud igitur leti praeclusa est ianua caelo
nec soli terraeque neque altis aequoris undis,
sed patet immani et vasto respectat hiatu.   375
quare etiam nativa necessumst confiteare
haec eadem ; neque enim, mortali corpore quae sunt,
ex infinito iam tempore adhuc potuissent
immensi validas aevi contemnere viris.

Denique tantopere inter se cum maxima mundi   380
pugnent membra, pio nequaquam concita bello,
nonne vides aliquam longi certaminis ollis
posse dari finem? vel cum sol et vapor omnis
omnibus epotis umoribus exsuperarint :
quod facere intendunt, neque adhuc conata patrarunt :   385
tantum suppeditant amnes ultraque minantur
omnia diluviare ex alto gurgite ponti,
nequiquam, quoniam verrentes aequora venti
deminuunt radiisque retexens aetherius sol,
et siccare prius confidunt omnia posse   390
quam liquor incepti possit contingere finem.
tantum spirantes aequo certamine bellum
magnis ⟨inter se⟩ de rebus cernere certant,
cum semel interea fuerit superantior ignis
et semel, ut fama est, umor regnarit in arvis.   395
ignis enim superat et lambens multa perussit,
avia cum Phaethonta rapax vis solis equorum
aethere raptavit toto terrasque per omnis.

---

369 pericli] per ictus *Bruno*   375 immani] immane *Bruno*   et
O corr.: e *O*: ac *Q*   383 omnis] amnis *Postgate*   385 patrarunt *Goebel*: patrantur *OQ*   393 inter se *hic add. Lachmann*,
post de rebus *L*   396 superat *Lachmann*: superauit *OQ*   lam-
be. s *Q corr.* : ambens *OQ*: ardens *Polle*: *alii alia*   397 petontana
rapax *O*: petonta rapax *Q*

at pater omnipotens ira tum percitus acri
magnanimum Phaethonta repenti fulminis ictu   400
deturbavit equis in terram, solque cadenti
obvius aeternam succepit lampada mundi
disiectosque redegit equos iunxitque trementis,
inde suum per iter recreavit cuncta gubernans,
scilicet ut veteres Graium cecinere poetae.   405
quod procul a vera nimis est ratione repulsum.
ignis enim superare potest ubi materiai
ex infinito sunt corpora plura coorta;
inde cadunt vires aliqua ratione revictae,
aut pereunt res exustae torrentibus auris.   410
umor item quondam coepit superare coortus,
ut fama est, hominum vitas quando obruit undis.
inde ubi vis aliqua ratione aversa recessit,
ex infinito fuerat quaecumque coorta,
constiterunt imbres et flumina vim minuerunt.   415
    Sed quibus ille modis coniectus materiai
fundarit terram et caelum pontique profunda,
solis lunai cursus, ex ordine ponam.
nam certe neque consilio primordia rerum
ordine se suo quaeque sagaci mente locarunt   420
nec quos quaeque darent motus pepigere profecto,
sed quia multa modis multis primordia rerum
ex infinito iam tempore percita plagis
ponderibusque suis consuerunt concita ferri
omnimodisque coire atque omnia pertemptare,   425
quaecumque inter se possent congressa creare,
propterea fit uti magnum vulgata per aevum
omne genus coetus et motus experiundo
tandem conveniant ea quae convecta repente
magnarum rerum fiunt exordia saepe,   430

399 tum *l 31*: cum *OQ*   400 fulminis *O corr.* : fluminis *OQ*
405 Graium *l 31* : gratum *OQ*   412 vitas *Purmann* : multas *OQ*
undis] urbis *Pontanus*   428 omne genus *Lachmann* : omnigenus
OQ   429 convecta *Lachmann* : conventa *OQ*   430 fiunt *l 31* :
fluunt *OQ*

terrai maris et caeli generisque animantum.

  Hic neque tum solis rota cerni lumine largo
altivolans poterat nec magni sidera mundi
nec mare nec caelum nec denique terra neque aer
nec similis nostris rebus res ulla videri,   435
sed nova tempestas quaedam molesque coorta
omne genus de principiis, discordia quorum   [440]
intervalla vias conexus pondera plagas   [441]
concursus motus turbabat proelia miscens,   [442]
propter dissimilis formas variasque figuras   440 [443]
quod non omnia sic poterant coniuncta manere   [444]
nec motus inter sese dare convenientis.   [445]
diffugere inde loci partes coepere paresque   [437]
cum paribus iungi res et discludere mundum   [438]
membraque dividere et magnas disponere partis, 445 [439]
hoc est, a terris altum secernere caelum,
et sorsum mare, uti secreto umore pateret,
sorsus item puri secretique aetheris ignes.

  Quippe etenim primum terrai corpora quaeque,
propterea quod erant gravia et perplexa, coibant   450
in medio atque imas capiebant omnia sedis ;
quae quanto magis inter se perplexa coibant,
tam magis expressere ea quae mare sidera solem
lunamque efficerent et magni moenia mundi.
omnia enim magis haec e levibus atque rotundis   455
seminibus multoque minoribu' sunt elementis
quam tellus.   ideo per rara foramina terrae
partibus erumpens primus se sustulit aether
ignifer et multos secum levis abstulit ignis,
non alia longe ratione ac saepe videmus,   460
aurea cum primum gemmantis rore per herbas

    433 altivolans *Pontanus* : alte volans *OQ*   437–445 *hunc versuum
ordinem restituit Reisacker*   437 omne genus de *Lachmann* : omni-
genis e *O* : omnigenus e *Q*   438 vias *Q corr.* : uia *OQ*   445
magnas *Macrobius* : magna *OQ*   447 umore *Q corr.* : umor *OQ*
458 se *L* : et *OQ*

matutina rubent radiati lumina solis
exhalantque lacus nebulam fluviique perennes,
ipsaque ut interdum tellus fumare videtur ;
omnia quae sursum cum conciliantur in alto   465
corpore concreto subtexunt nubila caelum.
sic igitur tum se levis ac diffusilis aether
corpore concreto circumdatus undique ⟨flexit⟩
et late diffusus in omnis undique partis
omnia sic avido complexu cetera saepsit.   470
hunc exordia sunt solis lunaeque secuta,
interutrasque globi quorum vertuntur in auris ;
quae neque terra sibi adscivit nec maximus aether,
quod neque tam fuerunt gravia ut depressa sederent,
nec levia ut possent per summas labier oras,   475
et tamen interutrasque ita sunt ut corpora viva
versent et partes ut mundi totius exstent ;
quod genus in nobis quaedam licet in statione
membra manere, tamen cum sint ea quae moveantur.
his igitur rebus retractis terra repente,   480
maxima qua nunc se ponti plaga caerula tendit,
succidit et salso suffudit gurgite fossas.
inque dies quanto circum magis aetheris aestus
et radii solis cogebant undique terram
verberibus crebris extrema ad limina in artum,   485
in medio ut propulsa suo condensa coiret,
tam magis expressus salsus de corpore sudor
augebat mare manando camposque natantis,
et tanto magis illa foras elapsa volabant
corpora multa vaporis et aeris altaque caeli   490
densabant procul a terris fulgentia templa.
sidebant campi, crescebant montibus altis

463 exalantque *OQ* : exalare *Lachmann*   468 flexit *Lachmann* :
saepsit *OQ* (*ex* 470)   482 salso suffudit *O corr.* : salso suffodit *O* :
salsos offudit *Q*   484 radii *Q* : radiis *O*   485 in artum *Munro* :
partem *OQ* : raptim *Bentley*   491 densabant] densebant *Lambinus*

ascensus ; neque enim poterant subsidere saxa
nec pariter tantundem omnes succumbere partes.

  Sic igitur terrae concreto corpore pondus   495
constitit atque omnis mundi quasi limus in imum
confluxit gravis et subsedit funditus ut faex ;
inde mare inde aer inde aether ignifer ipse
corporibus liquidis sunt omnia pura relicta,
et leviora aliis alia, et liquidissimus aether   500
atque levissimus aerias super influit auras,
nec liquidum corpus turbantibus aeris auris
commiscet ; sinit haec violentis omnia verti
turbinibus, sinit incertis turbare procellis,
ipse suos ignis certo fert impete labens.   505
nam modice fluere atque uno posse aethera nisu
significat Pontos, mare certo quod fluit aestu
unum labendi conservans usque tenorem.

  Motibus astrorum nunc quae sit causa canamus.
principio magnus caeli si vertitur orbis,   510
ex utraque polum parti premere aera nobis
dicendum est extraque tenere et claudere utrimque ;
inde alium supra fluere atque intendere eodem
quo volvenda micant aeterni sidera mundi ;
aut alium subter, contra qui subvehat orbem,   515
ut fluvios versare rotas atque haustra videmus.
est etiam quoque uti possit caelum omne manere
in statione, tamen cum lucida signa ferantur ;
sive quod inclusi rapidi sunt aetheris aestus
quaerentesque viam circum versantur et ignes   520
passim per caeli volvunt summania templa ;
sive aliunde fluens alicunde extrinsecus aer
versat agens ignis ; sive ipsi serpere possunt
quo cuiusque cibus vocat atque invitat euntis,

   500 leviora *Ital.*: leuior *OQ*   **503** commiscet *Naugerius*: com-
misci *OQ*   **507** Pontos *Lachmann*: ponto *OQ*: Ponti *Pontanus*
509–533 *uncinis incl. Lachmann, post* 563 *collocavit Brieger*   **514**
aeterni] nocturni *Merrill*   **515** qui *Marullus*: quis *OQ*   **516**
fluvios *Nonius*: fluuius *OQ*   **518** lucida *l 31*: lucia *OQ*   **521** sum-
mania] immania *Creech*

flammea per caelum pascentis corpora passim.					525
nam quid in hoc mundo sit eorum ponere certum
difficile est; sed quid possit fiatque per omne
in variis mundis varia ratione creatis,
id doceo plurisque sequor disponere causas,
motibus astrorum quae possint esse per omne;					530
e quibus una tamen siet hic quoque causa necessest
quae vegeat motum signis; sed quae sit earum
praecipere haudquaquamst pedetemptim progredientis.

Terraque ut in media mundi regione quiescat,
evanescere paulatim et decrescere pondus					535
convenit, atque aliam naturam subter habere
ex ineunte aevo coniunctam atque uniter aptam
partibus aeriis mundi quibus insita vivit.

propterea non est oneri neque deprimit auras;
ut sua cuique homini nullo sunt pondere membra					540
nec caput est oneri collo nec denique totum
corporis in pedibus pondus sentimus inesse;
at quaecumque foris veniunt impostaque nobis
pondera sunt laedunt, permulto saepe minora.

usque adeo magni refert quid quaeque queat res.					545
sic igitur tellus non est aliena repente
allata atque auris aliunde obiecta alienis,
sed pariter prima concepta ab origine mundi
certaque pars eius, quasi nobis membra videntur.

praeterea grandi tonitru concussa repente					550
terra supra quae se sunt concutit omnia motu;
quod facere haud ulla posset ratione, nisi esset
partibus aeriis mundi caeloque revincta.

nam communibus inter se radicibus haerent
ex ineunte aevo coniuncta atque uniter apta.					555

---

528 creatis (cf. 1345): creati OQ   530 omne Marullus : omnem OQ
531 siet Lachmann hic Bernays ; sit et hae O : sit et haec Q   532
vegeat Gifanius : uigeat OQ   536 subter l 31 : super OQ   545
magni Ital. : magi OQ   queat ed. Veronensis : quaeat OQ : aveat
Lachmann : obeat Munro : alii alia   549 videntur] videtur Brieger
553 aeriis Ital. : aeri OQ   555 apta Pontanus : aucta OQ

nonne vides etiam quam magno pondere nobis
sustineat corpus tenuissima vis animai
propterea quia tam coniuncta atque uniter apta est?
denique iam saltu pernici tollere corpus
quid potis est nisi vis animae quae membra gubernat?   560
iamne vides quantum tenuis natura valere
possit, ubi est coniuncta gravi cum corpore, ut aer
coniunctus terris et nobis est animi vis?

   Nec nimio solis maior rota nec minor ardor
esse potest, nostris quam sensibus esse videtur.   565
nam quibus e spatiis cumque ignes lumina possunt
adicere et calidum membris adflare vaporem,
nil illa his intervallis de corpore libant
flammarum, nil ad speciem est contractior ignis.
proinde, calor quoniam solis lumenque profusum   570 [573]
perveniunt nostros ad sensus et loca mulcent,   [570]
forma quoque hinc solis debet filumque videri,   [571]
nil adeo ut possis plus aut minus addere, vere.   [572]
lunaque sive notho fertur loca lumine lustrans   575
sive suam proprio iactat de corpore lucem,
quidquid id est, nilo fertur maiore figura
quam, nostris oculis qua cernimus, esse videtur.
nam prius omnia, quae longe semota tuemur
aera per multum, specie confusa videntur   580
quam minui filum. quapropter luna necesse est,
quandoquidem claram speciem certamque figuram
praebet, ut est oris extremis cumque notata,
quantaque quantast, hinc nobis videatur in alto.
postremo quoscumque vides hinc aetheris ignis;   585
quandoquidem quoscumque in terris cernimus ⟨ignis⟩,

558 apta Q corr. : rapta OQ   560 quid Lambinus : quis OQ
animae] animi Lachmann   564 ardor] ardens Bockemüller : alii
alia   567 adiicere Lambinus : adlicere OQ   568 nil illa his
Bernays : nihil nisi OQ   libant Marullus : librant OQ   570 [573]
huc transtulit Marullus   571 mulcent Lachmann : fulgent OQ :
tingunt Lambinus   572 filumque Turnebus : illumque O : ilumque Q
574 = 571 (570) secl. editores   581 minui Bentley : mi OQ   584
quantaque Eichstädt : quanto quoque OQ   586 ignes add. Marullus

dum tremor ⟨est⟩ clarus, dum cernitur ardor eorum,
perparvum quiddam interdum mutare videntur
alteram utram in partem filum, quo longius absunt:
scire licet perquam pauxillo posse minores   590 [594]
esse vel exigua maiores parte brevique.   [595]

   Illud item non est mirandum, qua ratione   [590]
tantulus ille queat tantum sol mittere lumen,   [591]
quod maria ac terras omnis caelumque rigando   [592]
compleat et calido perfundat cuncta vapore.   595 [593]
nam licet hinc mundi patefactum totius unum   597
largifluum fontem scatere atque erumpere lumen,
ex omni mundo quia sic elementa vaporis
undique conveniunt et sic coniectus eorum   600
confluit, ex uno capite hic ut profluat ardor.
nonne vides etiam quam late parvus aquai
prata riget fons interdum campisque redundet?
est etiam quoque uti non magno solis ab igni
aera percipiat calidis fervoribus ardor,   605
opportunus ita est si forte et idoneus aer,
ut queat accendi parvis ardoribus ictus;
quod genus interdum segetes stipulamque videmus
accidere ex una scintilla incendia passim.

forsitan et rosea sol alte lampade lucens   610
possideat multum caecis fervoribus ignem
circum se, nullo qui sit fulgore notatus,
aestifer ut tantum radiorum exaugeat ictum.

   Nec ratio solis simplex ⟨et⟩ recta patescit,
quo pacto aestivis e partibus aegocerotis   615
brumalis adeat flexus atque inde revertens
cancri se ut vertat metas ad solstitialis,

---

587 est *add. l 31*   588 uidentur *Q*: uidetur *O*   589 absunt
Lachmann: absit *OQ*: absint *Lambinus*   590, 591 [594, 595] *huc
transtulit Marullus*   596 = 584 *secl. editores*   599 vaporis
Lambinus: uapore *OQ*   601 hic] hinc *Merrill*   605 percipiat
Naugerius: percipitat *OQ*   609 accidere *Q*: accedere *O*   613
aestifer ut tantum *l 31*: aestiferi utantum *Q* (utantur *C*)   614 et
add. Marullus   recta] certa *Lambinus*   617 cancri se *Lachmann*:
canceris *OQ*

lunaque mensibus id spatium videatur obire,
annua sol in quo consumit tempora cursu.
non, inquam, simplex his rebus reddita causast.   620
nam fieri vel cum primis id posse videtur,
Democriti quod sancta viri sententia ponit,
quanto quaeque magis sint terram sidera propter,
tanto posse minus cum caeli turbine ferri.
evanescere enim rapidas illius et acris   625
imminui subter viris, ideoque relinqui
paulatim solem cum posterioribu' signis,
inferior multo quod sit quam fervida signa.
et magis hoc lunam : quanto demissior eius
cursus abest procul a caelo terrisque propinquat,   630
tanto posse minus cum signis tendere cursum.
flaccidiore etiam quanto iam turbine fertur
inferior quam sol, tanto magis omnia signa
hanc adipiscuntur circum praeterque feruntur.
propterea fit ut haec ad signum quodque reverti   635
mobilius videatur, ad hanc quia signa revisunt.
fit quoque ut e mundi transversis partibus aer
alternis certo fluere alter tempore possit,
qui queat aestivis solem detrudere signis
brumalis usque ad flexus gelidumque rigorem,   640
et qui reiciat gelidis a frigoris umbris
aestiferas usque in partis et fervida signa.
et ratione pari lunam stellasque putandumst,
quae volvunt magnos in magnis orbibus annos,
aeribus posse alternis e partibus ire.   645
nonne vides etiam diversis nubila ventis
diversas ire in partis inferna supernis?
qui minus illa queant per magnos aetheris orbis
aestibus inter se diversis sidera ferri?
    At nox obruit ingenti caligine terras,   650

---

623 sint *Ital.* : in *O* : sin *Q*   629 dimisior *OQ*   632 etiam]
etenim *Lachmann*   648 illa *l 31* : ille *OQ*

aut ubi de longo cursu sol ultima caeli
impulit atque suos efflavit languidus ignis
concussos itere et labefactos aere multo,
aut quia sub terras cursum convertere cogit
vis eadem, supra quae terras pertulit orbem. 655

    Tempore item certo roseam Matuta per oras
aetheris auroram differt et lumina pandit,
aut quia sol idem, sub terras ille revertens,
anticipat caelum radiis accendere temptans,
aut quia conveniunt ignes et semina multa 660
confluere ardoris consuerunt tempore certo,
quae faciunt solis nova semper lumina gigni;
quod genus Idaeis fama est e montibus altis
dispersos ignis orienti lumine cerni,
inde coire globum quasi in unum et conficere orbem. 665
nec tamen illud in his rebus mirabile debet
esse, quod haec ignis tam certo tempore possunt
semina confluere et solis reparare nitorem.
multa videmus enim, certo quae tempore fiunt
omnibus in rebus. florescunt tempore certo 670
arbusta et certo dimittunt tempore florem.
nec minus in certo dentis cadere imperat aetas
tempore et impubem molli pubescere veste
et pariter mollem malis demittere barbam.
fulmina postremo nix imbres nubila venti 675
non nimis incertis fiunt in partibus anni.
namque ubi sic fuerunt causarum exordia prima
atque ita res mundi cecidere ab origine prima,
conseque quoque iam redeunt ex ordine certo.

    Crescere itemque dies licet et tabescere noctes, 680
et minui luces, cum sumant augmina noctes,

651 sol ultima *C*: soluet ima *OQ*   656 roseam *Ital.*: rosea *OQ*
Matuta *Pontanus*: matura *OQ*: natura *Bockemüller*   657 et
O corr.: e *OQ*   667 possunt *Lachmann*: possit *OQ*   675 fulmina
Marullus: flumina *OQ*   679 conseque . . . redeunt *Lachmann*:
consequiae . . . rerum *OQ*: consequiae . . . suerunt *Merrill*

aut quia sol idem sub terras atque superne
imparibus currens anfractibus aetheris oras
partit et in partis non aequas dividit orbem,
et quod ab alterutra detraxit parte, reponit   685
eius in adversa tanto plus parte relatus,
donec ad id signum caeli pervenit, ubi anni
nodus nocturnas exaequat lucibus umbras.
nam medio cursu flatus aquilonis et austri
distinet aequato caelum discrimine metas   690
propter signiferi posituram totius orbis,
annua sol in quo concludit tempora serpens,
obliquo terras et caelum lumine lustrans,
ut ratio declarat eorum qui loca caeli
omnia dispositis signis ornata notarunt.   695
aut quia crassior est certis in partibus aer,
sub terris ideo tremulum iubar haesitat ignis
nec penetrare potest facile atque emergere ad ortus.
propterea noctes hiberno tempore longae
cessant, dum veniat radiatum insigne diei.   700
aut etiam, quia sic alternis partibus anni
tardius et citius consuerunt confluere ignes
qui faciunt solem certa de surgere parte,
propterea fit uti videantur dicere verum

*

Luna potest solis radiis percussa nitere   705
inque dies magis ⟨id⟩ lumen convertere nobis
ad speciem, quantum solis secedit ab orbi,
donec eum contra pleno bene lumine fulsit
atque oriens obitus eius super edita vidit;
inde minutatim retro quasi condere lumen   710
debet item, quanto propius iam solis ad ignem

684 et *O corr.*: e *OQ*   692 concludit *Lachmann*: contudit *OQ*
700 diei *L*: dici *OQ*   704 * 705 *lacunam indicavit Munro, versum
post 714 coll. Naugerius, Gifanius*   705 percussa *l 31*:
perculsa *OQ*   706 id *add. Lachmann*, hinc *Merrill*   708 donec
O corr.: doneque *O*: donique *Q*   711 iam *Marullus*: tam *OQ*

labitur ex alia signorum parte per orbem;
ut faciunt, lunam qui fingunt esse pilai
consimilem cursusque viam sub sole tenere.
est etiam quare proprio cum lumine possit   715
volvier et varias splendoris reddere formas.
corpus enim licet esse aliud quod fertur et una
labitur omnimodis occursans officiensque
nec potis est cerni, quia cassum lumine fertur.
versarique potest, globus ut, si forte, pilai   720
dimidia ex parti candenti lumine tinctus,
versandoque globum variantis edere formas,
donec eam partem, quaecumque est ignibus aucta,
ad speciem vertit nobis oculosque patentis;
inde minutatim retro contorquet et aufert   725
luciferam partem glomeraminis atque pilai;
ut Babylonica Chaldaeum doctrina refutans
astrologorum artem contra convincere tendit,
proinde quasi id fieri nequeat quod pugnat uterque
aut minus hoc illo sit cur amplectier ausis.   730
denique cur nequeat semper nova luna creari
ordine formarum certo certisque figuris
inque dies privos aborisci quaeque creata
atque alia illius reparari in parte locoque,
difficilest ratione docere et vincere verbis,   735
ordine cum ⟨possint⟩ tam certo multa creari.
it ver et Venus, et Veneris praenuntius ante
pennatus graditur, Zephyri vestigia propter
Flora quibus mater praespargens ante viai
cuncta coloribus egregiis et odoribus opplet.   740
inde loci sequitur calor aridus et comes una
pulverulenta Ceres ⟨et⟩ etesia flabra aquilonum.

727 Babylonica *l 31*: Babylonisa *OQ*   Chaldaeum *Avancius·*
Chaldeum *OQ*   736 possint *add. Lachmann*   737 Veneris] veris
Pontanus   738 Zephyri] Zephyrus *Pontanus*   742 pulverulenta
Pontanus: poluerunta *O* (pul- *Q*)   et *add. Marullus*

inde autumnus adit, graditur simul Euhius Euan.
inde aliae tempestates ventique sequuntur,
altitonans Volturnus et auster fulmine pollens.   745
tandem bruma nives adfert pigrumque rigorem
reddit hiemps, sequitur crepitans hanc dentibus algor.
quo minus est mirum si certo tempore luna
gignitur et certo deletur tempore rursus,
cum fieri possint tam certo tempore multa.   750
    Solis item quoque defectus lunaeque latebras
pluribus e causis fieri tibi posse putandumst.
nam cur luna queat terram secludere solis
lumine et a terris altum caput obstruere ei,
obiciens caecum radiis ardentibus orbem ;   755
tempore eodem aliud facere id non posse putetur
corpus quod cassum labatur lumine semper ?
solque suos etiam dimittere languidus ignis
tempore cur certo nequeat recreareque lumen,
cum loca praeteriit flammis infesta per auras,   760
quae faciunt ignis interstingui atque perire ?
et cur terra queat lunam spoliare vicissim
lumine et oppressum solem super ipsa tenere,
menstrua dum rigidas coni perlabitur umbras ;
tempore eodem aliud nequeat succurrere lunae   765
corpus vel supra solis perlabier orbem,
quod radios interrumpat lumenque profusum ?
et tamen ipsa suo si fulget luna nitore,
cur nequeat certa mundi languescere parte,
dum loca luminibus propriis inimica per exit ?   770
    Quod superest, quoniam magni per caerula mundi   772
qua fieri quicquid posset ratione resolvi,
solis uti varios cursus lunaeque meatus
noscere possemus quae vis et causa cieret,   775

743 euā Q : aeuom O   747 reddit l 31 : redit OQ : prodit Lach-
mann   crepitans l 31 : creditans OQ   hanc Q : ac O   algor
Gifanius: algi OQ: algu Vossius   750 fieri Marullus : fleri
OQ   753 solis Lambinus : possis OQ   756 eodem (cf. 765) :
eadem OQ   761 perire Marullus : periri OQ   771 = 764 secl.
Lambinus

quove modo ⟨possent⟩ offecto lumine obire
et neque opinantis tenebris obducere terras,
cum quasi conivent et aperto lumine rursum
omnia convisunt clara loca candida luce,
nunc redeo ad mundi novitatem et mollia terrae   780
arva, novo fetu quid primum in luminis oras
tollere et incertis crerint committere ventis.

   Principio genus herbarum viridemque nitorem
terra dedit circum collis camposque per omnis
florida fulserunt viridanti prata colore,   785
arboribusque datumst variis exinde per auras
crescendi magnum immissis certamen habenis.
ut pluma atque pili primum saetaeque creantur
quadrupedum membris et corpore pennipotentum,
sic nova tum tellus herbas virgultaque primum   790
sustulit, inde loci mortalia saecla creavit
multa modis multis varia ratione coorta.
nam neque de caelo cecidisse animalia possunt
nec terrestria de salsis exisse lacunis.
linquitur ut merito maternum nomen adepta   795
terra sit, e terra quoniam sunt cuncta creata.
multaque nunc etiam exsistunt animalia terris
imbribus et calido solis concreta vapore ;
quo minus est mirum si tum sunt plura coorta
et maiora, nova tellure atque aethere adulta.   800
principio genus alituum variaeque volucres
ova relinquebant exclusae tempore verno,
folliculos ut nunc teretes aestate cicadae
linquunt sponte sua victum vitamque petentes.
tum tibi terra dedit primum mortalia saecla.   805
multus enim calor atque umor superabat in arvis.
hoc ubi quaeque loci regio opportuna dabatur,

   776 possent *add. ed. Brixiensis*   782 tollere et *Pontanus* :
tolleret *OQ*   crerint *Orelli* : credunt *OQ*   800 maiora *Pontanus* :
maiore *OQ*

crescebant uteri terram radicibus apti;
quos ubi tempore maturo patefecerat aetas
infantum fugiens umorem aurasque petessens,   810
convertebat ibi natura foramina terrae
et sucum venis cogebat fundere apertis
consimilem lactis, sicut nunc femina quaeque
cum peperit, dulci repletur lacte, quod omnis
impetus in mammas convertitur ille alimenti.   815
terra cibum pueris, vestem vapor, herba cubile
praebebat multa et molli lanugine abundans.
at novitas mundi nec frigora dura ciebat
nec nimios aestus nec magnis viribus auras.
omnia enim pariter crescunt et robora sumunt.   820
    Quare etiam atque etiam maternum nomen adepta
terra tenet merito, quoniam genus ipsa creavit
humanum atque animal prope certo tempore fudit
omne quod in magnis bacchatur montibu' passim,
aeriasque simul volucris variantibu' formis.   825
sed quia finem aliquam pariendi debet habere,
destitit, ut mulier spatio defessa vetusto.
mutat enim mundi naturam totius aetas
ex alioque alius status excipere omnia debet,
nec manet ulla sui similis res: omnia migrant,   830
omnia commutat natura et vertere cogit.
namque aliud putrescit et aevo debile languet,
porro aliud succrescit et ⟨e⟩ contemptibus exit.
sic igitur mundi naturam totius aetas
mutat et ex alio terram status excipit alter,   835
quod tulit ut nequeat, possit quod non tulit ante.
    Multaque tum tellus etiam portenta creare
conatast mira facie membrisque coorta,

---

809 aetas *Marullus* : aestas *OQ* : aestus *Lachmann* : auctus *Merrill*
823 animal *Marullus* : anima *OQ* : animas *O corr.*   825 aeriasque
Marullus : aeriaeque *OQ*   833 succrescit *Lachmann* (*in commen-
tario*) : crescit *OQ* : clarescit *Lachmann*   e add. *Marullus*   836
tulit ut *Bentley* : potuit *OQ* : pote uti *Lachmann*   nequeat] nequit,
ut *Munro*   838 facie *l 31* : facit *OQ*

androgynum, interutrasque nec utrum, utrimque remotum,
orba pedum partim, manuum viduata vicissim,   840
muta sine ore etiam, sine vultu caeca reperta,
vinctaque membrorum per totum corpus adhaesu,
nec facere ut possent quicquam nec cedere quoquam
nec vitare malum nec sumere quod foret usus.

cetera de genere hoc monstra ac portenta creabat,   845
nequiquam, quoniam natura absterruit auctum
nec potuere cupitum aetatis tangere florem
nec reperire cibum nec iungi per Veneris res.
multa videmus enim rebus concurrere debere,
ut propagando possint procudere saecla;   850
pabula primum ut sint, genitalia deinde per artus
semina qua possint membris manare remissis;
feminaque ut maribus coniungi possit, habere
mutua qui mutent inter se gaudia uterque.

Multaque tum interiisse animantum saecla necessest   855
nec potuisse propagando procudere prolem.
nam quaecumque vides vesci vitalibus auris,
aut dolus aut virtus aut denique mobilitas est
ex ineunte aevo genus id tutata reservans.
multaque sunt, nobis ex utilitate sua quae   860
commendata manent, tutelae tradita nostrae.
principio genus acre leonum saevaque saecla
tutatast virtus, vulpis dolus et fuga cervos.
at levisomna canum fido cum pectore corda
et genus omne quod est veterino semine partum   865
lanigeraeque simul pecudes et bucera saecla
omnia sunt hominum tutelae tradita, Memmi.

839 androgynum interutraque nec utrum, utrimque *Lachmann* (interutrasque *Munro*): androgynem inter utras nec utramque utrumque *Q* (ut utrunque *O*)   841 muta *Naugerius*: multa *OQ*   844 foret *Lambinus*: uolet *OQ*   846 absterruit *Ital.*: abserruit *O*: abseruit *Q*   850 procudere *Ital.*: procludere *OQ*   852 remissis] remissa *Lachmann*   853 maribus *Ital.*: marius *OQ*   854 mutent *Bernays*: metuent *OQ*   859 tutata *ed. Brixiensis*: tuta *OQ*   863 et *Q*: ut *O*   865 veterino *Nonius*: ueteri non *OQ*

nam cupide fugere feras pacemque secuta
sunt et larga suo sine pabula parta labore,
quae damus utilitatis eorum praemia causa.					870
at quis nil horum tribuit natura, nec ipsa
sponte sua possent ut vivere nec dare nobis
utilitatem aliquam quare pateremur eorum
praesidio nostro pasci genus esseque tutum,
scilicet haec aliis praedae lucroque iacebant					875
indupedita suis fatalibus omnia vinclis,
donec ad interitum genus id natura redegit.

   Sed neque Centauri fuerunt, nec tempore in ullo
esse queunt duplici natura et corpore bino
ex alienigenis membris compacta, potestas					880
hinc illinc par, vis ut sat par esse potissit.
id licet hinc quamvis hebeti cognoscere corde.
principio circum tribus actis impiger annis
floret equus, puer haudquaquam ; nam saepe etiam nunc
ubera mammarum in somnis lactantia quaeret.					885
post ubi equum validae vires aetate senecta
membraque deficiunt fugienti languida vita,
tum demum puerili aevo florente iuventas
occipit et molli vestit lanugine malas.
ne forte ex homine et veterino semine equorum					890
confieri credas Centauros posse neque esse,
aut rabidis canibus succinctas semimarinis
corporibus Scyllas et cetera de genere horum,
inter se quorum discordia membra videmus ;
quae neque florescunt pariter nec robora sumunt					895
corporibus neque proiciunt aetate senecta
nec simili Venere ardescunt nec moribus unis
conveniunt, neque sunt eadem iucunda per artus.

---

   868 secuta *Lambinus* : secutae *OQ*			871 nil *Pontanus* : ni *O* :
in *Q*			881 par, vis ut sat par *Giussani* : paruis ut non sit pars *O*
(sat *Q*) : partis ut si par *Lachmann* : visque ut non sat par *Munro* :
alii alia			884 nam *Q* : om. *O*			885 lactantia *l 31* : laetantia
OQ			888 puerili] pueris *Avancius*			889 occipit *Marullus* : officit
OQ : sufficit *Merrill*			892 rabidis *Heinsius* : rapidis *OQ*			896
proiciunt *Turnebus* : proficiunt *OQ*

quippe videre licet pinguescere saepe cicuta
barbigeras pecudes, homini quae est acre venenum. 900
flamma quidem ⟨vero⟩ cum corpora fulva leonum
tam soleat torrere atque urere quam genus omne
visceris in terris quodcumque et sanguinis exstet,
qui fieri potuit, triplici cum corpore ut una,
prima leo, postrema draco, media ipsa, Chimaera 905
ore foras acrem flaret de corpore flammam?
quare etiam tellure nova caeloque recenti
talia qui fingit potuisse animalia gigni,
nixus in hoc uno novitatis nomine inani,
multa licet simili ratione effutiat ore, 910
aurea tum dicat per terras flumina vulgo
fluxisse et gemmis florere arbusta suesse
aut hominem tanto membrorum esse impete natum,
trans maria alta pedum nisus ut ponere posset
et manibus totum circum se vertere caelum. 915
nam quod multa fuere in terris semina rerum
tempore quo primum tellus animalia fudit,
nil tamen est signi mixtas potuisse creari
inter se pecudes compactaque membra animantum,
propterea quia quae de terris nunc quoque abundant 920
herbarum genera ac fruges arbustaque laeta
non tamen inter se possunt complexa creari,
sed res quaeque suo ritu procedit et omnes
foedere naturae certo discrimina servant.

At genus humanum multo fuit illud in arvis 925
durius, ut decuit, tellus quod dura creasset,
et maioribus et solidis magis ossibus intus
fundatum, validis aptum per viscera nervis,
nec facile ex aestu nec frigore quod caperetur
nec novitate cibi nec labi corporis ulla. 930

---

901 vero *add. ed. Juntina,* denique *ante* flamma *Lachmann* 904
una *ed. Brixiensis* : unam *OQ*   906 foras *Naugerius:* feras *OQ* 914
ponere *Q corr.* : pondere *OQ*   923 res *Munro:* si *OQ* : vis *Lachmann* : sibi *Merrill*   925 at *Lachmann* : et *OQ*

multaque per caelum solis volventia lustra
vulgivago vitam tractabant more ferarum.
nec robustus erat curvi moderator aratri
quisquam, nec scibat ferro molirier arva
nec nova defodere in terram virgulta neque altis   935
arboribus veteres decidere falcibu' ramos.
quod sol atque imbres dederant, quod terra crearat
sponte sua, satis id placabat pectora donum.
glandiferas inter curabant corpora quercus
plerumque; et quae nunc hiberno tempore cernis   940
arbuta puniceo fieri matura colore,
plurima tum tellus etiam maiora ferebat.
multaque praeterea novitas tum florida mundi
pabula dura tulit, miseris mortalibus ampla.
at sedare sitim fluvii fontesque vocabant,   945
ut nunc montibus e magnis decursus aquai
claru' citat late sitientia saecla ferarum.
denique nota vagi silvestria templa tenebant
nympharum, quibus e scibant umori' fluenta
lubrica proluvie larga lavere umida saxa,   950
umida saxa, super viridi stillantia musco,
et partim plano scatere atque erumpere campo.
necdum res igni scibant tractare neque uti
pellibus et spoliis corpus vestire ferarum,
sed nemora atque cavos montis silvasque colebant   955
et frutices inter condebant squalida membra
verbera ventorum vitare imbrisque coacti.
nec commune bonum poterant spectare neque ullis
moribus inter se scibant nec legibus uti.
quod cuique obtulerat praedae fortuna, ferebat   960
sponte sua sibi quisque valere et vivere doctus.

934 molirier *ed. Brixiensis* : mollerier *OQ* : mollirier *O corr.*   941
arbuta *O corr.* : aruita *OQ*   944 dura *Vat. 3276* : dira *OQ*   947
claru' citat *Forbiger* late *Bosius* : claricitati a te *OQ* : clarigitat late
Lachmann : *alii alia*   948 vagi *Lachmann* : uagis *OQ*   tenebant]
petebant *Brieger*   949 umori' *Bentley* : umore *OQ*

et Venus in silvis iungebat corpora amantum ;
conciliabat enim vel mutua quamque cupido
vel violenta viri vis atque impensa libido
vel pretium, glandes atque arbuta vel pira lecta.   965
et manuum mira freti virtute pedumque
consectabantur silvestria saecla ferarum
missilibus saxis et magno pondere clavae ;   [975]
multaque vincebant, vitabant pauca latebris ;   [968]
saetigerisque pares subus silvestria membra   970 [969]
nuda dabant terrae nocturno tempore capti,   [970]
circum se foliis ac frondibus involventes.   [971]
nec plangore diem magno solemque per agros   [972]
quaerebant pavidi palantes noctis in umbris,   [973]
sed taciti respectabant somnoque sepulti,   975 [974]
dum rosea face sol inferret lumina caelo.
a parvis quod enim consuerant cernere semper
alterno tenebras et lucem tempore gigni,
non erat ut fieri posset mirarier umquam
nec diffidere ne terras aeterna teneret   980
nox in perpetuum detracto lumine solis.
sed magis illud erat curae, quod saecla ferarum
infestam miseris faciebant saepe quietem.
eiectique domo fugiebant saxea tecta
spumigeri suis adventu validique leonis   985
atque intempesta cedebant nocte paventes
hospitibus saevis instrata cubilia fronde.

Nec nimio tum plus quam nunc mortalia saecla
dulcia linquebant lamentis lumina vitae.
unus enim tum quisque magis deprensus eorum   990
pabula viva feris praebebat, dentibus haustus,
et nemora ac montis gemitu silvasque replebat
viva videns vivo sepeliri viscera busto.

962 iungebat *L* : lugebat *O* : lucebat *Q*   968 [975] *huc trans-
posuit Naugerius*   970 subus] suibus *C*   971 nuda dabant *Lambinus* : nudabant *OQ*   976 rosea *l 31* : rotea *OQ*   979 posset]
possent *Brieger*   984 eiectique *l 31* : et lectique *O* : electique *Q*
989 lamentis] labentis *Muretus* : languentis *Merrill*   993 vivo *l 31* :
uino *OQ*

at quos effugium servarat corpore adeso,
posterius tremulas super ulcera taetra tenentes   995
palmas horriferis accibant vocibus Orcum,
donec eos vita privarant vermina saeva
expertis opis, ignaros quid vulnera vellent.
at non multa virum sub signis milia ducta
una dies dabat exitio nec turbida ponti   1000
aequora lidebant navis ad saxa virosque.
hic temere incassum frustra mare saepe coortum
saevibat leviterque minas ponebat inanis,
nec poterat quemquam placidi pellacia ponti
subdola pellicere in fraudem ridentibus undis.   1005
improba navigii ratio tum caeca iacebat.
tum penuria deinde cibi languentia leto
membra dabat, contra nunc rerum copia mersat.
illi imprudentes ipsi sibi saepe venenum
vergebant, nunc dant ⟨aliis⟩ sollertius ipsi.   1010
    Inde casas postquam ac pellis ignemque pararunt,
et mulier coniuncta viro concessit in unum

*

cognita sunt, prolemque ex se videre creatam,
tum genus humanum primum mollescere coepit.
ignis enim curavit ut alsia corpora frigus   1015
non ita iam possent caeli sub tegmine ferre,
et Venus imminuit viris puerique parentum
blanditiis facile ingenium fregere superbum.
tunc et amicitiem coeperunt iungere aventes
finitimi inter se nec laedere nec violari,   1020
et pueros commendarunt muliebreque saeclum,
vocibus et gestu cum balbe significarent

994 at] et *Brieger*   995 ulcera *l 31* : uicera *O* : uicerat *Q*   997
donec *Marullus* : denique *OQ*   1001 lidebant] ledebant *O corr.* :
laedebant *ed. Aldina*   1002 hic *Lachmann* : nec *OQ* : sed *Lambinus*   1003 ponebat *Marullus* : potebas *OQ*   1006 navigii]
navigiis *Bothe*   tum] cum *Munro*   1009 imprudentes *Marullus* :
prudentes *OQ*   1010 nunc dant aliis *ed. Juntina* : nudant *OQ* :
alii alia   1011 casas *l 31* : cassas *OQ*   1012 * 1013 *lacunam
indicavit Marullus*   1013 cognita sunt] conubium *Lachmann* : con-
iugium *Bernays*

imbecillorum esse aequum misererier omnis.
nec tamen omnimodis poterat concordia gigni,
sed bona magnaque pars servabat foedera caste;   1025
aut genus humanum iam tum foret omne peremptum
nec potuisset adhuc perducere saecla propago.

At varios linguae sonitus natura subegit
mittere et utilitas expressit nomina rerum,
non alia longe ratione atque ipsa videtur   1030
protrahere ad gestum pueros infantia linguae,
cum facit ut digito quae sint praesentia monstrent.
sentit enim vis quisque suas quoad possit abuti.
cornua nata prius vitulo quam frontibus exstent,
illis iratus petit atque infestus inurget.   1035
at catuli pantherarum scymnique leonum
unguibus ac pedibus iam tum morsuque repugnant,
vix etiam cum sunt dentes unguesque creati.
alituum porro genus alis omne videmus
fidere et a pinnis tremulum petere auxiliatum.   1040
proinde putare aliquem tum nomina distribuisse
rebus et inde homines didicisse vocabula prima,
desiperest. nam cur hic posset cuncta notare
vocibus et varios sonitus emittere linguae,
tempore eodem alii facere id non quisse putentur?   1045
praeterea si non alii quoque vocibus usi
inter se fuerant, unde insita notities est
utilitatis et unde data est huic prima potestas,
quid vellet facere ut sciret animoque videret?
cogere item pluris unus victosque domare   1050
non poterat, rerum ut perdiscere nomina vellent.
nec ratione docere ulla suadereque surdis,

1023 omnis *Marullus*: omni *OQ*   1025 caste *l 31*: casti *OQ*
1032 monstrent *Marullus*: monstret *OQ*   1033 vis] vim *ed.*
Brixiensis   suas *Müller*: suam *OQ*   quoad *Lambinus (in commen-*
tario): quod *OQ*   1035 infestus *Q*: infessus *O*   1038 etiam
Marullus: iam *O*: tiam *Q*   1039 porro *ed. Juntina*: proporro *OQ*
1040 pinnis *Q*: pennis *O*   1048 utilitatis *Marullus*: utilitas *OQ*

quid sit opus facto, facilest; neque enim paterentur
nec ratione ulla sibi ferrent amplius auris
vocis inauditos sonitus obtundere frustra.   1055
postremo quid in hac mirabile tantoperest re,
si genus humanum, cui vox et lingua vigeret,
pro vario sensu varia res voce notaret?
cum pecudes mutae, cum denique saecla ferarum
dissimilis soleant voces variasque ciere,   1060
cum metus aut dolor est et cum iam gaudia gliscunt.
quippe etenim licet id rebus cognoscere apertis.
irritata canum cum primum magna Molossum
mollia ricta fremunt duros nudantia dentis,
longe alio sonitu rabie restricta minantur,   1065
et cum iam latrant et vocibus omnia complent.
at catulos blande cum lingua lambere temptant
aut ubi eos iactant pedibus morsuque petentes
suspensis teneros imitantur dentibus haustus,
longe alio pacto gannitu vocis adulant,   1070
et cum deserti baubantur in aedibus aut cum
plorantes fugiunt summisso corpore plagas.
denique non hinnitus item differre videtur,
inter equas ubi equus florenti aetate iuvencus
pinnigeri saevit calcaribus ictus amoris   1075
et fremitum patulis sub naribus edit ad arma,
et cum sic alias concussis artubus hinnit?
postremo genus alituum variaeque volucres,
accipitres atque ossifragae mergique marinis
fluctibus in salso victum vitamque petentes,   1080
longe alias alio iaciunt in tempore voces,
et cum de victu certant praedaeque repugnant.

1053 facilest *Lachmann* : facile si *OQ*   1058 varia *Bentley* :
uarias *OQ*   1062 id *Gifanius* : in *OQ*   1064 fremunt *Marullus* :
premunt *OQ*   1065 alio *l 31* : alia *OQ*   restricta *Lachmann* :
stricta *OQ*   minantur *Pontanus* : minatur *OQ*   1067 at] et *Lachmann*   1068 iactant *Naugerius* : lactant *OQ*   petentes *l 31* :
potentes *OQ*   1071 deserti baubantur *L* : desertibus aubantur *OQ*
1072 plorantis *O corr.* : florantis *OQ*   1076 sub] ubi *Lachmann*
1082 praedaque *O corr. L* : predataque *OQ* : praedaeque *Avancius*

et partim mutant cum tempestatibus una
raucisonos cantus, cornicum ut saecla vetusta
corvorumque greges ubi aquam dicuntur et imbris   1085
poscere et interdum ventos aurasque vocare.
ergo si varii sensus animalia cogunt,
muta tamen cum sint, varias emittere voces,
quanto mortalis magis aequumst tum potuisse
dissimilis alia atque alia res voce notare!   1090
   Illud in his rebus tacitus ne forte requiras,
fulmen detulit in terram mortalibus ignem
primitus, inde omnis flammarum diditur ardor.
multa videmus enim caelestibus incita flammis
fulgere, cum caeli donavit plaga vapore.   1095
et ramosa tamen cum ventis pulsa vacillans
aestuat in ramos incumbens arboris arbor,
exprimitur validis extritus viribus ignis,
emicat interdum flammai fervidus ardor,
mutua dum inter se rami stirpesque teruntur.   1100
quorum utrumque dedisse potest mortalibus ignem.
inde cibum coquere ac flammae mollire vapore
sol docuit, quoniam mitescere multa videbant
verberibus radiorum atque aestu victa per agros.
   Inque dies magis hi victum vitamque priorem   1105
commutare novis monstrabant rebus et igni
ingenio qui praestabant et corde vigebant.
condere coeperunt urbis arcemque locare
praesidium reges ipsi sibi perfugiumque,
et pecus atque agros divisere atque dedere   1110
pro facie cuiusque et viribus ingenioque;
nam facies multum valuit viresque vigebant.
posterius res inventast aurumque repertum,

   1084 ut *Naugerius*: et *OQ*   1090 res *L*: re *OQ*   1091–1160 *uncinis incl. edd.*   1094 incita *Marullus*: insita *OQ*: inlita *Lachmann*
1095 vapore *Lachmann*: uaporis *OQ*   1096 et *Marullus*: ut *OQ*
1099 emicat] et micat *Marullus*   1105 hi victum *Naugerius*: inuictum *OQ*   1106 rebus et igni] rebu' benigni *Lachmann*: rebus et ipsi *Merrill*   1110 pecus *Lachmann*: pecudes *OQ*   1112
vigebant] vigentes *Faber*: vigorque *Lachmann*

quod facile et validis et pulchris dempsit honorem;
divitioris enim sectam plerumque sequuntur   1115
quamlibet et fortes et pulchro corpore creti.
quod siquis vera vitam ratione gubernet,
divitiae grandes homini sunt vivere parce
aequo animo; neque enim est umquam penuria parvi.
at claros homines voluerunt se atque potentis,   1120
ut fundamento stabili fortuna maneret
et placidam possent opulenti degere vitam,
nequiquam, quoniam ad summum succedere honorem
certantes iter infestum fecere viai,
et tamen e summo, quasi fulmen, deicit ictos   1125
invidia interdum contemptim in Tartara taetra;
invidia quoniam, ceu fulmine, summa vaporant   [1131]
plerumque et quae sunt aliis magis edita cumque;   [1132]
ut satius multo iam sit parere quietum   [1127]
quam regere imperio res velle et regna tenere. 1130 [1128]
proinde sine incassum defessi sanguine sudent,   [1129]
angustum per iter luctantes ambitionis;   [1130]
quandoquidem sapiunt alieno ex ore petuntque
res ex auditis potius quam sensibus ipsis,
nec magis id nunc est neque erit mox quam fuit ante.   1135
   Ergo regibus occisis subversa iacebat
pristina maiestas soliorum et sceptra superba,
et capitis summi praeclarum insigne cruentum
sub pedibus vulgi magnum lugebat honorem;
nam cupide conculcatur nimis ante metutum.   1140
res itaque ad summam faecem turbasque redibat,
imperium sibi cum ac summatum quisque petebat.
inde magistratum partim docuere creare
iuraque constituere, ut vellent legibus uti.

   1116 creti *l 31*: certi *OQ*   1122 placidam possent *Ital.*: placida
possunt *OQ*   1124 certantes iter *Marullus*: certantesque inter *O*
(*inter om. Q*)   1127–1132 *hunc versuum ordinem restituit Munro*
1128 [1132] aliis *Lambinus*: altis *OQ*   1141 redibat *l 31*: recidat *Q*:
recidit *O*   1142 petebat *O corr.*: patebat *OQ*

nam genus humanum, defessum vi colere aevum, 1145
ex inimicitiis languebat; quo magis ipsum
sponte sua cecidit sub leges artaque iura.
acrius ex ira quod enim se quisque parabat
ulcisci quam nunc concessumst legibus aequis,
hanc ob rem est homines pertaesum vi colere aevum. 1150
inde metus maculat poenarum praemia vitae.
circumretit enim vis atque iniuria quemque
atque, unde exortast, ad eum plerumque revertit,
nec facilest placidam ac pacatam degere vitam
qui violat factis communia foedera pacis. 1155
etsi fallit enim divum genus humanumque,
perpetuo tamen id fore clam diffidere debet;
quippe ubi se multi per somnia saepe loquentes
aut morbo delirantes protraxe ferantur
et celata ⟨diu⟩ in medium peccata dedisse. 1160
  Nunc quae causa deum per magnas numina gentis
pervulgarit et ararum compleverit urbis
suscipiendaque curarit sollemnia sacra,
quae nunc in magnis florent sacra rebu' locisque,
unde etiam nunc est mortalibus insitus horror 1165
qui delubra deum nova toto suscitat orbi
terrarum et festis cogit celebrare diebus,
non ita difficilest rationem reddere verbis.
quippe etenim iam tum divum mortalia saecla
egregias animo facies vigilante videbant 1170
et magis in somnis mirando corporis auctu.
his igitur sensum tribuebant propterea quod
membra movere videbantur vocesque superbas
mittere pro facie praeclara et viribus amplis.
aeternamque dabant vitam, quia semper eorum 1175
suppeditabatur facies et forma manebat,

1145 vi colere *l 31* : vicere *O* : vigere *Q* 1152 vis *C* : ius *OQ*
1160 diu *add. Marullus,* mala *Lachmann,* tot *Merrill* medium
et *OQ*: et *del. Marullus*

et tamen omnino quod tantis viribus auctos
non temere ulla vi convinci posse putabant.
fortunisque ideo ionge praestare putabant,
quod mortis timor haud quemquam vexaret eorum,   1180
et simul in somnis quia multa et mira videbant
efficere et nullum capere ipsos inde laborem.
praeterea caeli rationes ordine certo
et varia annorum cernebant tempora verti
nec poterant quibus id fieret cognoscere causis.   1185
ergo perfugium sibi habebant omnia divis
tradere et illorum nutu facere omnia flecti.
in caeloque deum sedis et templa locarunt,
per caelum volvi quia nox et luna videtur,
luna dies et nox et noctis signa severa   1190
noctivagaeque faces caeli flammaeque volantes,
nubila sol imbres nix venti fulmina grando
et rapidi fremitus et murmura magna minarum.
   O genus infelix humanum, talia divis
cum tribuit facta atque iras adiunxit acerbas!   1195
quantos tum gemitus ipsi sibi, quantaque nobis
vulnera, quas lacrimas peperere minoribu' nostris!
nec pietas ullast velatum saepe videri
vertier ad lapidem atque omnis accedere ad aras
nec procumbere humi prostratum et pandere palmas   1200
ante deum delubra nec aras sanguine multo
spargere quadrupedum nec votis nectere vota,
sed mage pacata posse omnia mente tueri.
nam cum suspicimus magni caelestia mundi
templa super stellisque micantibus aethera fixum,   1205
et venit in mentem solis lunaeque viarum,
tunc aliis oppressa malis in pectora cura
illa quoque expergefactum caput erigere infit,

1178 ulla *ed. Brixiensis* : illa *OQ*   1184 varia *Ital.* : uarias *OQ*
1189 nox] sol *Lambinus* : lux *Lachmann*   1198 ullast velatum *Lactantius* : ulla velatumst *OQ*   1203 pacata *ed. Juntina* : placata *OQ*

nequae forte deum nobis immensa potestas
sit, vario motu quae candida sidera verset.   1210
temptat enim dubiam mentem rationis egestas,
ecquaenam fuerit mundi genitalis origo,
et simul ecquae sit finis, quoad moenia mundi
solliciti motus hunc possint ferre laborem,
an divinitus aeterna donata salute   1215
perpetuo possint aevi labentia tractu
immensi validas aevi contemnere viris.
praeterea cui non animus formidine divum
contrahitur, cui non correpunt membra pavore,
fulminis horribili cum plaga torrida tellus   1220
contremit et magnum percurrunt murmura caelum?
non populi gentesque tremunt, regesque superbi
corripiunt divum percussi membra timore,
nequid ob admissum foede dictumve superbe
poenarum grave sit solvendi tempus adactum?   1225
summa etiam cum vis violenti per mare venti
induperatorem classis super aequora verrit
cum validis pariter legionibus atque elephantis,
non divum pacem votis adit ac prece quaesit
ventorum pavidus paces animasque secundas,   1230
nequiquam, quoniam violento turbine saepe
correptus nilo fertur minus ad vada leti?
usque adeo res humanas vis abdita quaedam
obterit et pulchros fascis saevasque securis
proculcare ac ludibrio sibi habere videtur.   1235
denique sub pedibus tellus cum tota vacillat
concussaeque cadunt urbes dubiaeque minantur,
quid mirum si se temnunt mortalia saecla
atque potestates magnas mirasque relinquunt
in rebus viris divum, quae cuncta gubernent?   1240

1214 solliciti *Bentley*: et taciti *OQ*   1220 fulminis *Marullus*:
fulmini *OQ*   1224 nequid *Lachmann*: nequod *OQ*   1225 adultum
Lachmann: adauctum *OQ*: adactum *Pontanus*   1226 summa *l 31*:
summe *O*: summet *Q*   1229 adit ac prece *l 31*: adita prece *O*
(praece *Q*)

Quod superest, aes atque aurum ferrumque repertumst
et simul argenti pondus plumbique potestas,
ignis ubi ingentis silvas ardore cremarat
montibus in magnis, seu caeli fulmine misso,
sive quod inter se bellum silvestre gerentes   1245
hostibus intulerant ignem formidinis ergo,
sive quod inducti terrae bonitate volebant
pandere agros pinguis et pascua reddere rura,
sive feras interficere et ditescere praeda.
nam fovea atque igni prius est venarier ortum   1250
quam saepire plagis saltum canibusque ciere.
quidquid id est, quacumque e causa flammeus ardor
horribili sonitu silvas exederat altis
ab radicibus et terram percoxerat igni,
manabat venis ferventibus in loca terrae   1255
concava conveniens argenti rivus et auri,
aeris item et plumbi. quae cum concreta videbant
posterius claro in terra splendere colore,
tollebant nitido capti levique lepore,
et simili formata videbant esse figura   1260
atque lacunarum fuerant vestigia cuique.
tum penetrabat eos posse haec liquefacta calore
quamlibet in formam et faciem decurrere rerum
et prorsum quamvis in acuta ac tenvia posse
mucronum duci fastigia procudendo,   1265
ut sibi tela parent, silvasque ut caedere possint
materiemque dolare et levia radere tigna
et terebrare etiam ac pertundere perque forare.
nec minus argento facere haec auroque parabant
quam validi primum violentis viribus aeris,   1270
nequiquam, quoniam cedebat victa potestas,

1241 aes atque *Marullus* : aeque *OQ*   1243 ingentis *Ital.* :
gentis *OQ*   1244 caeli *Q* : caelo *O*   1253 altis *O corr.* : ? alas *O* :
altas *Q*   1254 ab ed. *Juntina* : a *OQ*   1258 terra *Lachmann* :
terras *OQ* : terris *Lambinus*   1259 capti *I 31* : capiti *OQ*   1260
videbant *Ital.* : uidebat *OQ*   1266 ut *Lachmann* : et *OQ*   1267
dolare et levia *Marullus* : dolaret levare ac *OQ* : *alii alia*

nec poterant pariter durum sufferre laborem.
nam fuit in pretio magis ⟨aes⟩ aurumque iacebat
propter inutilitatem hebeti mucrone retusum.
nunc iacet aes, aurum in summum successit honorem.   1275
sic volvenda aetas commutat tempora rerum.
quod fuit in pretio, fit nullo denique honore;
porro aliud succedit et ⟨e⟩ contemptibus exit
inque dies magis appetitur floretque repertum
laudibus et miro est mortalis inter honore.   1280
    Nunc tibi quo pacto ferri natura reperta
sit facilest ipsi per te cognoscere, Memmi.
arma antiqua manus ungues dentesque fuerunt
et lapides et item silvarum fragmina rami,
et flamma atque ignes, postquam sunt cognita primum.   1285
posterius ferri vis est aerisque reperta.
et prior aeris erat quam ferri cognitus usus,
quo facilis magis est natura et copia maior.
aere solum terrae tractabant, aereque belli
miscebant fluctus et vulnera vasta serebant   1290
et pecus atque agros adimebant. nam facile ollis
omnia cedebant armatis nuda et inerma.
inde minutatim processit ferreus ensis
versaque in opprobrium species est falcis aenae,
et ferro coepere solum proscindere terrae   1295
exaequataque sunt creperi certamina belli.
et prius est armatum in equi conscendere costas
et moderarier hunc frenis dextraque vigere
quam biiugo curru belli temptare pericla.
et biiugos prius est quam bis coniungere binos   1300
et quam falciferos armatum escendere currus.
inde boves lucas turrito corpore, taetras,
anguimanus, belli docuerunt vulnera Poeni

    1272 poterant] poterat *Lambinus*   1273 nam] tum *Lachmann*
aes *add. l. 31*   1278 e *add. ed. Brixiensis*   1285 flamma atque
Q corr. : flammatque *OQ*   1294 ahenac *Ital.* : athenae *O* : athene *Q*
1300 biiugos *Faber* : biiugo *OQ*   1302 lucas *Q corr.* : cas *OQ*
taetras *Lachmann* : tetras *OQ*

sufferre et magnas Martis turbare catervas.
sic alid ex alio peperit discordia tristis,　　　　　　1305
horribile humanis quod gentibus esset in armis,
inque dies belli terroribus addidit augmen.
　Temptarunt etiam tauros in moenere belli
expertique sues saevos sunt mittere in hostis.
et validos partim prae se misere leones　　　　　　1310
cum doctoribus armatis saevisque magistris
qui moderarier his possent vinclisque tenere,
nequiquam, quoniam permixta caede calentes
turbabant saevi nullo discrimine turmas,
terrificas capitum quatientes undique cristas,　　　1315
nec poterant equites fremitu perterrita equorum
pectora mulcere et frenis convertere in hostis.
irritata leae iaciebant corpora saltu
undique et adversum venientibus ora petebant
et nec opinantis a tergo deripiebant　　　　　　　1320
deplexaeque dabant in terram vulnere victos,
morsibus adfixae validis atque unguibus uncis.
iactabantque suos tauri pedibusque terebant
et latera ac ventris hauribant subter equorum
cornibus et terram minitanti mente ruebant.　　　1325
et validis socios caedebant dentibus apri
tela infracta suo tingentes sanguine saevi,
permixtasque dabant equitum peditumque ruinas.　1329
nam transversa feros exibant dentis adactus　　　1330
iumenta aut pedibus ventos erecta petebant,
nequiquam, quoniam ab nervis succisa videres
concidere atque gravi terram consternere casu.
siquos ante domi domitos satis esse putabant,
effervescere cernebant in rebus agundis　　　　　1335

1307 belli *Ital.* : bellis *OQ*　　1310 partim] Parthi *C*　　1319 petebant *Vat. 640*: patebant *OQ*　　1320 deripiebant *O* : diripiebant *Q*
1323 suos] sues *Q corr.*　　1325 mente] fronte *Lachmann*　　1328
in se fracta suo tinguentes sanguine tela *om. Mon.*　　1330 dentis
adactus *Marullus* : dentis adauctus *Q* : dentibus adauctus *O*

vulneribus clamore fuga terrore tumultu,
nec poterant ullam partem redducere eorum;
diffugiebat enim varium genus omne ferarum;
ut nunc saepe boves lucae ferro male mactae
diffugiunt, fera facta suis cum multa dedere.   1340
si fuit ut facerent. sed vix adducor ut, ante
quam commune malum fieret foedumque, futurum   [1343]
non quierint animo praesentire atque videre;   [1342]
et magis id possis factum contendere in omni,
in variis mundis varia ratione creatis,   1345
quam certo atque uno terrarum quolibet orbi.
sed facere id non tam vincendi spe voluerunt,
quam dare quod gemerent hostes, ipsique perire,
qui numero diffidebant armisque vacabant.

Nexilis ante fuit vestis quam textile tegmen.   1350
textile post ferrumst, quia ferro tela paratur,
nec ratione alia possunt tam levia gigni
insilia ac fusi radii scapique sonantes.
et facere ante viros lanam natura coegit
quam muliebre genus; nam longe praestat in arte   1355
et sollertius est multo genus omne virile;
agricolae donec vitio vertere severi,
ut muliebribus id manibus concedere vellent
atque ipsi pariter durum sufferre laborem
atque opere in duro durarent membra manusque.   1360
At specimen sationis et insitionis origo
ipsa fuit rerum primum natura creatrix,
arboribus quoniam bacae glandesque caducae
tempestiva dabant pullorum examina subter;
unde etiam libitumst stirpis committere ramis   1365
et nova defodere in terram virgulta per agros.
inde aliam atque aliam culturam dulcis agelli

1340 facta] fata *Q corr.*   1341-6 *secl. Munro*, 1344-6 *Lachmann*
1343 *ante* 1342 *posuit Lachmann*   1361 at *Q corr.* : a *OQ*

temptabant fructusque feros mansuescere terra
cernebant indulgendo blandeque colendo.
inque dies magis in montem succedere silvas   1370
cogebant infraque locum concedere cultis,
prata lacus rivos segetes vinetaque laeta
collibus et campis ut haberent, atque olearum
caerula distinguens inter plaga currere posset
per tumulos et convallis camposque profusa;   1375
ut nunc esse vides vario distincta lepore
omnia, quae pomis intersita dulcibus ornant
arbustisque tenent felicibus obsita circum.

At liquidas avium voces imitarier ore
ante fuit multo quam levia carmina cantu   1380
concelebrare homines possent aurisque iuvare.
et zephyri, cava per calamorum, sibila primum
agrestis docuere cavas inflare cicutas.
inde minutatim dulcis didicere querelas,
tibia quas fundit digitis pulsata canentum,   1385
avia per nemora ac silvas saltusque reperta,
per loca pastorum deserta atque otia dia.
haec animos ollis mulcebant atque iuvabant   1390
cum satiate cibi; nam tum sunt omnia cordi.
saepe itaque inter se prostrati in gramine molli
propter aquae rivum sub ramis arboris altae
non magnis opibus iucunde corpora habebant,
praesertim cum tempestas ridebat et anni   1395
tempora pingebant viridantis floribus herbas.
tum ioca, tum sermo, tum dulces esse cachinni
consuerant. agrestis enim tum musa vigebat;
tum caput atque umeros plexis redimire coronis
floribus et foliis lascivia laeta monebat,   1400
atque extra numerum procedere membra moventis

1368 terra] terram *Lachmann*   1386 reperta] repertas *Bockemüller: alii alia*   1388-1389 = 1454, 1455 ^seci. *Lachmann*
1391 *post* tum *Lambinus* haec *inseruit*   omnia]otia *Faber*: carmina
Lachmann   1393 propter aquae *O corr.*: proptereaque *OQ*   1397
ioca *l 31*: loca *OQ*   1400 monebat *l 31*: mouebat *OQ*

duriter et duro terram pede pellere matrem ;
unde oriebantur risus dulcesque cachinni,
omnia quod nova tum magis haec et mira vigebant.
et vigilantibus hinc aderant solacia somno,　　　　　1405
ducere multimodis voces et flectere cantus
et supera calamos unco percurrere labro ;
unde etiam vigiles nunc haec accepta tuentur
et numerum servare genus didicere, neque hilo
maiorem interea capiunt dulcedini' fructum　　　　　1410
quam silvestre genus capiebat terrigenarum.
nam quod adest praesto, nisi quid cognovimus ante
suavius, in primis placet et pollere videtur,
posteriorque fere melior res illa reperta
perdit et immutat sensus ad pristina quaeque.　　　　1415
sic odium coepit glandis, sic illa relicta
strata cubilia sunt herbis et frondibus aucta.
pellis item cecidit vestis contempta ferinae ;
quam reor invidia tali tunc esse repertam,
ut letum insidiis qui gessit primus obiret,　　　　　1420
et tamen inter eos distractam sanguine multo
disperiisse neque in fructum convertere quisse.
tunc igitur pelles, nunc aurum et purpura curis
exercent hominum vitam belloque fatigant ;
quo magis in nobis, ut opinor, culpa resedit.　　　　1425
frigus enim nudos sine pellibus excruciabat
terrigenas ; at nos nil laedit veste carere
purpurea atque auro signisque ingentibus apta,
dum plebeia tamen sit quae defendere possit.
ergo hominum genus incassum frustraque laborat　　　1430
semper et ⟨in⟩ curis consumit inanibus aevum,
nimirum quia non cognovit quae sit habendi

1405 somno] somni *Lambinus*　　　1409 genus] sonis *Lachmann* :
recens *Munro* : genis *Everett*　　　1410 maiorem *l 31* : maiore *OQ*
dulcedini' *Lambinus* : dulcedine *OQ*　　　1418 ferinae *ed. Juntina* :
ferina *OQ*　　　1419 tunc *editio Brixiensis* : nunc *OQ*　　　1428 ingentibus]
rigentibus *Jortin (apud Wakefield)*　　　1431 in *add. l 31*

finis et omnino quoad crescat vera voluptas.
idque minutatim vitam provexit in altum
et belli magnos commovit funditus aestus.   1435
  At vigiles mundi magnum versatile templum
sol et luna suo lustrantes lumine circum
perdocuere homines annorum tempora verti
et certa ratione geri rem atque ordine certo.
  Iam validis saepti degebant turribus aevum   1440
et divisa colebatur discretaque tellus ;
tum mare velivolis florebat †propter odores†
auxilia ac socios iam pacto foedere habebant,
carminibus cum res gestas coepere poetae
tradere ; nec multo priu' sunt elementa reperta.   1445
propterea quid sit prius actum respicere aetas
nostra nequit, nisi qua ratio vestigia monstrat.
  Navigia atque agri culturas moenia leges
arma vias vestis ⟨et⟩ cetera de genere horum,
praemia, delicias quoque vitae funditus omnis,   1450
carmina picturas, et daedala signa polire,
usus et impigrae simul experientia mentis
paulatim docuit pedetemptim progredientis.
sic unumquicquid paulatim protrahit aetas
in medium ratioque in luminis erigit oras.   1455
namque alid ex alio clarescere corde videbant,
artibus ad summum donec venere cacumen.

1442 tum] iam *Lachmann*   propter odores *OQ*: puppibus et res
Lachmann : puppibus ; urbes *Munro* : *alii alia*   1449 et add *l jı*
1451 polire *l jı* : polito *OQ*   1456 corde videbant] conveniebat
Lachmann : et ordine debet *Munro* : cordi' videbant *Polle*

COMMENTARY

The introduction to Book 5 (1–90) falls into two sections: a eulogy of
Epicurus (1–54) and an outline of the plan of the book (55–90).

1–54. Epicurus. There are four extended panegyrics of Epicurus in the
DRN (1.63–101, 3.1–30, 5.1–54, 6.1–42): they serve to give intensity and elevation to the openings of the books in which they occur
and to remind the reader of the continued personal dominance of
the master in subsequent Epicureanism and of L.'s unswerving
devotion to him. Common to all four eulogies is the claim that
Epicurus first brought salvation to men (9n.): this passage is distinctive in claiming divinity for him and asserting that the blessings he
brought are superior to the gifts of Ceres and Bacchus and the feats
of Hercules. Thus the Epicurean removal of ignorance and fear is
elevated far above the so-called essentials corn and wine and the
fame of the (significantly Stoic) hero Hercules. (For further discussion on this proem see D. E. W. Wormell *ap.* Dudley, 47–8.)

1. quis potis . . .: L. echoes Ennius *Ann.* 174V 'quis potis ingentes oras
evolvere belli?' He had a very high regard for 'Ennius noster' (see
1.117–19), and there is abundant evidence in the *DRN* of the older
poet's influence on L.'s poetic diction and verbal technique in
general: see Merrill, *Parallels and Coincidences in Lucretius and
Ennius*, Berkeley, 1918; O. Gigon in *Entretiens Fondation Hardt*,
xxiv, 1977, 167–96.

   dignum: to be taken either absolutely or loosely attached to
pro, as *laudes/pro* are similarly linked in the parallel lines 3–4.

   pectore: regularly the seat of the intellect, as at 5 below: see *OLD*
s.v. 3b.

2. rerum: 'nature' or 'the world', and the subject-matter of the *carmen*.

   maiestate hisque: Lambinus's generally accepted correction
(*maiestatis atque* OQ), *his* being an oblique reference to Epicurus,
like 'eius' 4, 'virum' 6.5. Epicurus is named only once in the whole
poem, at 3.1042.

3. valet verbis tantum: 'has such power of language'.

5. parta . . . quaesita: the sentence, like many cases of so-called ὕστερον
πρότερον, puts the dominant idea first (131 n.): 'won by hard
mental searching'.

6. A blunt end-stopped reply to what sounded like rhetorical questions.
   corpore cretus is a favourite Lucretian phrase, e.g. below 60, 1116.

   These lines incensed Lactantius (*Inst.* 3.14), who quotes 6–8 and
50–1 ('nonne decebit . . . dignarier esse?') and takes L. to task for

deifying Epicurus. He adds however: 'verum potest ut poetae dari venia.'

7. **sī ut:** hiatus and syllable-shortening in thesis or the unaccented part of the metrical foot: more commonly with a relative word (e.g. 74 below), but elsewhere with *si* at 4.1061, 6.796 (Bailey, i, 128).

cognita: 'known' through Epicurus. The grandeur, *maiestas*, of our knowledge of the world reflects the grandeur of the world itself (2).

8. **deus ille . . . deus:** cf. 51. Epicurus is deified as the εὑρετής of discoveries that bring freedom from human misery. So the Epicurean Velleius in Cic. *ND* 1.43 speaks of venerating (*venerari*) Epicurus, though the expositor in *Tusc.* 1.48 criticizes the practice of regarding as divine a leader of scientific inquiry. Epicurus himself encouraged the identification of divinity with the philosophic life: *Ep. Men.* 135 ζήσεις δὲ ὡς θεὸς ἐν ἀνθρώποις; and in Diogenes of Oenoanda (fr. 52 IV 2-3 Chilton) the writer tells his mother of his 'godlike condition'. The claim was not new, and Epicurus might have pointed to Empedocles who had boasted ἐγὼ δ' ὑμῖν θεὸς ἄμβροτος, οὐκέτι θνητός/πωλεῦμαι (B112.4-5 D-K). See further Kenney, *DRN* 3, pp. 1-2.

Virgil seems to remember the line at *E.* 5.64 'deus, deus ille, Menalca'.

inclute: Memmius is in good company: the epithet is applied elsewhere by L. only to Venus 1.40 and Epicurus 3.10. Memmius is named more often (five times) in this book than in any other, but it is scarcely to be regarded as more personally addressed to him than the others. (On the frequency of addresses to Memmius in the six books see G. B. Townend, *CQ* 28 (1978), 267 ff.)

9. **princeps:** so *primum* 1.66, *primus* 3.2, *primae* (*Athenae*, i.e. Epicurus) 6.4: though Epicurus did not invent atomic physics he first drew from it the ethical inferences which free men from fear, and so propounded the first philosophy worthy of the name, – a practical philosophy of *living* (*vitae rationem*).

10. **sapientia:** σοφία, 'philosophy' – but not used again by L.

per artem: τέχνη, 'by his technical skill', 'scientific method'.

11-12. A good example of Lucretian *ars*, with the staccato *t*s and sibilants of 11 succeeded by the peaceful vowels and liquids of 12. The two images of darkness/light and storm/calm are here powerfully combined. Both occur elsewhere: for the darkness of ignorance and fear see 2.15, 3.1, and for the storm see the opening passage of Book 2. The latter seems to have been a favourite metaphor with Epicurus, e.g. *Ep. Men.* 128 (without pain and fear λύεται πᾶς ὁ τῆς ψυχῆς χειμών), *Ep. Hdt.* 83 (the use of the word γαληνισμός for peace of mind), Usener 544 τἀγαθὸν ἐν τῷ βαθυτάτῳ τῆς ἡσυχίας ὥσπερ ἐν ἀκλύστῳ λιμένι καὶ κωφῷ τιθέμενος. See too Cic. *Tusc.* 5.16 and

M. F. Smith in *CR* 16 (1966), 265.

13-14. divina . . . antiqua reperta: the use of two adjectives without *et* or an equivalent is a mannerism of L. and a characteristic of early Latin poetry: Hofmann–Szantyr, 160–1: Munro has an extensive list of examples.

    enim/namque: not an inelegant repetition: *namque* (καὶ γάρ, 'for instance') has its common function of introducing *exempla* or precedents, here the frequently coupled Ceres and Liber.

14-15. liquoris vitigeni laticem: a similar periphrasis for 'wine' at 6.1072, these being the only extant occurrences of *vitigenus* (for the unmetrical *vitigeneus* – and L. is fond of *-gen-* compounds). Here there may be a parody of priestly cult titles as L. is deflating the alleged achievements of mythological benefactors (West, 28).

16-17. Varro expressed the more usual view: '. . . Cererem et Liberum, quod horum fructus maxime necessari ad victum' (*RR* 1.1.5), but editors quote Caesar (*BG* 6.22.1) on the Germans whose diet was predominantly milk, cheese, and meat.

18. This paraphrases a famous dictum of Epicurus: οὐκ ἔστιν ἡδέως ζῆν ἄνευ τοῦ φρονίμως καὶ καλῶς καὶ δικαίως (Κ.Δ.5 = *Ep. Men.* 132). It was much quoted, e.g. Cic. *Tusc.* 3.49, *Fin.* 1.57, and the Epicurean concept of the pleasant life was the focus of attack in one of Plutarch's anti-Epicurean pieces, *Moralia* 1086C ff. L.'s *vita/bene vivi* (ζῆν/εὖ ζῆν) is a stock contrast: cf. Sen. *Ep.* 90.1: 'quis dubitare . . . potest quin deorum inmortalium munus sit quod vivimus, philosophiae quod bene vivimus?'

    poterat: the idiomatic use of the imperfect for present, as at 2.1035 'quid magis his rebus poterat mirabile dici': see K-S i, 173.

    puro: 'clean' i.e. untainted by fear and wrong desire, the same sense as in the stronger phrase *purgatum pectus* 43, *purgavit pectora* 6.24; cf. too *voluptatem puram* 3.40.

21. dulcia . . . solacia vitae: the phrase (again at 6.4) could be the poem's motto, and *vitae* must be interpreted 'life with its fears and problems'.

22 ff. There is special point in singling out Hercules' exploits for derisive treatment as he was an ideal saviour-hero of the Stoics and other moralists. Why should we be impressed by the victories of this muscleman over monsters which would be no threat to us even if he had not disposed of them? All that pales into insignificance when compared with Epicurus' victory over fear in the human heart (43 ff.). It is a sardonic passage, with the labours of Hercules ironically described in turgid and inflated language: *Nemeaeus magnus hiatus* 24, *venenatis vallata colubris* 27, *tripectora tergemini vis Geryonai* 28, and so on: cf. 14–15 n. As Merrill points out the eight labours singled out involved the more obviously dangerous 'threats' to mankind. The series of questions beginning with *quid* 24 is finally answered bluntly and unequivocally with *nil, ut opinor* 39. Then at 43 ff., balancing the list of unreal dangers conquered by Hercules, there follows a list of the genuine cares, fears, and vices that would bedevil mankind untaught by Epicurus.

22. antistare: 'excel' (sc. the *facta* of Epicurus).

    autem: 'again', 'moreover'.

23. ratione: 'insight', 'reasoning': *vera ratio* often suggests more or less pointedly, the Epicurean philosophy (cf. 1117).

24–5. Nemeaeus . . . hiatus . . . leonis: the mannered hypallage is part of the mock-inflated flavour of the passage and reflects Homeric phrases like Γοργείη κεφαλὴ δεινοῖο πελώρου (*Il.* 5.741), though L. is fond of the mannerism elsewhere without intending parody (e.g. 1.10, 474; 2.501: Bailey, i, 144).

    -us sus: the jingle may be another deflating effect (like Horace's famous 'ridiculus mus' *Ars* 139), though in itself the monosyllabic line-ending is fairly common in L. and usually not significant.

26. denique: 'again', 'furthermore'.

27. vallata: 'palisaded', 'fenced': a striking image. The Senecan *Herc. Oet.* recalls L.'s gaping Nemean lion and serpent-girdled hydra, 'utinam meo cruore satiasset suos / Nemeaea rictus pestis aut centum anguibus / vallatus hydram tabe pavissem mea' 1192–94 (cf. too 1789–90 with 31 below). See also *Ciris* 79 for another possible echo.

28. tripectora: a ἅπαξ λεγόμενον probably coined by L., as Virgil coined *tricorpor*, also for Geryon (see Austin on *A.* 6.289).

    t. t. vis Geryonai: an elaborate example of the periphrasis *vis* + genitive often found in L., 'the mighty so-and-so': below 397 *rapax vis equorum, fortis equi vis* 3.8, *promissa canum vis* 4.681. It is a feature of early Latin and reflects the Greek ἴς or βία + genitive. L. is also fond of the impressive effect of a single five-syllabled word (Gēr̆y̆ōnāī) occupying the last two feet of the line (so *materiai, militiai*, and others: see Bailey, i, 114 ff).

29–31. A vexed and much discussed passage. The tradition has:

> et Diomedis equi spirantes naribus ignem   29
> tanto opere officerent nobis Stymphala colentes   30
> Thracia Bistoniasque plagas atque Ismara propter   31

It is universally agreed that 30 must be misplaced as it interrupts the references to Thrace in 29 and 31, and it is generally agreed that the dislocation also involves the loss of a line. For an account of earlier attempts to deal with the problem see Bailey's note. The best suggestions are: (1) transpose 29 and 30 (Munro, assuming a preceding lost line, e.g. 'quid volucres pennis aeratis invia stagna'); (2) put 30 after 25, whether or not there is a lacuna between them (Büchner, *Hermes* 84 (1956), 230–1, D. A. West, *Hermes* 93 (1965), 499–502). It seems certain that something is lost before 30 (the alternative to assuming that is to make a gratuitous emendation in 30 to fill out its meaning, like Lachmann's *et aves* for *nobis*), and the accidental inversion of 29-30 is the simplest diagnosis of the trouble. The OCT follows Munro: in any case his correction *Thracis* (with *Diomedis*) must be regarded as certain.

29[30] . officerent, obesset 34, nocerent 38: 'what harm could all these monsters do to us? '

30[29]. spirantes naribus ignem: the phrase stuck in Virgil's memory: *G.* 2.140 (cf. 3.85), *A.* 7.281; he similarly borrowed *asper acerba tuens* 33 at *A.* 9.794 and slightly varied it at *G.* 3.149.

31. A resounding and pictorial line giving the range of Diomedes' horses along the south coast of Thrace.

> **propter:** like many other prepositions *propter* is frequently postponed by L., but only when it is local in sense.

34. denique: virtually temporal, 'after all', 'in the end'.

35. pelagique severa: 'the harsh tracts of the sea', 'the grim sea': a favourite type of circumlocution for L. (neuter plural + genitive); cf. *pontique profunda* 417, *cava calamorum* 1382, *saepta domorum* 1.489, *caelique serena* 2.1100, *rara viarum* 6.332. For *severa* cf. 1.1190.

36. barbarus: i.e. not Greek or Roman. The line has a sardonic edge ('Who would be fool enough to go there anyway? '), and, like 42 below, is a deliberate stylistic let-down after the inflated tone of the preceding lines.

39-40. nil: the blunt monosyllabic answer is the more effective after the rhetorical expansiveness of the questions: in any case the world is still full of horrific beasts.

> **satiatem:** a by-form, found also at 1391 and 2.1038, for the unmetrical *satietas.*

> **ferarum . . . scatit:** 'teems with wild beasts'. The genitive, again with *scatit* 6.890-91, is on the analogy of the genitive with words of 'fulness', e.g. *abundans, dives, complere, plenus.* L. uses only third-conjugation forms of *scatere.*

41. nemora, montes, silvas: almost a routine collocation: cf. 955, 992.

43-54. By contrast the real dangers are within us, the lusts and fears which Epicurus has shown us the way to conquer. There is a similar panegyric of this achievement of Epicurus at 6.9-34: note the repetition of key words in 24-5, 'veridicis igitur purgavit pectora dictis / et finem statuit cuppedinis atque timoris.'

43-4. quae proelia . . . insinuandum?: the meaning seems to be 'what battles and dangers must we then get involved in even against our will?' with *nobis* the usual dative of the agent and L.'s frequent construction with gerund + accusative instead of nominative gerundive (Bailey, i, 103-4). For intransitive *insinuare* with accusative see 73 below and *OLD* s.v. 2 b and c: the word perhaps suggests the difficulty of extricating oneself from the perils, hence the translation offered, 'involved in'. *sunt* OQ must be wrong and editors generally opt for Lachmann's *tumst,* or *tunc* (first printed by Lambinus, but it is

uncertain whether he or Marullus first thought of it: see Munro's
apparatus and M. F. Smith's Loeb note ad loc.). For further discussion
see also C. N. Cole, *CR* 19 (1905), 205–6 and W. R. Hardie, *CQ* 5
(1911), 105–6.

45–6. cuppedinis, timores: cf. 6.25, quoted above. The lines also recall
3.994 'aut alia quavis scindunt cuppedine curae'. *cuppedinis = cupid-
inis*, a metrically different form that occurs several times elsewhere
in L.

47–8. D. E. W. Wormell (*ap.* Dudley, 48) discusses this passage and
suggests that the list of vices, *superbia, spurcitia, petulantia, luxus,
desidiae*, together with *avarities* and *honorum caeca cupido* (= *am-
bitio*) referred to at 3.59, correspond to the seven deadly sins and
provide evidence of the influence of Epicureanism on early Christian
moral thinking. Perhaps some Epicureans did have a list of cardinal
vices, but clear evidence is lacking, and the suggestion entails interpre-
ting *spurcitia* as 'sordid lust' (it might be 'sordid avarice') and *luxus*
in the restricted sense of 'gluttony'.

    petulantia: 'insolence', 'aggressiveness'. The plurals *luxus* (if
plural) and *desidiae* suggest acts or manifestations of these moral
failings, much like *laetitiae*, 'feelings of pleasure', at 3.142.

    superbiă sp-: L. several times allows a short vowel before initial
double consonant (so *liberă sponte* 79). Augustan and later poets
clearly felt this to be metrically anomalous (e.g. in Virgil only at
A. 11.309), and generally avoided such a collocation of words. For a
discussion and statistics see Bailey, i, 126–7.

49–54. Epicurus deserves to be regarded as a god (8n.) for showing us
how to banish these vices and fears, especially as he himself spoke so
eloquently about the gods. His reasoning and teaching powers are
stressed in the repetition of *dictis* 50, *dicta* 53, *dictis* 54, and contrasted with purely physical conquests, *armis* 50 (like those of
Hercules derided above). It is likely that 53–4 contain specific references to Epicurus' treatises περὶ θεῶν and περὶ φύσεως. These lines
form the climax to the panegyric of Epicurus and are written with
elegance and care: note the contrasts *dictis/armis* 50 and *hominem/
divum* 51, and the extended interwoven alliteration of *m*s and *d*s in
51–4.

51. dignarier: passive, as normally in Cicero and occasionally elsewhere:
'be held worthy'.

49. qui: for the oblique reference to Epicurus see 2n.

55–90. The second section of the introduction contains a recapitulation
of previous conclusions (55–63), an outline of the teaching of this
book (64–77), and a reminder that the purpose of this teaching is to
show that gods are not needed to explain the functioning of the
universe (78–90). This reminder is of crucial importance to L.'s
message and is found in the three other books (1.146–58, 2.167–81,

6.50-79) which, like 5, are concerned to show that natural phenomena do not require divine assistance.

55 ff. The enormous sentence continues to 75 and has its main clause in 64, with an extended parenthesis at 59-63. This parenthesis refers to the content of Books 3 and 4, and on the likely assumption that 5 was written before 3 and 4 Bailey might be right in suggesting (iii, 1330) that the lines might have been added later to this summary after the composition of those two books.

55-6. L. stresses the closeness and fidelity with which he follows the master's teaching: similarly he says at 3.3-4 'te sequor . . . inque tuis nunc / ficta pedum pono pressis vestigia signis.'

   rationes: 'his (detailed) reasonings': the plural of *ratio* is rare in the *DRN*, the singular of course extremely common in the sense of 'principle', 'system'.

56-8. A summary survey of the arguments of Books 1 and 2 which describe the fixed and binding law or terms (*foedere, leges*) by which matter is created. *quo* is relative after *eo*: 'how all things must abide under the law by which they were created'. *nec . . . valeant* is loose syntax equivalent to 'et quam non valeant'.

   aevi leges: 'the laws of time', the limits appointed to the lifetime of each created thing. L. uses *aevum* to mean (1) 'time' generally (1.1004, 5.314), (2) 'time of existence', 'lifetime' (5.537, 1440), (3) 'life', 'existence' (3.357). Our passage seems to link the first two senses.

59-63. A rather awkward parenthesis (see above) covering roughly the contents of Books 3 and 4.

59. quo genere in primis: 'wherein most importantly': the same phrase at 3.296, 4.855. (*in*) *quo genere* and other phrases with *genus* (*id genus, quod genus*) are Lucretian stereotypes serving to link stages in arguments, and translation has to be adjusted to the context.

   animi: 'mind'. In strict Lucretian usage *animus* is the rational part of the soul, *anima* the irrational part (see 3.94 ff.).

60. nativo: 'that has birth': the main lesson of Book 3 is that the soul is corporeal and therefore mortal.

61. incolumis: 'intact'. But Marullus's conjecture for *incolumem* (from *incolumen* O) is unnecessary.

62-3. We should not imagine that the soul is immortal because we see visions of the dead in our sleep: these are just 'images' which deceive us because our sleeping senses and memory do not distinguish them from reality. This is the argument in 4.757-76, reflected also in a fragmentary text of Diogenes of Oenoanda, New fr. 5 Col IV 3 – New fr. 6 Col II 1. (For text, translation, and discussion see M. F. Smith in *AJA* 75 (1971), 360 and 363-5.)

64 ff. The programme of this book, though the topics do not all follow the sequence given here. Robin suggested that L. may be influenced by the philosophical subjects covered in the Doxographies. These were collections of the opinions of philosophers based mainly on Theophrastus, which were current from the fourth century BC onwards. One of them, named by Diels the *Vetusta Placita* (now lost), was probably compiled in the first century BC and thus may have been known to L. See Robin's note here, and for the doxographic tradition Kirk–Raven, *The Presocratic Philosophers*, 3 ff., Guthrie, i, xiii–xiv.

64. rationis: 'plan', 'design'.

　　detulit: sc. *me.*

65–6. mortali/nativum: the world is subject to the limits of death and birth. There is a similar emphatic statement about souls at 3.417–8: 'nativos animantibus et mortalis / esse animos'.

67. Nearly repeated at 416. *congressus* here and *coniectus* at 416 represent the Epicurean συμφόρησις and ἄθροισμα – the fusion of atomic particles which create the constituent parts of the cosmos.

69. quae: *animans* is fem. in L. wherever the gender is detectable, and generally when referring to other creatures than man (presumably sc. *fera* or the like): see Neue–Wagener, *Formenlehre*, i, 916.

70. It is important for L. to establish that there are practical limits to the processes of atomic combination, or outlandish results would follow. Hence he is at pains to prove the impossibility of freaks and hybrids like Scylla, Centaurs, and Chimaeras: see the discussion at 878 ff. and cf. 2.700–17 and 4.732–48 (where it is explained how we come to envisage such non-existent monsters through the coalescing of disparate *imagines* from different creatures).

71–2. variante loquela . . . vesci per nomina rerum: 'to use a variety of utterances by naming things': cf. 'varios linguae sonitus' 1028.

　　vesci: an interesting old verb which, as the grammarian Nonius remarked (415.31), meant both 'feed on' and 'use', 'enjoy' (much like Greek ἐστιῶμαι and English 'feast on'). Both meanings go back at least to Accius (frs. 218, 145R), and it is not clear which derived historically from the other. Here the sense is clearly 'use'; in the other two Lucretian occurrences (2.1127, 5.857) the two meanings merge into one another.

73. insinuarit: 44 n.

74. quī in: 7 n.

75. lacus: the most famous lakes with divine associations were Lake Nemi at Aricia (Diana) and one at Henna in Sicily (Ceres).

76. meatus: a favourite word for the movement or path of a heavenly body: apart from the other Lucretian examples (1.128, 2.208, 5.774) see Virg. *A.* 6.849, Lucan 1.663, 9.6, Pliny *HN* 2.67.

77 ff. One of the most difficult problems in Epicurean and Lucretian cosmology is the relation between necessity (ἀνάγκη, *vis*) and chance (τύχη, *casus*) in the formation and operation of the world. For clues

to Epicurus' thinking see *Ep. Men.* 113–4 (with Bailey's note on
133.8); Diogenes of Oenoanda, New frs. 7 and 8 (text and discussion
by M. F. Smith in *AJA* 75 (1971), 367–71); J. M. Rist, *Epicurus, an
Introduction*, 51–2. L. perhaps had not made up his mind firmly on
this problem. *Natura*, usually regarded as here as a controlling principle in the world, seems to allow for the operation of both *vis* and
casus: thus at 2.1048–76 two consecutive and alternative accounts
of the formation of the world seem to be given, one based on chance
(see esp. 1058–60) and one on necessity (see esp. 1072 'visque eadem
et natura' — like 'vi . . . natura' here). So too evil in human life
arises 'naturali . . . / seu casu seu vi' 6.30–1. Elsewhere it is stressed
that the original fusion of atoms in creation happened *casu* (1.1021–
23 = 5.419–21); while in our passage the *vis* of nature has taken
over and governs the movements of bodies after they have been
formed: we are not to think of them as operating 'libera sponte sua'.

79. liberā sponte: 47 n.

  perennis: 'yearly' or 'constant', 'endless'.

80–1. Neither of their own intent nor aided by the gods do sun and
moon course the heavens for our benefit.

  morigera: 'with the obliging intention of': L. is ironic. So in 2.167
ff. he attacks the theological view that it is the gods who cause crops
and seasons to operate 'humanis rationibus admoderate' (where
admoderate means much the same as *morigera* here). Epicurus spelled
out very clearly that the movements of the heavenly bodies were
independent of divine guidance (*Ep. Hdt.* 76–7), and L.'s similar
crisp statement (81) about the gods rounds off the programme of
the book and leads into the warning against weak-willed superstition
with which the introduction closes.

82–90. Repeated at 6.58–66 — a good example of a thematic repetition
of a point essential to the poem's message: a correct apprehension
of the existence of the gods and grasp of the workings of the universe
stops us from cowering in fear of divine powers. So Epicurus stresses
the need for φυσιολογία, natural science, to dispel our fears: Κ.Δ. 11
and 12.

82. Quoted in part light-heartedly by Horace, *Sat.* 1.5.100, as his Epicurean *credo*.

83. tamen interea: a strong phrase: 'if they *still* nevertheless persist in
wondering'.

85. supera: L. uses this earlier form of *supra* several times, e.g. 1407.

86. religiones: 'religious fears', 'superstitions', the regular meaning of
the plural in the poem: 1.109, 932; 2.44.

87. dominos acris: cf. 2.1091, where nature is said to be 'dominis privata
superbis'.

89–90. These lines occur also at 1.76–7, 595–6 and drive home one of
the strongest principles of Epicurean physics, that everything has its

powers defined and immovably limited. The idea is vividly reinforced by the memorable metaphor of the 'deep-set boundary mark' (*haerens* means planted firm and there to stay), dividing the possible from the impossible, which L. used again at 2.1087, 'vitae depactus terminus alte', and which was picked up by Virgil for one of Dido's most passionate speeches, 'et sic fata Iovis poscunt, hic terminus haeret', *A.* 4.614. Editors quote Accius fr. 481R 'veter fatorum terminus sic iusserat', which may have influenced L.'s phrase.

Take *finita sit* together, the subjunctive, like the others, being dependent on *ignari*.

91-508. The world. In the first main section of the book L. discusses the world as a whole, i.e. the earth, sky, and heavenly bodies. (1) The world will one day perish because it is mortal (91-109, 235-415). This subsection is interrupted by a long digression which attacks the belief that any part of the world is divine, or that the gods either dwell anywhere in the world or had a share in its creation (110-234). (2) The world was created out of original chaos by the haphazard union of atoms. Gradually as like atoms joined to like the elements earth, air, fire, and water were formed, and the divisions of the world as we see them came into being, earth, sea, sky, sun, and moon (416-508).

91-109. It is a new and strange idea that destruction awaits the world, but let reason prove that this is true.

91. quod superest: 'next', 'to proceed': a common transition formula (also at 261, 772, 1241). *moremur* suggests that L. is conscious of an over-long preamble to the book: cf. 6.245 'neque te in promissis plura morabor.'

92-4. As he opens the subject L. is non-technical in stressing sea, earth, and sky as the three divisions of the world: it is these which are obvious and visible to everyone. (When he comes to proving the proposition he isolates and discusses the traditional four physical elements, earth, air, fire, and water (247-305).) Yet the atomic structure of matter is kept in view here with *texta*, 'interwoven fabrics' (94), which is used repeatedly in this sense (4.743, 6.997, 1054).

95. una dies: *dies* meaning a specific day is usually masc. in early Latin and in prose, but L. may prefer to write *-a dies* for metrical reasons: cf. 1000 below, 3.899 (with Kenney's note). Ovid adroitly adapts the line in his praise of L.'s poem: 'carmina sublimis tunc sunt peritura Lucreti, / exitio terras cum dabit una dies' (*Am.* 1.15.23-4).

96. moles et machina mundi: one of L.'s resonant alliterative phrases, which links closely the concepts of the universe as a bulky mass and also a contrivance that works (*machina*): 'the massive, complex structure of the world'. L. seems to have given the lead to other writers in using *machina* of the fabric of the universe: see *OLD* s.v.6.

97. nec me animi fallit: a formula (cf. 1.136, 922), in which *fallit* is impersonal and *animi* a genitive of reference (as in phrases like *miser animi, incertus animi* etc.).

97-8. quam ... futurum: 'how strange and startling a thought is the future destruction of heavens and earth.'

99. pervincere: 'to prove conclusively'. L. is very fond of words compounded with intensive *per-*, though by other writers with literary pretensions they were usually avoided as colloquialisms: see Axelson, *Unpoëtische Wörter*, 37-8, Hofmann-Szantyr, 164.

100-1. apportes, possis: the generalizing second person present subjunctive, common in the *DRN* (e.g. 2.314, 3,213, 854: see Bailey, i, 99).

101-3. The highway to the mind recalls Empedocles (on apprehending divinity): οὐκ ἔστιν πελάσασθαι ἐν ὀφθαλμοῖσιν ἐφικτὸν / ἡμετέροις ἢ χερσὶ λαβεῖν, ᾗπέρ τε μεγίστη / πειθοῦς ἀνθρώποισιν ἀμαξιτὸς εἰς φρένα πίπτει, 'it is not possible to approach god for him to be accessible to our eyes, nor to grasp him with our hands — and that is the chief highway of persuasion leading to the mind of men' (B133 D-K), though L. alludes of course to the Epicurean theory of knowledge. For the paramount importance of touch (*manus*) in sense-perception see 2.434 ff.

102. indu: an archaic form of *in*, sometimes used in compound words for metrical reasons (see 876, 1227). Here it is probably a preposition, as at 2.1096 'indu manu', though many editors take *iacere indu* as an inverted tmesis = *inicere*.

    via munita: 'a paved road', 'highway': cf. the variant phrase 'munita viai' 3.498.

103. pectus: the abode of the *animus* and *mens* (3.139-40).

    templa mentis: 'regions *or* precincts of the mind'. For the various meanings of *templum* in the *DRN* see Bailey on 1.120. The other occurrences in this book also mean something like 'region' or 'abode' (491, 521, 948, 1188, 1205, 1436), but the nearest parallel to its use here of the body is 4.624 'linguai ... templa'.

104 ff. effabor: 'I shall speak out': the verb is often used of solemn, oracular utterance (see *OLD* s.v.), and this tone is carried on in the prophetic style of 110-12. Yet there seems also to be a touch of sardonic humour in what follows here: 'it may take a real earthquake to make you believe me, but let us hope it won't come to that and I can persuade you just by reason.'

    ipsa res: (and below 108) 'actual events' — like terrible earthquakes.

107. flectat fortuna gubernans: fortune here replaces nature in the same phrase at 77: see note there for the role of chance in human life.

108. horrisono: a vivid compound in L.'s manner (previously in Cic. *Arat.* 13) and probably popularized by him. Cf. *raucisonos* 1084.

109. omnia: 'the whole world'.

110–234. L. defers his promised *ratio* in order to make an extensive and
strongly argued attack on the 'theological' view of the world and its
creation. This is the longest of the many digressions in the poem
(see Introduction, xvi), and it differs from others in being explicitly
marked as one (*prius adgredior quam*) – in contrast, for example,
with the digression on Cybele at 2.600–60. Our digression is a long
and important one because L. clearly felt that at the outset of the
book's argument it was vital to reassure people about the gods:
the world is not divine, the gods have no dwelling in it – and therefore you will not be punished for throwing off such superstitious
beliefs. The main points are: (1) the world cannot be divine as no
animus can exist in the natural elements (110–45); (2) gods cannot
live in the world as it is physically unsuited to their bodies (146–55);
(3) they did not make the world – why should they? (156–94); (4) no
divine plan would have produced such a faulty world, and an earth
so ill-planned and intractable (195–234).

Here as elsewhere (2.167 ff., 644 ff.; 5.1183 ff.; 6.43 ff.) L.'s
main object of attack is the Aristotelian world-picture, which was
strongly teleological and saw the cosmos as largely divinely controlled.
To a lesser extent there may also be a hit at the Stoic *anima mundi*
theory (e.g. 140–3), but the Stoics were not the main opposition to
the Atomists' physical theories: see Introduction, xvii.

110–12. L. adopts the pose of a prophet far more reliable than the oracles
of Greece's most famous shrine at Delphi (which of course he would
regard as worthless). 111–12 are repeated from 1.738–9 where they
refer to Epicurus' own utterances. Epicurus himself said that in
studying nature he would like to speak like an oracle (*Sent. Vat.* 29),
and this gave a lead to Cicero to refer, no doubt satirically, to Epicurus uttering *quasi oracula* (*Fin.* 2.20 and 102). Diogenes Laertius
(10.12) quotes an epigram of Athenaeus praising Epicurus, who
learnt wisdom Πυθοῦς ἐξ ἱερῶν τριπόδων. L. builds up the impressive-
ness of the lines with the oracular expressions *fundere fata* (cf. Cat.
64.321 'fuderunt carmine fata'; Cic. *ND* 1.66 'oracula fundo') and
profatur, while the tripod and bay-leaves add the traditional equipment of the Pythia, the Delphic priestess.

113. solacia: the 'comfort' is addressed to men's fears (117 ff.) that if
they question the divinity of the world they will be punished for
impiety. Similarly at the outset of his work L. counsels the student
of philosophy not to feel that his speculations are impious (1.80 ff.).
He had a point: we know that Anaxagoras, like Galileo, was accused
of impiety because of his scientific insights, and Plutarch (*Mor*. 923a)
quotes a similar attitude towards Aristarchus of Samos. The link
here with Anaxagoras is close, as he was charged in particular with
denying the divinity of the sun (Diog. Laert. 2.12; Plato *Apol*. 26d).

116. manere: as *meare* OQ suits only *sidera lunam* the Juntine correction *manere* is generally accepted, though, as Bailey pointed out, the proximity of *sidera lunam* at the end of the previous line may have led L. to write *meare*, which is regularly used of heavenly bodies: *OLD* s.v. 1.b.

117. Gigantum: the story of the Giants and their punishment for attacking the Olympian gods was one of the most popular myths of antiquity. Apollodorus (1.6.1–2) gives the details of the legend, which was much used in the imagery of the poets (e.g. by Horace in one of his most complex and serious odes, 3.4.42 ff.). Here the Olympian battlements attacked by the Giants are as it were the *moenia mundi* penetrated by rational thought.

119. disturbent moenia mundi: 'demolish the walls of the world', just as the genius of Epicurus 'extra / processit longe flammantia moenia mundi / atque omne immensum peragravit mente animoque' (1.72-4). *moenia mundi* is a recurrent phrase (in this book also at 371, 454, 1213) meaning the outer boundary enfolding the world, consisting of the lightest particles of fire and air. (The process of its formation is described below 452 ff.). Epicurus taught men to speculate boldly on what lies beyond our world.

121. notantes: 'degrading', the word used of the official stigmatizing by Roman censors.

122-5. 'although these things are so very far removed from divine power and so unworthy to be imagined among the number of the gods, that they should rather be thought able to give us an idea of what is devoid of living movement and feeling'. *usque adeo . . . distent . . . sint* (concessive subjunctives) is picked up by *ut . . . putentur*, but the construction is complicated by the unnecessary repetition of *quae* in 123. *notitia* seems here to have a general sense, 'idea', 'conception', and not the technical meaning = πρόληψις, as at 182, 1047.

126-7. non est . . . ut esse posse . . . putetur: the language is prosaic as L. drives home a fundamental point before elaborating it.

  quovis: 'any and every': it must be the human body.

128-41. These lines are repeated from 3.784-97 with minor rewording at beginning and end to adjust them to their new context. It is clear that they were written first for Book 3, where their theme (everything has its place and the soul cannot exist outside of the body) is integral to the argument there, and re-used to add a supporting point in our passage. See the discussion in Boyancé, *Lucrèce et l'Épicurisme*, 217-18, and contrast the other extensive repeat, 5.351-63 = 3.806-18, where the transfer has probably been from Book 5 to Book 3.

128-30. These five absurdities of the natural world are examples of a type of exaggeration common in Greek and Latin literature (and perhaps proverbial in origin), the *adynaton* or impossibility, by which writers make an emphatic point: 'sooner will trees grow in the sky than will so-and-so happen.' L. used the device also at 1.161-6 (arguing that nothing can arise out of nothing, or else anything could be produced from anything), and 1.881–92 (attacking doctrines of Anaxagoras and adducing the similar absurdity of blood in a stone). Wood and stone (130) are often quoted as symbols of hardness and solidity: see West on Hes. *Th*. 35, Nisbet–Hubbard on Hor. *C*. 1.3.9.

131. quicquid: 'each thing' = *quicque*, as often (264, 284, 304, 773).

    crescat et insit: 'grow and have its place': a so-called ὕστερον πρότερον or inversion of the logical order, like 6.527 'sursum crescunt sursumque creantur' and in contrast with 'esse et crescere' 139. L. is sparing in his use of it, and in any case many such examples are best explained as simply putting the more important or emphatic idea first: see 5 n., Hofmann–Szantyr, 698–9, Austin on Virg. *A*. 2. 353.

133. longius: 'very far', 'too far'. *longius* is used (as at 3.676) in the idiomatic, not strictly comparative, sense in which other comparatives like *citius*, *saepius* occur: see Hofmann–Szantyr, 168–9.

134–43. If the *animus* could exist outside the human body it would yet rather dwell in one or other part of the body; but in fact it can occupy only one fixed part of the body (the *pectus*): therefore it cannot exist outside the body. The argument is a rather tortuous one and this may account for the difficulties of 134–7 – the combination *quod . . . enim* and the awkward construction of *manere* in asyndeton. Cf. too the confusing introduction of the *anima* in 140.

134. quod . . . enim: an awkward fusion of *quod si posset* and *hoc si posset enim* (which L. could have written). The only quoted parallel is Varro *RR* 2.4.8 'ut volutentur in luto, quae enim illorum requies' (perhaps it is an archaic use of *enim*), but Bailey here notes L.'s fondness for connecting with a relative.

    prius: 'sooner', 'rather'.

137. 'at any rate remain in the same man and the same container', i.e. linked firmly with one man, in whatever part of him. The image of the body as the container (*vas*) of the *animus* appears at 3.440, 555 and in Cicero (*Tusc*. 1.52).

138–40. This is carefully explained at 3.140 ff., and the marked alliteration of 138–9 hammers home the important point. But the mention of *anima* introduces a confusion, as strictly speaking we have been concerned only with the *animus*, which is localized firmly in the *pectus* (the *anima* being diffused throughout the body). Perhaps L. just likes pairing the words, for this elsewhere too leads to a lapse in logic: see Kenney on 3.705–8.

138–9. quoque . . . certum / dispositumque: cf. 131.

140–3. Perhaps a side-swipe at the Stoic doctrine of the all-pervading *anima mundi*: see introductory note to 110–234 and Robin on 140–5.

141. totum . . . extra corpus: 'completely outside the body': this is impossible *a fortiori*, since even within the body the mind's location is firmly fixed.

144. constant: sc. the natural elements just mentioned.

145. vitaliter ... animata: 'quickened with the breath of life'. *vitaliter* illustrates one of L.'s favourite adverbial formations: cf. *innumerabiliter* 274.

146–55. The gods could not physically live in the world. The argument is based on the Epicurean theory of the physical nature of the gods: their forms are of such a rarefied and tenuous structure that any bodily contact with the grosser world would be impossible. Our only apprehension of them is by our minds, and that with difficulty (149). The Epicureans supposed the gods to live in the spaces between the different worlds, μετακόσμια, *intermundia*, where they enjoy a blissful detachment from the lives of men (Usener 359, Cic. *ND* 1.18). In a famous passage based on Homer, L. pictures the peace and beauty of their dwelling-place (3.18–22); and Tennyson in turn wrote of 'The Gods, who haunt / The lucid interspace of world and world, / Where never creeps a cloud, or moves a wind, / . . . Nor sound of human sorrow mounts to mar / Their sacred everlasting calm!' (*Lucretius* 104 ff.).

148–9. See n. on 1169 ff. and cf. esp. 1170 'egregias animo facies vigilante videbant.' The phrase *animi mens* occurs also at 3.615, 4.758, 6.1183, and distinguishes the *mens* as the strictly intellectual element of the *animus* (which also includes the emotions).

150. suffugit: 'has (always) escaped' through its tenuousness: a sort of 'gnomic' or generalizing perfect. For this sense cf. 4.360 'hoc ubi suffugit sensum simul angulus omnis'.

154. de: 'conforming to', 'in accord with': for this meaning of *de* see *OLD* s.v. 5.

155. This line offers us the clearest proof that L. did not complete his poem: there is no extended (*largo sermone*) treatment elsewhere of the nature of the gods. An attempt has been made by U. Pizzani (*Il problema del testo e della composizione del DRN di Lucrezio*, 174–80) to reconcile L.'s promise here with other references to the gods in the poem, but this is unpersuasive: see Boyancé, *Lucrèce et l'Épicurisme*, 80.

156–94. It is foolish to imagine that the gods created the world for man's sake: they had neither motive nor model for doing so. This is central Epicurean doctrine, attacking the teleological view of the creation of the world and the idea of the gods as caring beings (Epic. *Ep. Hdt*. 76–7, Cic. *ND* 1.19–23). Again it is stressed that everything has come into being merely by the chance combinations of atoms (187–94).

156–65. dicere ... putare ... adfingere et addere ... desiperest: 'to say ... to think ... to keep on adding fictions ... is sheer lunacy.' L. sets up a series of untenable ideas and then gives them a crisp and pungent dismissal. For similar, shorter examples of the same technique see

1041-3 and 3.800-2, where as here *desiperest* gains force from its position at the beginning of the line and followed by a pause. The reader has to thread his way through a welter of infinitives: *dicere, putare, adfingere, addere* are substantivized infinitives subject to *desiperest*, and there is a further syntactical subordination whereby *dicere* governs *voluisse parare* and *laudare decere*, and *putare* governs *fas esse* (which in turn governs *sollicitare, vexare, evertere*).

156. voluisse: sc. *deos.*

159. aeternum: this cannot relate to the past (Bailey, Ernout-Robin), as *fundatum* 161 presupposes a beginning in time of the world.

161. perpetuo aevo: 'with everlasting life': a sort of loose descriptive ablative.

162-3. On this view it is against the principles of divine law, *fas* 160, that the god-created world should be physically disturbed, or should be attacked with arguments seeking to overthrow its immortal nature. *ab imo evertere summa*, explaining *verbis vexare*, means literally 'to overturn the top from the bottom', i.e. 'to turn (the world) completely upside down' by proving that it is created by chance and doomed to ultimate destruction.

165. This line illustrates what has been called a 'quasi-caesura', i.e. the main third-foot caesura divides a compound word after its prefix, which is also preceded by an elided syllable: 'desiperest quid en(im) im|mortalibus atque beatis'. There are several other examples in the poem, e.g. 2.1059, 3.174 (where see Kenney's note), 3.612, 6.197.

165-6. quid ... emolumenti: 'what advantage could our gratitude bestow ... ?'

168. post ante: There seems to be no serious point in the juxtaposition: *post* goes with *tanto, ante* with *quietos.*

170-1. nam ... obsunt: A variant of the proverbial commonplace of discontent with one's lot illustrated by 3.957 'semper aves quod abest, praesentia temnis', and providing the theme of Hor. *Sat.* 1.1. See Otto, *Sprichwörter* s.v. *certus.* But the gods, having suffered no distress, have no desire for novelty (171-3).

175-6. With the traditional line-order (followed here) *vita* is man's life; but many editors from Lambinus onwards have supposed the gods to be referred to, and have transposed the lines accordingly (see apparatus). This may well be right, not so much because very similar wording is used of the gods by the Epicurean speaker in Cic. *ND* 1.22, as because of the difficulty of conceiving, however sardonically, what could have been man's *vita* before the *rerum genitalis origo*, and how his creation is to be considered as separate from that of the world. If the lines do belong after 173 (Lambinus) and refer to the gods, the idea would be (ironically) that the gods' life was previously so dull and miserable that they created the world just for something to do. (The dislocation presumably arose when the copyist's eye moved from *quid* 173 to *quidve*, leaving out the intervening two lines, which were subsequently restored in the wrong sequence. Note also that *enim* 177 follows 174 more naturally than 176.)

an, credo: a parenthetic *credo* in an interrogative sentence is very unusual (hence Lachmann's *at*), and editors have cited only Cic. *Fam.* 4.5.3. 'an illius vicem, credo, doles?'

iacebat: 875 n.

genitalis origo: 'creative beginning': 324, 1212.

180. **in numero:** 'enrolled' (among the living) as *vitae* indicates, just as at Virg. *A.* 6.545 'explebo numerum' the context shows that the dead are referred to.

quid . . . creatum?: the near repetition of 174 hammers home the unanswerable question.

181-6. A further argument: the gods had no pattern or concept to follow in creating the world and mankind. *notities* here is the technical Epicurean πρόληψις, the conception or general idea of a class of things built up in the mind by past perceptions of individual objects in that class, to which further perceptions are referred, as it were, for identification. The same argument is applied below to the origin of language (see 1046-9 n.), and in the refutation of scepticism at 4.473-7.

183. Virtually repeated at 1049.

184-6. A more precise rewording of the question: what could the gods know of the power of the atoms (the constituents of things) and their creative rearrangements?

187-94. The true cause of creation was the haphazard meetings and combinations of atoms. This is a routine description of atom-behaviour: hence the general similarity to 1.1024-8, and the repetition of 187-91 (apart from the first two words) at 422-6.

187. **namque:** '(No, it was nature's doing) for . . . '. *Natura* (186) includes the operation of chance: see notes to 77 ff., 107. *ita* is picked up by *ut* 192.

189. **ponderibusque . . . concita:** 'carried along by their own weight' (cf. 2.239 'aeque ponderibus non aequis concita ferri'). *percita / concita* give a touch of *variatio*.

190. **omnimodis:** 'in all sorts of ways': a formation which L. liked (again at 425, 718, 1024) but which does not recur in Classical Latin.

193. **deciderunt:** Ernout-Robin point out that the verb suggests the casual and haphazard nature of the atomic combinations. Note the original quantity *decidĕrunt*, regular in the *DRN* (e.g. *fuĕrunt* 474). The form *-ērunt* is probably a fusion of *-ĕrunt* and *-ēre* (L. R. Palmer, *The Latin Language*, 275).

194. **haec rerum . . . summa:** 'our world', as below 237, 368 and 1.235, 1028. Bailey on 1.235 discusses L.'s use of this and related phrases.

novando: 'by renewal'. Similarly 2.75-6 'sic rerum summa novatur / semper', in a passage explaining how the constant movement of atoms keeps the sum of the world's physical structure unchanged, though individual combinations of matter come and go.

195-234. Climate and other physical conditions on the earth prove that it was not divinely made for man. Much of the earth's surface is useless for agriculture, and even when crops are laboriously produced they are ravaged by bad weather (200-17). Fierce beasts and diseases take their toll of us (218-21). The new-born human child is helpless to face his surroundings compared with the young of other animals (222-34).

195-9. These lines are repeated with minor alterations from 2.177-81, where they occur in a passage similarly attacking the belief that the gods created the world for man (see introductory note to 110-234). It is hard to say which book they were originally written for, but in any case 5.195-234 in effect fulfil the promise made following these lines in Book 2, 'quae tibi posterius, Memmi, faciemus aperta' (2.182).

195. iam: 'for the sake of argument', 'even' (*OLD* s.v. 7d).

 ignorem: the present subjunctive in unfulfilled conditions is regular in early Latin, and used several times by L. (E. C. Woodcock, *A New Latin Syntax*, 153, Bailey, i 99-100): cf. 276-8 and for other kinds of 'irregular' sequence see 211-12 n. and 1266 n.

196. caeli rationibus: 'the workings of the sky', here weather or climate, as the following passage indicates. Cf. 1183, where the phrase alludes to the heavenly bodies.

197. reddere: 'explain', 'prove', as at 1.566: the full phrase is *rationem reddere*, which occurs frequently in the poem.

199. tanta ... culpa: a crisp and scornful indictment, which L. develops in three proofs (*principio* 200, *praeterea* 218, *tum porro* 222). The phrase *praedita culpa* is edged and startling, as *praeditus* normally refers to fine, praiseworthy, attributes.

200. impetus: 'expanse', 'sweep': for this sense see 505, 913, and *OLD* s.v. 8.

201. avide: Bernays's conjecture for the MSS *avidam* (which many editors retain and explain as a sort of hypallage for *avidi montes* etc.). Purmann's *amplam* is worth considering.

 ferarum: 'belonging to wild beasts' — a further restriction on man's share of the earth.

204. duas ... partis: 'two-thirds': the equatorial and arctic zones. This refers to a belief that there were torrid, temperate, and arctic belts or zones in the heavens which caused corresponding ones on the earth, only the temperate one being habitable by man: see Virg. *G.* 1.233 ff., Macrobius, *Somnium Scipionis* 2.7 (an extensive discussion).

205. geli casus: frost 'falls' because it is formed in the sky: 6.527 ff. (and cf. *Ep. Pyth.* 108-9).

206-9. Virgil's *Georgics* show several echoes of these lines: see 1. 45–6, 198, 2. 237, 411.

206-7. vi / vis: it is a physical tussle for survival between man and nature.

210-11. Repeated from 1.211–12, except for *si non* replacing *quae nos*. This change has caused the loss of an object for *cimus* (and thus too a subject for *nequeant*), and we have therefore to supply something like *fruges* or *fetus* from the context; but L. may have intended to tidy up the passage. (Bockemüller deleted 210–12, which at any rate gives a smooth transition from 209 to *tamen* 213.)

211. subigentes: 'digging', 'drilling': a farming term, e.g. Cato, *Agr*. 45.1, Virg. *G*. 1.125; see *OLD* s.v. 7b.

211-12. cimus / nequeant: for the mood-sequence (logically, 'if we do not actually . . . , they would not . . . ') cf. 1.805–8 and see 1266 n.

213. tamen: 'even so'.

215. aetherius sol: This line-ending recurs at 267, 281, 389, and (probably) 3.1044.

217. ventorum violento . . . vexant: L. similarly uses *v*-alliteration to describe the violence of winds at 957 'verbere ventorum vitare' and 6.114–15 'vestem chartasque volantis / verberibus venti versant'; and *violento turbine* recurs at 368, 1231.

218-20. The argument from wild beasts dangerous to man was traditional, and used by Cicero in defence of scepticism in *Ac. Pr.* 120: 'cur deus, omnia nostra causa cum faceret (sic enim vultis), tantam vim natricum viperarumque fecerit, cur mortifera tam multa ac perniciosa terra marique disperserit?' (see Reid's note for other passages on this controversy). Some commentators have been troubled by elements of un-Epicurean pessimism in these and the following lines, but L. is here appealing to non-philosophical common sense to assist his argument, and there are hints too of the commonplaces of the traditional *consolatio* (see Robin's note here).

222 ff. The helpless human baby has good reason to wail as it emerges new-born into a world of troubles. This is another commonplace idea ([Plato] *Axiochus* 366d, Sen. *Ep.* 102.26, *Cons. Polyb.* 4, Pliny *HN* 7.2; later parallels are cited in Munro), here developed by L. into a virtuoso passage, blending pathos (inevitable sorrows awaiting the baby), scornful humour (no rattles for the animal young) and irony (the paraphernalia man needs to protect his own), and ending on the quiet cadence *naturaque daedala rerum* 234.

223. infans: literally 'speechless': cf. *infantia* 1031.

224. in luminis oras: 'onto the shores (or boundaries) of light', i.e. the light of day, life: an Ennian phrase (*Ann*. frs. 114, 131 V) which L. made his own (again at 781, [1389], 1455 and several times elsewhere in the poem). Here it brilliantly continues the image of the *proiectus navita*: the new-born child is shipwrecked into life.

226. aequum: 'reasonable': you cannot blame the baby.

228 ff. By contrast animals cope far better than man (so why not say the world was created for them?). 228–30 deal with animal young, with *crescunt* implying 'grow up' without man's attendant difficulties, and the rattles and baby-talk symbolizing the care taken of tender, helpless creatures. 231–4 switch to adult animals.

230. infracta loquela: 'baby-talk': *infractus* is used of a mincing, effeminate style of speech or song (Sen. *Ep.* 90.19, 114.1), and Porphyrion comments on Hor. *Sat.* 1.3.48 (*balbutit*) 'blandientes infantibus infringere linguam solent ut quasi eos imitentur.' L. uses the phrase *infringi linguam* (3.155) of faltering speech.

231. tempore caeli: 'season'.

233. qui: 'with which': an archaic instrumental abl. (cf. 854), used in both sing. and pl.

234. daedala rerum: 'skilful creator of things'. *daedalus* (δαίδαλος) is a favourite word of L. in both active and passive senses ('artful', 'artfully made'): see 1451 n.

235–415. After the digression L. resumes the arguments for the mortality of the world, which are signposted in his usual way by *principio, praeterea, praeterea, denique.* (1) The elements composing the world are mortal and therefore the world itself is mortal (235–323). (2) The world must have had a beginning and also be still young because our records do not go back beyond a certain point (324–50). (3) The world does not satisfy the conditions of immortality, e.g. the solidity of the atoms and the intangibility of the void (351–79). (4) It is quite possible that some day one of the elements will overmaster the others and thus destroy the world (380–415).

235–46. A general statement of the first argument, which is followed by discussions of the elements separately (earth, water, air, fire). Mortality entails birth and dissolution, and Epicurus had argued (*Ep. Hdt.* 73) that worlds are created and destroyed as their constituent matter comes together and subsequently dissolves. It should be noticed that though the atomists did not of course accept the traditional four 'elements', earth, water, air, fire (apparently first distinguished by Empedocles), as the truly fundamental constituents of the cosmos – these were atoms and void – they seem to have regarded them at least as basic observable components whose atomic composition could be distinguished. (See Guthrie, ii, 413–14.) So too at 1.705 ff. L. firmly rejects the notion that the Empedoclean elements could be the fundamental material of the world, while here allowing that together they make up the visible 'sum of things' (237).

235–6. L. formulates the list more briefly at 1.715: 'ex igni terra atque anima procrescere et imbri.' For *anima* = 'breeze' (the most obvious manifestation of this element) see also 1230 and 6.578.

238. nativo / mortali: 65–6 n., 321.

239. eodem: sc. *corpore.*

242. ferme: emphatic rather than qualifying, 'always', 'invariably'; apparently a rare meaning, but cf. 2.218 'incerto tempore ferme'.

243-4. maxima mundi / . . . membra: the elements, as at 380-1. Cicero speaks of '(mundi) membra, caelum terras maria' (*ND* 1.100).

regigni: probably this compound and *egigni*, 2.703, are Lucretian coinages as neither is found elsewhere.

247-60. The earth diminishes and increases in turn.

247-8. corripuisse me mihi: literally 'that I have taken for myself', i.e. 'assumed arbitrarily', 'begged the question'. This meaning is hard to parallel and may reflect somewhat similar senses of συναρπάζειν (Eur. *IA* 531, 'Longinus' 16.2) and *arripere* (Cic. *ND* 1.77).

253 ff. Not only is part of the earth lost but it seems to change into air or water, and change proves mortality − an axiom of Epicurean physics, as laid down at 3.517-18: 'at neque transferri sibi partis nec tribui vult / immortale quod est quicquam neque defluere hilum.'

255. revocatur: 'is reduced to'; cf. 6.292 'ad diluviem revocare'.

257-8. 'moreover whatever the earth nourishes and increases is in due proportion restored to it': earth affords nourishment for the growth of plants and creatures which it receives back equivalently when they die and decompose into it. But the construction is certainly abrupt (Brieger, Giussani, and Müller assumed a lacuna after 257), and *terra* must be understood from the context as the subject of *alit auget*. The thought is illustrated also at 322-3 and 2.999-1000 'cedit item retro, de terra quod fuit ante / in terras.'

259. The idea was a commonplace: Xenophanes fr. B27 D-K ἐκ γαίης γὰρ πάντα καὶ εἰς γῆν πάντα τελευτᾷ, Eur. fr. 195N ἄπαντα τίκτει χθὼν πάλιν τε λαμβάνει, Eur. *Suppl.* 536, Aesch. *Ch.* 127-8, Ennius *varia* fr. 48V.

omniparens (cf. 2.706 'per terras omniparentis') is a conventional epithet in line with phrases like Aesch. *Pr.* 90 παμμῆτόρ τε γῆ, *h. Hom.* 30.1 γαῖαν παμμήτειραν, and reflecting the ancient belief, adopted by the Epicureans, in the earth as mother of all living things: see introductory note to 783-836.

260. tibi: 'you see': the so-called 'ethic' dative; cf. 294, 805, 1209.

261-72. Water constantly perishes and is re-created. It is everywhere apparent that waters flow ceaselessly, but surface evaporation and underground seepage both (*partim, partim*) cause a counterbalancing loss (or transformation into another element: see n. on 253 ff.). These two types of water-loss are discussed again at 6.608-38 to show why the bulk of the sea remains constant.

262. latices: 'waters' generally, comprising the specific kinds in 261.

263. decursus aquarum / aquai: occurs also at 946, 1.283, 6.609.

264-5. primum quicquid aquai: 'each foremost part of water' in the advancing flow successively evaporates or seeps away, so that the total volume remains constant.

266-7. verrentes . . . sol: are repeated at 388-9 (at 267 *deminuunt*
('lessen') should be read for *diminuunt* ('break up') OQ).

> **verrentes:** the verb is used always of wind in the *DRN*: cf. 1227.
>
> **radiis:** it has been suggested by B. Farrington (quoted by Bailey,
> iii, 1756) and D. A. West (*The Imagery and Poetry of Lucretius*, 82)
> that L. intends a pun here, involving *radius* in the sense of 'shuttle'
> linked with the literal meaning of *retexens*: 'unweaving the water
> with the shuttles of his rays'. Given L.'s characteristically associative
> technique of composition this may well be right.

269-72. The water which seeps away is purified and returns through the
earth to feed the springs. (L. does not here describe the corresponding
process by which the evaporated water returns from the clouds as
rain: for this see 6.495 ff., 627 ff.) These lines recur with minor
changes at 6.635-8: see n. to 261-72. This and related theories of
the cycle of waters had a long history before and after L.: Xenophanes B30 D–K, Anaxagoras A42.4–5 D–K, Sen. *NQ* 3.4 ff., Pliny *HN*
2.166. Aristotle thought the subject important enough to give a very
extensive discussion of the origin of the sea, *Meteor.* 353 a 32 ff.

269. percolatur . . . virus: 'the saltness is strained off': the same process
of filtering salt water through earth is described at 2.473-7.

270. materies umoris: 'the substance of the water', without the extran-
eous salt.

271-2. agmine: often used of flowing water (see *OLD* s.v. 1), and L.
may here be remembering Ennius, 'leni fluit agmine flumen' (*Ann.*
fr. 173V). The image is continued with the 'liquid step' in 272. Elsewhere streams have a *pes* at Hor. *Epode* 16.48, Sil. It. 6.140, *Culex*
17, and we speak of 'running' water.

> **via secta semel:** the existing river course.

273-80. Air changes by absorbing matter from things and discharging it
back to them. This is as it were the reverse process of the changes
undergone by earth (erosion) and water (evaporation), though from
the nature of air L. can make only a theoretical statement about it
without the physical illustrations he gives for the other three elements.
Though short, the section strongly emphasizes the unremitting inter-
flow between elements by the repetition *fluit fluentis fluere*, and
perhaps too the alliterative *re- re- re-* (277, 279-80).

273. corpore: air is just as material as the other elements.

274. innumerabiliter: 145 n.

> **privas:** = *singulas*, which is unmetrical: cf. 733.

276. aeris . . . mare: the metaphor may partly suggest the interchange
of elements under discussion, just as the similar image at 2.550
'materiae tanto in pelago' certainly looks ahead to the shipwreck
two lines later. Editors quote Ennius *scen.* fr. 382V 'caeli fretum',
Shakespeare *Timon* 4.2.21–2 'We must all part / Into this sea of air.'

276-8. nisi . . . retribuat / forent: for the 'irregular' sequence see 195 n.

fluentis: sc. *res*, which like these effluent *corpora* are also said to be in a state of flux.

278. See 380 ff. for the possible dominance of one of the elements.

281-305. Fire in its visible manifestation, light, streams forth in a succession of particles which constantly perish and are replaced. This is proved by the fact that clouds which intercept sunbeams create shadows under them: light needs constant renewal from its source. The argument here is similar to the account of the evaporation of the surface particles of water: cf. *primum quicquid fulgoris / flammarum* (284, 304) with *primum quicquid aquai* (264), and note the use of words applicable also to water — *liquidi fons irrigat caput*. L. adds a further argument by analogy from the appearance of the light continuously emitted by lamps and torches. (At 4.185-90 the atomic nature of the sun's light and heat is carefully described — a stream of minute particles, each kept moving by pressure from the one behind it.)

281-2. fons: used of the sun also at 598, while *irrigat . . . caelum* is varied as *caelumque rigando* 594.

283. Very similar is 4.189 'suppeditatur enim confestim lumine lumen.'

284. ei: sc. *lumini*. All nine occurrences of *ei* in the *DRN* are at the end of a line and scanned as a spondee (e.g. below 300, 754). The oblique cases of *is* were generally avoided as colourless in verse, especially from the Augustan poets onwards: see Axelson, *Unpoetische Wörter*, 70 ff., Austin on Virg. *A*. 4.479.

287. inter quasi rumpere: (cf. 299) Note the effect of the tmesis. Such separation of the elements of a compound verb was a favourite mannerism of Ennius. It was used with more restraint by L., who was particularly fond of dividing the word so as to illustrate visibly, as it were, the intended meaning. Other examples are: 3.262 'inter enim cursant', 3.860 'inter enim iectast', 4.948 'inter enim saepit', 5.1374 'inter plaga currere', 6.332 'inter enim fugit'.

290. novo: the constant fresh supply of light-particles from their source (293) which the clouds have intercepted.

295-6. The description of the torches is carefully balanced: *clarae . . . fulguribus / pingues . . . caligine* ('rich with murky smoke').

295. lychni: (Gk. λύχνοι) lamps hung from the ceiling: cf. Virg. *A*. 1.726 'dependent lychni laquearibus'.

297. ardore ministro: 'supplied by their flames', as if the *ardor* were an attendant mending the fire.

298-9. instant / instant: for the repetition see 950-1 n. Here it stresses the ceaseless uninterrupted stream of light. For the tmesis in 299 see 287 n.

300-1. 'so quickly is its (*ei = luci*) extinction hidden by the swift birth of flame from all the fires (which are its source).'

303. subortu: 'fresh supply', 'store springing up'. The word occurs only here and it illustrates L.'s strong partiality for fourth-declension abstract nouns, many of which he apparently coined: see 1040, 1142, Bailey, i, 135.

306-23. Two supplementary observations (*denique* 306, *denique* 318), which seem designed to confirm the proofs of the mortality of earth and air. In 306-17 L. varies the previous argument by citing observable decay alone, rather than a cycle of change, as a proof of mortality. 318-23 round off this section by briefly considering the sky which envelops the earth and is similarly mortal.

306. non: for *nonne*, as often (1073, 1222, 1229). *nonne* is generally avoided by poets: see Hofmann–Szantyr, 462. Time as an overmastering force is virtually personified here and at 314, 317.

308. fessa fatisci: (also at 3.458) 'are weakened and crack': perhaps an intentional 'figura etymologica', as the words seem to have a common root (see Ernout–Meillet s.v. *fatis*). There is a sardonic touch in the idea that the shrines and images of the gods share the general mortality.

312. The line is probably corrupt beyond redemption: see Bailey's discussion and Martin's (Teubner) apparatus for a selection of the large number of suggested restorations, e.g. Munro's 'quaerere proporro sibi sene senescere credas ('asking whether you believe that they in turn grow old'). The sense seems to be an ironic contrast between the visible ruins of the monuments (311) and some claim they themselves make to eternity.

313. silices: particularly hard stone, coupled with iron at 1.571, 2.449.

314. Cf. 379 [1217], 58 n.

315. finiti: '(even) limited' time – emphatically placed in the sentence and in the verse.

317. tormenta: a vivid image: Time batters the rocks with its siege-engines.

    privata fragore: 'without breaking up'.

318-23. The sky must be mortal if it is true that it creates all things and receives them back when they perish (as it will thus suffer the change of decrease and increase). The paragraph is curiously vague – the imprecise *hoc* (reflecting Pacuvius: see below) and the allusive *quidam* – and we might assume that the mortality of the sky was disposed of in the passage on air (273-80); but the theory of the sky as universal parent offers L. a supporting proof similar to that in 257-60. This theory is a variation of the ancient notion of father-sky impregnating mother-earth (cf. 1.250-1, 2.991 ff., Diels, *Doxographi Graeci*, 296), and contrasts with earth alone as universal mother (259 n.). Who were the *quidam* is hard to say: presumably thinkers like Diogenes of Apollonia (fifth century) who adopted Anaximenes' doctrine of air as the primary substance and origin of all things. More particularly L. is following quite closely some lines of Pacuvius (fr. 86 ff. R, perhaps based on Euripides' *Chrysippus*): 'hoc vide circum supraque quod complexu continet / terram . . . id quod nostri caelum memorant . . . omnia animat format alit auget creat / sepelit recipitque in sese omnia, omniumque idem est pater, / indidemque eadem aeque oriuntur deintegro atque eodem occidunt.' (It is interesting that there seems to be another link with tragedy in the similar context at 2.991 ff., which is reminiscent of Euripides fr. 839N.)

321. Cf. 238.

323. The double alliteration concludes the section with a flourish.

324–50. The world must have had a beginning and be still young because we have no records prior to the wars at Thebes and Troy; and the arts, and indeed philosophy, are recent developments. Even if we suppose that some natural disaster wiped out all traces of earlier generations it would follow that a greater disaster would have destroyed the world altogether.

There is some contradiction between the youth of the earth asserted here, and the picture of her as an exhausted mother past her child-bearing at 826–36 (see n. there) and 2.1150–74: L. in fact is blurring the distinction between the history of the physical earth and that of man and his activities.

324–7. Editors quote Macrobius using a similar argument in his commentary on Cic. *Somn. Scip.* 2.10.

326–7. The *Iliad* and the (lost) *Thebais*, both forming part of the early Greek Epic Cycle, represent the oldest known record of human activity. The idea that poets enshrine and immortalize men's achievements goes back at least to Pindar (Gow on Theocr. 16.30 f. collects references), and was itself given immortality by Horace, *C.* 4.8.28 'dignum laude virum Musa vetat mori', 4.9.25 ff.

supera: 'earlier than'.

329. 'flower grafted on to everlasting monuments of fame', i.e. recorded in immortal poetry. For this highly evocative image cf. Tac. *Dial.* 10.3 'nomen inserere possunt famae', and West, 2–3, who points to 'the juxtaposition of stone and flower, the fragility of fame and flower, the seeming durability of monuments, the immortality of poetry, and man's elaborate operations to procure immortality for himself'.

330. summa: = *summa rerum*: see 194 n.

332 ff. For progress in arts and crafts cf. 1448–57, where however a greater perfection of achievement is suggested. Here the repeated *nunc, modo*, and *nuper* stress that progress though good is still in comparatively early stages.

334. modo . . . sonores: see introd. n. to 1379–1435 for Democritus' view that music was a comparatively recent development in man's history. The Greek words *melicos, organici* (cf. 1036 n.) reflect the influence of Greek musical theory in the Roman world.

335-7. ratio: the Epicurean philosophy. The repetition *repertast* / *repertus* stresses the double importance of Epicurus' discoveries and of the appearance of L. himself to make them known in Latin. It is hard to test L.'s very emphatic claim (*primus cum primis*) to be the first to expound Epicureanism in Latin. We hear from Cicero that a certain Amafinius was the first to write in Latin on Epicureanism (*Tusc.* 4.6, *Fam.* 15.19.2): he does not mention L. in this connection, and we do not know exactly when Amafinius lived. But Cicero was very scathing in general about the quality of the writings of the Latin popularizers of philosophy, and L. may have shared his opinion and regarded himself as the first worthy exponent in his native tongue. Perhaps too Amafinius had concentrated on Epicurean ethics, while it is clear that L. thought it fundamental to clarify the physical theory. (See further Boyancé, *Lucrèce et l'Épicurisme*, 8 ff., H. M. Howe in *AJP* 72 (1951), 57-62, Robin on 336.)

337. The monosyllabic elision *s(um) in* is fairly common: Soubiran, 412-13, and cf. 1142 n. Surprisingly this is the only occurrence of *sum* in the poem.

338 ff. L. is thinking of legends like the exploits of Phaëthon and Deucalion, and his argument here is clearly part of the Epicurean response to Plato and Aristotle, whose works show these stories used in philosophical arguments (Plato, *Tim.* 22a ff., *Laws* 677a ff., Arist., περὶ φιλοσοφίας fr. 13R). L. develops the thought of overwhelming fires and floods in accordance with his own argument at 380-415.

340. vexamine: 'upheaval': ἅπαξ λεγόμενον. L. is particularly fond of -*men* formations, several of which occur only in the *DRN* (Bailey, i, 134-5).

343. tanto quique magis: 'all the more': an obscure phrase (recurring only at 3.700) in which *quique* is an abl. (233 n.).

   necessest: the usual form, but L. also has *necessumst* (376) and *necessust* (351) without any distinction in meaning.

344. Cf. 98.

345-7. Granted all this it would have needed only a more serious (*tristior*) affliction to bring the whole world to ruin. It is an argument from probability: given a set of conditions which produce a result, an extension of the conditions must lead to an extension of the result. (For a very similar argument see 3.484-6.)

348-50. To corroborate the last point L. adds an analogy, though this is not made explicit: our illnesses prove our mortality (so too natural disasters prove the world's mortality).

349. inter nos . . . aegrescimus: 'we see one another fall sick' (Rouse).

351-79. The world cannot be immortal: to be so it would have to be either solid (like atoms) or intangible (like void) or to have no space around it (like the universe). This reasoning is based on the axiom that destruction of anything can be caused only by an external blow or an inter-penetrating force (1.221–4), which can only be avoided by one or other of the conditions stated here. 351–63 recur at 3.806–18 (with minor variants in 351, 362) as one of the proofs of the mortality of the soul. As the argument is more relevant and more fully worked out here it is probable that the lines originated in Book 5: see 128–41 n.

351 ff. The construction is *necessust aut* (352) . . . *aut* (356) . . . *aut* (359) . . .

353–4. sibi: dat. of disadvantage instead of the more usual (*in*) *se* with *penetrare*.

  artas . . . partis: 'closely-packed parts': not having such parts atoms cannot suffer dissolution.

355. corpora: the atoms.

  ante: at 1.503–50: note especially 528–9 'haec neque dissolui plagis extrinsecus icta / possunt nec porro penitus penetrata retexi.'

358. neque ab ictu fungitur hilum: 'and is not in any degree at all affected by blows'. *fungitur* (πάσχει) regularly takes the acc. in old Latin.

  hilum: (cf. 1409) adverbial acc.: an obscure word used, generally after a negative, to mean 'very little', 'a tiny bit' (cf. *floccus, naucus* in a similar sense).

359. fit: Lachmann's correction of *sit* OQ to match the indicative *sunt* in 352 and 357.

360. quo: 'into which'.

  dissŏlŭĭque: to give a fifth-foot dactyl the *u* is frequently treated as a vowel: cf. 1.223, 559, 6.446, and contrast *dissŏlvĕrĕ* 363.

361–3. See also 2.303–7 for an emphatic statement of the same ideas.

  summarum summa: 'the universe', the complete totality of existence: an emphatic variant of expressions like *summa, omnis summa, rerum summa*. (Similar phrases with *haec* specify 'our world': 194 n.) For this type of intensifying genitive (somewhat rare in classical Latin) see Hofmann–Szantyr, 55–6, Kenney on 3.816. *neque extra* . . . depends on *sicut*, not on *quia*, with something like *res* ('its elements') understood as subject to *dissiliant*.

362. qui: adjectival 'any' after *neque*, for *ullus*.

364 ff. But none of these conditions is satisfied.

364. uti docui: at 1.329–69.

368. corruere: the transitive sense is rare: cf. Plautus *Rud.* 542 and perhaps Cat. 68.52.

369. cladem . . . pericli: 'dangerous disaster': the gen. is used adjectivally. For this kind of expression cf. Cic. *Clu.* 31 'poculo mortis', Hofmann–Szantyr, 64.

370. natura loci spatiumque profundi: the same phrase occurs at 1.1002.

373. leti . . . ianua: this vivid phrase is repeated at 1.1112 and varied at 2.960 'leti limine', 3.67 'leti portas', 6.762 'ianua Orci'. Death is virtually identified with Hades, and the expression derives from the

Homeric πύλαι Ἀΐδαο (*Il.* 5.646, *Od.* 14.156; cf. Aesch. *Ag.* 1291, with Fraenkel's note). It remained popular with later Latin poets: Virg. *A.* 2.661, Ovid *M.* 1.662, Statius *Silv.* 5.3.257, *Theb.* 3.68, Val. Fl. 3.386.

375. 'but it stands open and awaits them with a frightful huge chasm': note the yawning effect of the *a*-sounds (and another Virgilian echo at *A.* 6.237). For this sense of *respectare* ('await') cf. 975, 6.1234.

379. Repeated at 1217.

contemnere: 'defy'.

380–415. The fourth argument is from probability: it is quite possible that some day one of the elements will acquire such a preponderance over the others that it will overwhelm the world — look at the stories of Phaëthon's exploit, which nearly scorched the earth, and of the great flood. L.'s point is that the balance of elements which keeps the world going as we know it cannot be assumed to continue for ever, and his use of the illustrative myth of Phaëthon is interesting. He does not of course believe a word of it, but he introduces it as very picturesque decoration for his argument, he seems to think of it as a sort of allegory of the phenomenon he is envisaging — and he then with a sardonic *scilicet* (405) dismisses it as nonsense. The flood is treated more briefly and non-committally, perhaps because it was hallowed by a very strong and widespread tradition (see note below).

380–1. maxima ... membra: cf. 243–4 n. Because they are all *membra* of the world the elements' strife is called civil war, *pio nequaquam bello*. We regularly find *impius* (or an equivalent) used of civil war: Virg. *A.* 1.294, 6.613, Hor. *C.* 3.24.25, Lucan 1.238.

382. ollis: archaic form of *illis* used often by L. (see 1291, 1390).

383 ff. vel cum ... : the sentence rambles: there is no correlative *vel* (though we could take this one in the sense 'for instance'), and a new and extended thought takes off with *nequiquam* at 388.

385. patrarunt: Goebel's conjecture for the MSS *patrantur* gives the required perfect tense and avoids treating the verb as an unparalleled deponent. The reading may have arisen from the similar ending in the following line.

386. ultra: 'further', 'what is more'.

387. diluviare ... ponti: the rivers pour into the sea in such increased volume that the sea rises and floods the land. *diluviare* occurs only here.

388–9. Cf. 266–7.

392–3. spirantes ... bellum: cf. Cic. *Att.* 15.11.1 'Martem spirare diceres', and Greek phrases like the Homeric μένεα πνείοντες, Aesch. *Cho.* 33 κότον πνέων, Eur. *IT* 288 πνέουσα φόνον.

certamine ... cernere certant: another 'figura etymologica'. *cernere* is an archaic usage for *decernere* (cf. 782).

394. interea: adversative, 'nevertheless': cf. 83.

superantior: Ernout-Robin suggest a contrast between this comparative (apparently unique), suggesting a partial victory, and the emphatic *exsuperarint* 384.

396 ff. The Sun god allowed his son Phaëthon to drive his chariot for a day, but Phaëthon could not control the horses, which ran wildly off-course and approached too close to the earth. To prevent the earth being incinerated Jupiter blasted Phaëthon with a thunderbolt. (See Ovid's account at *M.* 2.1–328.) L.'s full-blown, elevated tone here suggests tongue-in-the-cheek parody of the epic style: see West, 52-3, and cf. 22 ff. n.

396. The text is uncertain (see apparatus): with this reading *superāt* is so scanned and taken as a contracted perfect (cf. similar examples at 1.70, 6.587).

397. avia: 'going astray': contrast 1386.

avia . . . rapax vis . . . equorum: for the complex periphrasis see 28 n.

399-400. Both epithets *omnipotens* and *magnanimum* are sardonic: Jupiter and his power are a myth, and is Phaëthon not 'great-spirited' but 'over-ambitious'?

402. succepit: 'caught from below', the literal sense associated with this form of the verb: see *OLD* s.v., Austin on Virg. *A.* 1.175.

lampada: also of the sun at 610, 6.1198.

403. trementis: from the panic of their own stampede.

404. 'then guiding them along their proper path restored all things'.

405. The sarcastic comment dismisses the childish fairy-tale. Similarly the account of Cybele is introduced at 2.600 with 'hanc veteres Graium docti cecinere poetae', and dismissed at 2.645 with 'longe sunt tamen a vera ratione repulsa' (cf. 406 here).

Graium: e.g. lost plays by Aeschylus (*Heliades*) and Euripides (*Phaëthon* – from which a number of lovely fragments survive: see the edition of J. Diggle (Cambridge, 1970)).

407 ff. ignis enim superare: lines with similar openings (cf. 396) frame the Phaëthon story, but this one introduces the real reason. Such a conflagration could arise only when an unusually large number (*plura*) of fire-particles collect from infinite space. Then either something happens to quell their force (such an occurrence might be enshrined in the Phaëthon myth), or the world perishes in flames (still a possibility).

411-15. L. treats the legend of the flood implicitly with more respect. More or less severe floods from rain or rivers are in any case a familiar experience, and there was a strong and widespread tradition of a great cataclysmic flood found in many versions in Near Eastern records, both Mesopotamian and Hebrew. These may have inspired to some extent the myth of Deucalion, the most famous of several

flood stories current in the Greco-Roman world (Pindar *O*. 9.41 ff.,
Apollodorus 1.7.2). See further *Encyclopaedia Britannica* (ed. 1968)
s.v. 'Flood (in Religion and Myth)'.

412. vitas: Purmann's conjecture for *multas* OQ (which some editors
retain with *urbis* (Pontanus) for *undis*). We might also consider
multos C 131, not recorded or discussed by Bailey, but adopted by
some early editors, and Wakefield and M. F. Smith. (For the partitive
gen. *hominum multos* cf. Virg. *A*. 2.398 'multos Danaum'.)

416–508. The formation of the world from a state of original chaos by
the chance grouping of atoms (416–48). First earth was formed,
then air and fire, and thus the sky (449–70); then sun and moon
(471–79); then the earth contracted and settled into shape and the
sea filled its hollows (480–94). Thus the elements settled into their
relative places as we know them (495–508).

In this section L. follows orthodox Epicurean physics: see, for
example, Epic. *Ep. Pyth*. 89–90, Aëtius 1.4.1 ff. (Usener 308), Robin
on 416 ff. As always his primary aim is to show that the formative
accumulations of atoms were entirely fortuitous and in no way due
to design (*neque consilio* 419: cf. Aëtius, loc. cit., τῶν ἀτόμων
σωμάτων ἀπρονόητον καὶ τυχαίαν ἐχόντων τὴν κίνησιν). Many of
the ideas here developed have been at least touched on before, for
which reason the introductory paragraph 416–31 consists almost
entirely of lines from elsewhere in this and other books (see below:
as Bailey rightly says, repetition was L.'s only means of giving a
cross-reference to a similar argument elsewhere).

416–31. Introductory statement: atoms created the world by chance.
The lines either vary or repeat earlier lines as follows: 416 (5.67),
417 (5.68), 418 (5.76), 419–21 (1.1021-3), 422 (5.187, 1.1024),
423 (5.188, 1.1025), 424–6 (5.189-91), 428 (1.1026), 429–31
(2.1061-3).

416. coniectus: cf. 67 n., 600: 'throwing together' suggests the haphazard nature of the process.

417. pontique profunda: for this type of expression see 35 n.

420–1. *sagaci mente* and *pepigere* are an obvious irony: there is neither
an over-all divine plan (*consilio*) nor intelligent thinking and bargain-
ing by individual atoms.

424–5. See notes to 189–90.

428. omne genus: 'of all kinds' (cf. 437): an 'internal' accusative used
adjectivally with *coetus* and *motus* (acc. plurals).

429. ea: 'those particular ones' which happen to form the first clusters
of matter.

432–48. There was an original state of confusion and discord among
the atoms; then they began to sort themselves out into groups, like
joining like, so as to form eventually the four elements of the world.

L. has already at 2.62-332 given an extensive general account of

the movements and combinations of atoms: here he concentrates on
how these have produced the visible phenomena of our world.

432. hic: 'in these circumstances': cf. 1002.

   rota: 'disc', 'orb' of the sun, rather than his chariot wheel, as is
clear from 564 and the regular use of κύκλος for the sun's disc in
Greek poetry (Aesch. *Pr.* 91, *Pers.* 504, Soph. *Ant.* 416).

434. caelum: used as often for *aether*, the outer, more rarefied air extending to the bounds of the world, opposed to *aer*, the nearer
atomsphere around the earth.

   denique: 'indeed', adding a slight emphasis to *terra*.

436-7. nova . . . principiis: 'a sort of strange turbulence in the primeval
mass composed of all kinds of rudimentary particles': for this sense
of *moles* cf. Ovid *Ars* 2.467, *M.* 1.7, *F.* 1.111.

437-45. Reisacker's transposition of the lines makes them synchronize
far better with the stages of the argument, and has been widely
accepted.

437-9. The construction is 'quorum discordia, proelia miscens, intervalla
. . . motus turbabat'. *intervalla . . . motus* is repeated from 2.726-7
– a catalogue of terms describing the relative positions and behaviour
of the atoms.

440-1. propter . . . figuras belongs within the *quod* clause: 'because
owing to . . . they could not all when joined together remain so'.

443. inde loci: 'then', 'next' (cf. 741, 791): *loci* is a partitive genitive
as in the similar expressions *ubi loci, eo loci* etc. (*OLD* s.v. 25).

444-5. discludere, dividere, disponere: an emphatic tricolon, varying
the same idea. The emphasis continues with the repeated *secernere,
secreto, secreti, sorsum, sorsus*.

447-8. The construction is uncertain but it seems simplest to take *mare*
(like *caelum*) as acc. with *secernere*: 'to separate the sea too, so that
it might spread out with its waters kept apart'. Otherwise take *mare*
as nom. and parallel with *ignes* after *facere* understood: '(facere)
mare uti pateret, . . . (paterent) ignes'. Similarly, *ignes* could be acc.
with *secernere* (taking *puri secretique* with *aetheris*), or nom. subject
of *paterent* understood.

449-70. The formation of earth, air, fire, and consequently the sky.

450. gravia et perplexa: in contrast with *levibus atque rotundis* 455. At
2.333-477 L. explains in detail how the characteristics of different
things are due to the shape of their constituent atoms.

451. medio / imas: the earth took shape in the middle of the spherical
world (cf. 534), and at 'the bottom position' relative to the upper
hemisphere of the world, which is all that we see of it.

453. expressere: 'squeezed out'.

454. moenia mundi: the *aether* (467-70): see 119 n. Part of the Epicurean definition of a world is περιοχή τις οὐρανοῦ . . . καταλήγουσα
ἐν πέρατι ἢ ἀραιῷ ἢ πυκνῷ, 'a certain portion of sky . . . terminating

in a boundary either rare or dense' (*Ep. Pyth.* 88). Our particular
world has a rare-textured boundary: Aëtius 1.4.2.

456. There is some ambiguity in the terms *seminibus* and *elementis*, which
can mean not only 'atoms' strictly, but 'particles' compounded of
the appropriate atoms (as at 3.187, 374).

457–8. per rara . . . erumpens: 'bursting out from the parts of the earth
through its loose-knit pores': *terrae* goes with both *foramina* and
partibus. Cf. 811, 6.592.

460–6. A beautiful and elaborate simile which goes poetically far
beyond the simple illustration of exhalations from the earth: a good
example of L.'s enjoyment of painting a picture for its own sake.
Strictly, *videmus* has no construction, being followed by a series of
cum-clauses and then a main finite verb *subtexunt* 466: we can
translate equally loosely 'this is very like what we often see: when
. . .'.

461. gemmantis rore per herbas: cf. 2.319 'herbae gemmantes rore
recenti'.

462. radiati . . . solis: cf. 700.

464. 'and even as the earth itself sometimes seems to smoke': the *ut*
construction slightly distorts the run of the sentence. (Some early
editors read *ipsa quoque* (Pius) or *ipsaque et* (Wakefield).) Cf. 6.523
'terraque cum fumans umorem tota redhalat'.

465. The OCT comma after *conciliantur* was rightly removed by Bailey
in his later edition: *in alto* reinforces *sursum*, and no ancient reader
of the unpunctuated text, with only the sense and rhythm of the
line to guide him, would have taken the phrase with the following
line.

466. subtexunt: all the exhalations becoming clouds literally 'weave a
texture under' the sky: cf. 6.482 'et quasi densendo subtexit caerula
nimbis' (in an account of the formation of clouds).

467. diffusilis: 'spreading', 'expansive': ἅπαξ λεγόμενον.

468. flexit: Lachmann's conjecture for *saepsit* OQ (a likely dittography
from 470) is widely accepted as giving the required sense. Stampini's
fudit is also attractive.

470. avido complexu: the *aether* is almost personified: cf. 2.1066 'hic
est avido complexu quem tenet aether.'

471–9. Then the sun and moon were formed (from particles which were
forced out from among the earth-particles: cf. 453–4 and 480 'his
. . . retractis').

472. interutrasque: 'between the two', earth and sky. This adverb
(*-utrasque* is formed like *alias, foras*) is used only by L., e.g. 476,
839 (by conjecture).

473. quae: sun and moon.

474. fuĕrunt: 193 n.

476. corpora viva: this is strictly a simile based on the fact that they move (*versent*), like *vivit* 538 used of the earth: the parts of the world are emphatically stated to be inanimate at 124-5.

477-9. Their positions and movements are such that they still remain genuine members of the world, just as our moving members are as much part of our bodies as those at rest. There are similar comparisons with the human body at 540 ff., 556 ff.

   quod genus: 'just as': cf. 59 n., 428 n.

480-94. Then the earth contracted into its present shape while the sea filled its hollows.

480. his: the particles listed at 453-4.

482. The *s*-alliteration no doubt echoes the flooding waters.

483 ff. More contraction of the earth's surface was caused by constant bombardment from winds from the *aether* and from the rays of the sun. This too caused further exuding of water particles to increase the seas, and of fire and air particles into the sky, and the earth's contours became firm.

483. aestus: 'tide', 'current'.

485. extrema ad limina: 'upon its outer edges'.

   in artum: 'into a dense mass': Munro's conjecture for *partem* OQ; but we should seriously consider Bockemüller's *terrae* (484) . . . *partes*, a simple change which also avoids the awkwardly juxtaposed adverbial phrases.

486. 'so that under this battering it was compressed and contracted upon its own centre': i.e. presumably, it formed a hard core within itself, if *medio* means the middle of the earth. But *medio suo* might mean 'its proper position in the centre' of the world, as at 451.

487. sudor: L. may recall a phrase of Empedocles, who is alleged to have called the sea the sweat of the earth (γῆς ἱδρῶτα θάλασσαν B55 D-K). Cf. the phrase *sudor maris* for 'brine' at 2.465.

488. camposque natantis: a picturesque phrase, repeated at 6.405, 1142, and imitated by Virgil at *G*. 3.198.

491. templa: 'regions': 103 n. Cf. 6.387-8 'fulgentia . . . caelestia templa'. 'Regions of the sky' is a typical periphrasis for the *aether*.

495-508. Summary and recapitulation of the relative positions of the elements after their formation.

495-6. terrae . . . constitit: 'the heavy earth was formed with its dense structure.'

   omnis mundi quasi limus: 'all the muddy part, as it were, of the world'.

   in imum: 451 n.

497. The line's stolid rhythm and heavy monosyllabic cadence carefully reflect the sense. Contrast the effect of 498: the repeated *i*-sounds and the three elisions make it much lighter and smoother.

498. ipse: the *aether* is seen as the climax of the elements, and the rest of the paragraph concentrates on its particular characteristics as an introduction to the next section on celestial phenomena.

499. liquidis / pura: in contrast with the earth and its constituent particles. *corporibus liquidis* is a descriptive ablative loosely attached to all the nouns in the previous line.

500–3. For the relative positions of *aether* and *aer* see 434 n.

503. haec omnia: 'all things below': *haec* from the viewpoint of someone on earth, like 'in hoc caelo qui dicitur aer' 4.132.

504–5. incertis / certo: the turbulence of the lower elements is contrasted with the smooth-flowing serenity of the *aether*.

    impete: 'sweep': an abl. form of *impetus* which L. regularly uses for metrical reasons. Cf. 200 n., 913.

    suos ignes: the heavenly bodies. The subject of their movements is taken up in detail in the next section.

507–8. L. argues from the steady flow of one element to that of another. Ancient geographers believed that the Pontus (Black Sea) flowed in one direction only into the Propontis (Sea of Marmara): Sen. *NQ* 4.2.29, Strabo 1.3.12. The idea survives as a simile in Shakespeare: Othello's urge for revenge is 'like to the Pontic sea, / Whose icy current and compulsive course / Ne'er feels retiring ebb, but keeps due on / To the Propontic and the Hellespont' (*Othello* 3.3.457 ff.).

    unum labendi ... tenorem: 'its single gliding course' – reflected in the spondaic rhythm of the line.

509–770. After discussing the world as a whole L. in this second main section of the book turns to astronomical phenomena – the movements and sizes of the heavenly bodies, the power of the sun, the origin of moonlight, day and night, eclipses. This is technically the most difficult part of the book to understand, and the interpretation of some passages is necessarily very speculative.

    The main statement of Epicurus' beliefs about astronomy is to be found in the *Letter to Pythocles*, from which it is clear that L. follows his theories more or less closely. Epicurus' own debt to earlier thinkers is harder to trace: we know that in some details he followed the earlier Atomists, and presumably he did so in others which we cannot check. We should remember too that the fourth century BC was particularly fertile in astronomical speculation based on the application of mathematical principles to the study of celestial phenomena. Eudoxus of Cnidus, Callippus of Cyzicus, Heraclides Ponticus, and Aristotle all attacked the problem of explaining the movements of the heavenly bodies, and some of them produced solutions using a variety of complex models based on revolving spheres. (See G. E. R. Lloyd, *Early Greek Science: Thales to Aristotle*, Chap. 7.) Epicurus' and Lucretius' picture of the world is recognizably derived from this kind of speculation. The world, *mundus*, is a hollow sphere with the earth, fixed and stationary, in the centre. Around the earth is the denser atmosphere, *aer*, and further out is the pure rarefied *aether*, extending to the boundary of the *mundus*. The heavenly bodies – sun,

moon, stars, and the five known planets – are seen to move in complex orbits through the *aer* or *aether* (it is not clear which), and it is
on these beautiful and dramatic objects that attention is mainly
focused. In view of the assumption of a central and unmoving earth
we should also remember that two brilliant insights had corrected
this picture long before L.'s time. Heraclides Ponticus in the fourth
century had postulated the axial rotation of the earth, and Aristarchus
of Samos in the third century had put forward a heliocentric model
of the world in place of the geocentric one. It is one of the ironies
of the history of science that most subsequent thinkers – like
Lucretius – rejected both these theories (Lloyd, op. cit., 95). A
separate question is raised by what L. thought to be the actual shape
of the earth (see introductory note to 534-63).

It is notable in this section how often L. is at pains to give alternative explanations of phenomena: see 526-33. In this he is following a firm principle of Epicurus' theory of knowledge: in areas
of investigation which are not fully open to sense-perception we
must accept as possible all solutions which are not contradicted by
our sensations (and in this connection arguments from analogy with
what we do know are valuable). See *Ep. Hdt.* 79-80, *Ep. Pyth.* 86-8,
Diog. Oen. fr. 8 col. III Chilton; and another clear statement of the
principle by L. at 6.703-11. The essential point throughout is that
whatever explanation we accept in no way derives from divine action.

509-33. The heavenly bodies move because either (1) the whole sphere
of the sky rotates, driven by air currents; or (2) the sky is stationary
and they move independently, driven by air currents or their own
desire for nourishment.

(Some editors have bracketed these lines as out of place on the
erroneous assumption that *astra* means only stars: see Bailey's sensible
arguments ad loc. in favour of keeping them here.)

509. astrorum: 'heavenly bodies' in general.

canamus: a touch of the high style (he could have said *docebo*) to
introduce a major topic: cf. *canenda* at 6.84, also referring to
heavenly phenomena.

511-12. If the sphere of the sky rotates (taking the stars etc. with it),
peripheral air pressure is required at both poles of its axis in order to
keep it, as it were, poised and steady.

utrimque: 'from both directions', i.e. at the poles of the axis,
repeating the idea in *ex utraque . . . parti.*

513-16. 'then another air flows above and keeps moving in the same
direction in which the stars of the eternal world roll in their sparkling
course; or yet another air flows beneath to push the sphere from
below in the opposite direction, just as we see rivers turn the scoops
of a water-wheel.' To keep the spherical *mundus* revolving there
must be a wind current acting upon it from outside. If such a current

is above the upper hemisphere it will of course be moving in the same direction as we see the stars moving; if it is below the lower hemisphere it must be moving in the opposite direction.

514. aeterni: a poetic, not (in L.'s view) scientifically true, adjective: cf. 476 n. Yet in 516 we have a scientific rather than poetic simile: contrast the almost impressionist picture of dawn mists at 460–6.

516. rotas atque haustra: 'the scoops of water-wheels' (hendiadys) – almost the only occurrence of *haustra*.

519 ff. Assuming a stationary *mundus*, the stars may be moved along by air currents either within the *mundus* (*inclusi* 519) or blowing in from outside it (*extrinsecus* 522).

519. inclusi: enclosed within the world, rather than within the stars as some editors take it.

521. caeli . . . summania templa: 'the night-thundering regions of the sky': Summanus was a Roman god (perhaps a form of Jupiter) who caused thunder at night (see Pliny *HN* 2.138).

522. aliunde . . . alicunde extrinsecus: 'from some place elsewhere and outside (the world)'.

523–5. sive . . . : Or the stars may themselves move over the sky in search of fresh fuel for their fires: a memorable image (recalling 2.317–19), in which the heavenly bodies are seen as sheep browsing in their pasture. L.'s artistry is obvious when we compare this picture with the corresponding laconic statement in *Ep. Pyth.* 93 κατά τινα ἐπινέμησιν τοῦ πυρὸς ἀεὶ ἐπὶ τοὺς ἑξῆς τόπους ἰόντος, 'owing to the spreading of the fire which always moves on to successive regions'. The stars' *cibus* is of course the fiery particles supplied by the *aether*: for *pascentis* see 1.231 'unde aether sidera pascit?', 1.1090. *serpere* is used of the sun below 692.

526–33. We must consider many possible causes in this and other worlds.

526. eorum: the above explanations.

527. per omne: 'throughout the universe': cf. 530, 1344.

528 = 1345.

531. hic: 'in our world'.

532. vegeat: 'give force to': an archaic transitive form of *vigeo*.

533. pedetemptim progredientis: 'one who advances gradually in knowledge': cf. 1453.

534–63. The earth is at the centre of the world and it is at rest. This is possible because it is joined to the atmosphere below it by a 'different substance', which thus prevents it from pressing down as a weight upon this nether air. This has been so since creation, so that the earth is organically linked with the *aer* just as our limbs are part of ourselves.

　　We cannot be sure what Epicurus or Lucretius thought of the shape of the earth (though L. presumably did not think it spherical as he rejects the notion of an antipodean part of the earth at 1.1058–67);

but it is a reasonable guess that they accepted the earlier Atomists' picture of the earth as flat and round (Leucippus said it was tambourine-shaped, and Democritus disc-shaped, A26, A94 D–K). A flat earth floating motionless on air was also a widely held theory, adopted by Anaximenes, Anaxagoras, and Democritus, according to Aristotle, *de caelo* 294 b 13 ff. L.'s rather obscure *alia natura* seems to add a refinement to this earlier picture in order to explain further the motionless stability of the earth, but this hypothesis too may derive from Epicurus, if some scrappy fragments from his περὶ φύσεως have been correctly interpreted: see frs. [26] [22], [26] [41] Arrighetti, and Bailey, iii, 1756-7. The meaning of 535 ff. seems to be that there is no sharp contrast under the earth between its own firm, dense texture and the adjacent air, but a gradual lessening of density away from the earth's surface which creates a sort of intermediate belt between earth and *aer*. This can be called a 'different nature' or 'substance', (i.e. neither earth nor air), and it is this which offers a firm prop to the weight of the earth.

534. media / quiescat: the two key concepts under discussion.

536. convenit: 'it is natural' or 'proper'.

537. ex ineunte aevo: 'from its earliest existence': cf. 859.

　　　uniter aptam: 'united into a single being': cf. 555, 558.

538. vivit: 'dwells': 476 n.

544. permulto . . . minora: '(although) very much smaller' than our limbs.

545. For the idea of the relative powers of individual things see 89-90 and n.

546-7. The alliteration is noteworthy, and also the emphatic *aliena, aliunde, alienis*, and the four elisions in 547.

548. pariter: sc. *cum auris*, i.e. *aere*.

549. The OCT comma after *membra* is a slip, and could only be acceptable with Brieger's *videtur*. Take *quasi . . . videntur* together, and understand *est* from 546 with *concepta* and *certa*.

550 ff. Proof of the earth's close links with the air above as well as below it (*supra* 551 as well as *subter* 536); but the phenomenon is hard to visualize, and one would think that shock-waves from thunder would be seen to travel from air to earth rather than vice versa.

554 = 3.325, in a passage describing the indissoluble link between soul and body: an explicit analogy follows (556-63) between this link and the close interconnection between earth and air.

556-63. The human body again illustrates a point (cf. 540 ff.). L. describes the mechanism by which the mind and the soul move the body at 4.877-906. Both play their part, the mind acting on the soul which in turn acts on the body: so here we have both *anima* (557, 560) and *animus* (563). The analogy is worked out in the form of three questions, the third of which makes the comparison explicit.

563. terris: 'the earth': *terrae* pl. (as in *orbis terrarum*) = *tellus* sing., whether for reasons of metre or just verbal variety.

564–91. The sun, moon, and stars are all about the same size as we see them. The arguments are from analogy. (1) Distant fires on earth, so long as they are bright and warm to us, never look smaller because of their distance: therefore sun and stars must really be the size we see them. (2) All things which we see at a distance begin to lose their clear outline before they look smaller: therefore the moon is the size it seems because it has a clear outline to our view.

L. derives both his statements and his basic argument from Epicurus (*Ep. Pyth.* 91), who made his own contribution to a much debated subject. Ancient philosophers differed widely about the size of the sun, though Heraclitus came close to Epicurus' view in his belief that the sun was a foot wide (B3 D–K). On the other hand, Cicero repeatedly jeered at Epicurus' simple-minded theory that the sun is about as big as it looks (*Fin.* 1.20, *Ac. Pr.* 2.82 and 123), and it must be taken as the *reductio ad absurdum*, however logical in Epicurean terms, of the unswerving reliance on sense-perception (see on *sensibus* below).

564. rota: 432 n.

565. sensibus: though further arguments will be from analogy (566 ff.) the inference is based on sense-perception, which cannot be questioned, as in the Epicurean source (see *Ep. Pyth.* 91, with Bailey's note).

566. quibus . . . cumque: tmesis.

568–9. For the phraseology cf. 3.213–14 'nil ibi libatum de toto corpore cernas / ad speciem', of soul-atoms leaving a corpse.

570 [573]. A certain transposition: the misplacement of the line also led to the repetition of 571 as 574, which must be deleted.

571. mulcent: Lachmann's emendation. Bailey in his later edition perhaps rightly reverted to the MSS *fulgent*, though we need not take it as 'a unique transitive use'. *loca* could be nom.: 'the world is bright'.

572. hinc: 'from earth': 503 n.

filum: 'outline', hence 'size', 'bulk' as at 581, 589.

573. vere: this has more point if taken with *videri*, in spite of the gap between them, than with *possis*.

575–6. For theories on the source of the moon's light see introductory note to 705–50.

notho: νόθῳ, 'borrowed' (properly 'bastard', 'spurious'): used of moonlight also by Catullus (34.15–16).

lumine lustrans: 'spreading her light over': a memorable alliterative phrase which L. uses again of heavenly bodies at 693, 1437, 6.284 (a thunderbolt). Cf. also *lustrare* by itself at 79.

578. The construction is 'quam ⟨haec figura⟩ esse videtur, qua nostris oculis cernimus ⟨eam ferri⟩'.

579 ff. Distant things lose their distinctness before they look smaller, but the moon looks quite distinct. The reason for the blurred appearance of things seen *aera per multum* is explained at 4.353-63 as the damage done to the edges of the *simulacra* before they reach us: the intervening air subjects them to a constant battering, so that they lose their clarity of outline and, for example, square buildings at a distance look round to us.

583-4. ut . . . alto: 'is seen on high by us from earth in just the outline which defines her shape and exactly the size she is'. The indefinites *utcumque* and *quanta quanta* ('however big') probably refer to the varying shape and size of the moon at different phases.

585 ff. The construction is suspended, *quoscumque* . . . not being picked up until *scire licet* . . . 590, with the argument from earthly fires in between. In this way L. juxtaposes the *quoscumque* clauses and stresses the closeness of the parallel. (But Cartault might have been right in transposing [594-5] to follow 585.)

   aetheris ignes: i.e. stars.

587. 'so long as their flickering is clear and their glow can be seen'.

589. alteram utram in partem: i.e. becoming greater or less (cf. 685). Metrically we have here a type of 'quasi-cretic' elision (-u-), *alter(am) utram*, which occurs a few times in the *DRN* but was on the whole avoided by the Augustan poets (Bailey, i, 129, Soubiran, 222 ff., 236).

590-1. Marullus's transposition of the clearly misplaced [594-5]: but see 585 n.

590. perquam pauxillo: 'by an exceedingly tiny amount': for the emphatic phrase cf. 3.229-30 'perquam pauxillis . . . seminibus' (of soul-atoms).

592-613. How can so small a sun give out so much light and heat? (1) Particles of heat may gather there from all over the world, so that as from one single fountain it can lavishly pour forth light and heat; or (2) the sun's own fire may be small but its heat particles may increase their force by kindling the air as they pass through it; or (3) perhaps much of the heat surrounding it is invisible but none the less powerful.

   This passage is an attempt to reconcile two apparently conflicting data of sense-perception: the tiny sun and its enormous power to produce heat and light. We do not know if the Epicureans asked L.'s question, but it is likely that this disparity struck them, and there is some scrappy evidence that Epicurus (Usener 343) and Diogenes of Oenoanda (fr. 8 cols. III-IV Chilton) had a view of the sun's source of power comparable to L.'s first suggestion.

592-3. mirandum . . . tantulus . . . tantum: for the phrasing cf. 4.898-900 'nec tamen illud in his rebus mirabile constat, / tantula quod tantum corpus corpuscula possunt / contorquere'.

594. rigando: 'flooding': 281-2 n.

596. Deleted as an obvious dittography of 584.

597. hinc: i.e. from the sun.

598. fontem: cf. 281.

    scatere atque erumpere lumen: 'to gush out and send forth a flood of light': the verbs are combined also at 952, 6.895–6, and cf. 40 above. Transitive *erumpere* is not rare: see *OLD* s.v.

600–1. conveniunt . . . confluit: cf. 660–1.

    coniectus: cf. 67, 416.

602–3. The explicit comparison with a spring brings together, as it were, the many words applicable also to water which have been used in the last few lines (*rigando, perfundat, largifluum fontem scatere, confluit, capite, profluat*). Cf. 281–305 n.

606. opportunus . . . et idoneus: almost 'ready and able' to be kindled by the small bits of heat passing through it.

608–9. Another comparison from common observation to make the point (cf. 602–3).

    quod genus: 478 n.

610. lampade: cf. 402.

612. nullo . . . notatus: 'with no clearly seen radiance'.

613. tantum: either (1) 'only' with *aestifer* (not bringing light too), or (2) 'so great a' with *ictum*. The subject of *exaugeat* is *ignis*.

614–49. The courses of the sun, moon, and stars. Possible explanations for (1) the apparently different speeds of the orbits of the heavenly bodies: the nearer they are to the earth the more slowly the revolving sky carries them round, so that the moon is slower than the sun (though she looks faster) and the sun slower than the stars; (2) the slanting plane of the sun's orbit (i.e. the ecliptic): this may be due to the action of alternating air currents, which may also be responsible for the orbital movements of the moon and stars.

    This is a difficult passage, chiefly because, as many editors have shown (see especially Bailey and Ernout–Robin), L. has confused the logical progression of his arguments. After stating the two phenomena to be discussed (614–19), he gives one possible explanation of one of them (varying orbital speeds: 621–36). He then begins at 637 with what should be an alternative cause (*fit quoque ut*) of the same phenomenon, but actually goes on to discuss the cause of the other one, the sun's ecliptic. This suggestion – air currents – is then offered too as an alternative cause of the movements of moon and stars, which brings us, partially at least, back to the subject of 621–36. Subsequent revision might have tidied up the logical precision of this section: probably L. was diverted by the realization that he must say something about the sun's ecliptic, and this distorted the symmetry of his arguments.

    The phenomenon referred to at 637–42 is the inclination of the ecliptic (the sun's apparent yearly path among the stars) at an angle to the plane of the celestial equator. This is in fact caused by the inclination of the earth's own axis, but to a geocentric viewpoint the sun's orbit seems to move up in the sky until at the summer solstice it reaches the Tropic (or 'turning-point') of Cancer (617), and then down until at the winter solstice it reaches the Tropic of Capricorn (615). Other Epicureans commented with interest on the ecliptic. Epicurus discussed it at *Ep. Pyth.* 93, and suggested various causes, one of which is the theory of air currents offered by L. Diogenes of Oenoanda too (fr. 8 col. I Chilton) noted that the sun and moon have oblique courses.

615-16. aegocerotis brumalis . . . flexus: 'the midwinter turning-point of Capricorn': the Greek form of Capricornus being more unusual gives a picturesque touch. *flexus* (616, 640) and *meta* (617 and perhaps 690) are used technically for 'tropics': see *OLD flexus* 4, *meta* 3.

617. cancri se: Lachmann's emendation of *canceris* OQ, to avoid the archaic genitive and the intransitive *vertat*; but neither is a compelling reason to alter the text (see Bailey's later thoughts in his note here).
> **ut:** 'how', parallel to *quo pacto* 615.

618-19. The moon's apparently greater orbital speed is shown to be illusory: what really happens is that being the slowest she is overtaken more quickly by the stars, not that she 'moves back more quickly' to them (635-6).

618. mensibus: 'month by month'.

619. Cf. 692.

621. vel cum primis: 'perhaps among the most likely causes'.

622 = 3.371: L. showed marked respect for Democritus' views. (Since appositional *vir* normally has an adjective, *sancta* is probably a 'transferred' epithet, the whole phrase standing for *Democriti sententia, viri sancti.*) The theory here mentioned may be referred to in a short comment of Aëtius on Democritus (A89 D-K).

623 ff. For the theory of a rotating sky see 510-16. The idea here is that the sky revolves more quickly the further it is from the earth, so that the stars move faster than the sun and the sun faster than the moon. So to an observer on the earth the sun is 'left behind' (626) by the stars; while the moon is so much slower that she seems to be 'reversing' towards the stars as they 'catch up' and 'return' to her at each of their revolutions (633-6): they are in effect 'lapping' the moon. (L. discusses at 4.387 ff. the optical illusions which can arise from the relative positions of moving and stationary objects.)

623. terram . . . propter: 31 n.
> **sidera:** 'heavenly bodies' generally (as at 649), while throughout the paragraph *signa* means strictly 'stars' or 'constellations'.

625-6. rapidas illius et acris . . . viris: 'the swiftness and forcefulness in the power of that whirling'.

627. posterioribu' signis: 'the stars still behind him' – though they will in due course overtake him.

629. lunam: sc.*relinqui*. The statement of Democritus' theory continues to 631 (*posse*), and the subordinate verbs *abest* and *propinquat* should strictly be subjunctive, but L. occasionally ignores this rule (see Bailey, i, 97).

632–6. Another, more detailed, statement of the same point.

634. hanc adipiscuntur circum: 'catch her up as they move round'.

635–6. L. concludes by picking up the point of the moon's apparent swiftness: see notes on 618–19, 623 ff.

637–42. The slanting of the ecliptic may be caused by alternating wind currents which push the sun to each of the tropics in turn: see introductory note to 614–49; and for air currents cf. 513–23.

637–8. transversis: 'across the sun's (normal equatorial) course'.

  aer . . . alter: 'each of two air currents' picked up by *qui* (639) . . . *qui* (641).

639. aestivis . . . signis: i.e. the stars or constellations which the sun passes through in summer. By a natural extension the sun is said to experience the same temperatures as the earth at corresponding times of the year (*gelidum, gelidis, frigoris, aestiferas, fervida*).

642. fervida signa: = *aestivis signis* 639: *fervida* here has a more precise application than in the same phrase at 628.

643–9. Consideration of air currents brings us back to the question of lunar and stellar orbits (see introductory note). Such currents may cause the heavenly bodies to move in directions contrary to one another, as we see happens with different layers of cloud.

643–4. It seems simplest to take *stellas* as 'stars' generally, and *magnos annos* as the great lengths of time taken by their individual orbits. Some editors and translators restrict *stellas* to 'planets', and raise the question whether 644 refers to the 'Great Year' – the period which it takes them to return simultaneously to their original starting-points (Plato *Tim.* 39d, Aratus *Phaen.* 458–9, Cic. *Arat.* 232–3: see in general *RE* 20.2095–6). But the 'Great Year', with its mystic and astrological implications, seems alien and irrelevant to L.'s thinking.

645. alternis: probably with *aeribus* as well as with *partibus.*

647. supernis: dat. after *diversas*: 'lower clouds move in directions contrary to (the directions of) upper ones'; a compendious expression of a fairly common type, like 4.1174 'eadem facit . . . omnia turpi'.

648. aetheris: if this is not a slip for *aeris* the heavenly bodies are also in the *aether* (see 509–770 n.).

650–5. Night comes because (1) the sun is extinguished each day; or (2) he passes under the earth. Again we are offered theories which derive from Epicurus (*Ep. Pyth.* 92, where the second explanation suggests that the sun disappears behind the edge of the earth, not actually under it); and the first suggestion of daily extinction (and rekindling) goes back to Xenophanes (A33 D–K), Heraclitus (B6 D–K), and Metrodorus of Chios (A4 D–K).

651. ultima caeli: the western horizon.

652–3. Cf. 758–61 on the cause of solar eclipses, especially the phrases *dimittere languidus ignis* and *per auras*. The latter suggests that *aere multo* here means 'by the long journey through the air', though it might mean, as Metrodorus thought (see above), that the air condensed into water and so quenched the sun.

   itere: an archaic form of the abl. L. has another old form *itiner* (acc.) at 6.339. The classical *iter, itineris* is thus a hybrid formation: see Ernout-Meillet, s.v. *eo* (*iter*).

655. vis: whether the rotating sky or something else (621 ff.).

656–79. Dawn comes because (1) the sun's rays light up the sky in advance of his own reappearance; or (2) at fixed times heat particles gather together to re-create a new sun, just as we see many natural phenomena occur at fixed times and in regular sequence.

   The issue here is not just the reappearance of the sun, which is accounted for by implication in the previous discussion of its disappearance, but the cause of the glow we see in the sky before we see the sun. The reasons offered follow logically (in reverse order) on the two theories just given about nightfall.

656. Matuta: an old Italian goddess of the dawn, identified with the Greek Ino or Leucothea (Cic. *Tusc.* 1.28, Ovid *F.* 6.479 ff.).

658. ille: 'the very one', emphasizing *idem*: contrast the *solis nova lumina* 662 of the other theory.

659. anticipat: 'occupies in advance' of his own appearance in the sky.

660–1. For the repeated *con- con- con-* words cf. 600–1.

662. faciunt . . . gigni: the infinitive after *facere* is rare in classical Latin and perhaps colloquial (K-S i 694, Hofmann-Szantyr, 354): cf. 703, 761.

663–5. quod genus: 478 n. L. illustrates the point with a story of the dramatic appearance of dawn as seen from Mount Ida in Phrygia. We have similar accounts of this phenomenon from Diodorus Siculus (17.7.5–7) and Pomponius Mela (1.18.94–5), and Euripides refers to it in *Tro.* 1066–70. The origin of the description is quite uncertain, but perhaps it derives from travellers' tales of what the sunrise looked like at what was thought to be the eastern boundary of the earth: see K. H. Lee on *Tro.* 1069–70.

665. i.e. the scattered fires unite into the ball of the fully formed sun.

667. certo tempore: the frequent repetition of the phrase in the next few lines shows that this daily re-creation of the sun (if the right explanation) would be just one more example of the many regular cycles and sequences in nature.

670–1. L. stresses the regularity of seasonal growth in a different context at 1.174 ff.

673-4. impubem ... pubescere: a typical play on words, rather like 'in tenero tenerascere corpore' 3.765. For the youthful beard cf. 888-9.

675. Cf. the list of weather features at 1192.

676. non nimis incertis: 'fairly certain' — the weather is not quite so predictable as the other events mentioned.

677-9. This fixed regularity in nature's course was established at the first creation of the world. These lines summarize the argument, and here we again have implicitly the difficult link between chance creation and a fixed order of subsequent events. All things were first formed by chance (cf. 416-31), but thereafter the 'laws of nature' (cf. 310, 924) took over and continue to govern the succession of phenomena, as Epicurus put it, κατὰ τὴν ἐξ ἀρχῆς ἐν τῇ γενέσει τοῦ κόσμου ἀνάγκην ἀπογεννηθεῖσαν, 'according to the natural law which was produced at the beginning of the world' (*Ep. Pyth.* 92). See note on 77 ff.

677-8. The chain of *causae* was initiated at the time that things first 'fell' into place: for the haphazard *cecidere* cf. 193 n.

    fuĕrunt: 193 n.

679. conseque ... redeunt: Lachman's emendation (*consequiae ... rerum* OQ), usually printed *faute de mieux*. The scansion *cōnsĕquĕ* is in line with L.'s regular scansion of *rēlĭquĭ* and *rēlĭquŏ*.

680-704. Day and night vary in length because (1) the sun varies the length of the arcs of his orbit proportionately above and below the earth, making them equal at the equinoxes; or (2) the air is thicker in certain parts of the sky and therefore delays his reappearance from under the earth in winter; or (3) at alternate seasons of the year the fires which gather to re-form the sun flow together more or less quickly.

    This topic is discussed in *Ep. Pyth.* 98, an obscure passage which seems, however, to offer at least the first two of L.'s explanations. In relation to L.'s own previous arguments, causes (1) and (2) assume a continuing sun which travels under the earth (654-5), while cause (3) assumes a daily re-created sun (660-2). The argument up to 688 is reasonably clear: more than half of the sun's daily orbit is visible in summer, less than half of it in winter (making days and nights proportionately longer and shorter), and at the two equinoxes half of his orbit is visible (making day and night equal). An equinox occurs at the point (*nodus* 688) when his ecliptic intersects the celestial equator. Lines 689-93 are difficult and have been much discussed. They are clearly an explanatory expansion on the previous statements, and the likeliest interpretation is that they refer to the theory that wind currents cause the slanting of the ecliptic (637-42). When each of the winds which alternately blow the ecliptic to the tropics has blown for half its time, the ecliptic, being then half-way towards a tropic, cuts the celestial equator and day equals night. On this interpretation *metas* (690) means 'tropics' as at 617, and 690-1 mean that the sun is equidistant from the two tropics because of the position of the zodiac.

(The above is the interpretation adopted by Bailey: see his commentary for further helpful details, and also a discussion of other interpretations of these lines. Their obscurity may be due to L.'s using a source which he himself did not fully understand.)

681. augmina: the word may be a Lucretian coinage as it occurs only in the *DRN* in the classical period: cf. 1307, 340 n.

682. sol idem: cf. 658.

682-4. 'in his swift course above and below the earth divides the regions of ether in unequal curves and separates his daily orbit into unequal parts'. The *anfractus* are the sections, above and below the earth, of the sun's whole *orbis*: for this sense see *OLD* s.v. 2 a.

686. eius: sc. *orbis.*

relatus: 'as he comes round' in turn from below to above the earth and vice versa.

687-8. id signum caeli: at the spring equinox (March) the sun is in the constellation Aries, at the autumn equinox (September) in Libra. *nodus*, like σύνδεσμος, is a technical term for the point at which the ecliptic cuts the celestial equator (cf. Cic. *Arat.* 243, Manil. 3.622): see introductory note.

689-91. 'For half-way through the course of the blast of the north wind and of the south wind the sky holds apart the tropics equally distant (from where the sun then is) owing to the position of the whole zodiac.' Essentially this means that at each equinox the sun is half-way between the two tropics: see introductory note. 691-2 refer to the zodiac, or belt extending across the sky, 8 degrees either side of the ecliptic, and containing the constellations through which the sun passes in his annual course. Cicero defines the phrase *orbis signifer* at *Div.* 2.89, *Arat.* 317-8.

692. Cf. 619.   **serpens:** cf. 523.

693. obliquo ... lumine: because of the tilt of the ecliptic relative to the celestial equator. For *lumine lustrans* cf. 575-6 n.

694-5. 'as the calculation of those men reveals who have mapped out all the regions of the sky, with the stars (or constellations) clearly marked in their separate places'. Simple descriptive lists of constellations had been drawn up perhaps as early as the fifth century BC: at any rate – and this may be significant for our context – Vitruvius (9.5.4) attributes one to Democritus. Hipparchus (second century BC) was the first to produce a real catalogue of stars, giving their positions based on calculations like their distances from the poles. So much for what was available to L. It was left to Ptolemy (second century AD) to draw up the first star catalogue in the modern sense of the term, based on a more sophisticated use of spherical co-ordinates.

For details and a technical discussion see O. Neugebauer, *A history of ancient mathematical astronomy* (1975), 277–88, 577.

696–700. Denser air under the earth could affect the sun (*tremulum, haesitat*) in his winter course and slow down his daily reappearance.

696. certis in partibus: i.e. around the Tropic of Capricorn.

700. radiatum insigne diei: 'the radiant emblem of the day' (cf. 462) – a majestic phrase for a majestic sight. For this use of *insigne* cf. Cic. *ND* 1.100 'horum (sky, earth, sea) insignia solem lunam stellasque'.

701–4. The fires which re-form the sun may come together more quickly and more slowly at alternate seasons of the year.

701. sic: 'for the same reason' – the *crassior aer*.

704. The line is incomplete in sense, whether we take it as attached to the preceding lines or as starting a new thought. The likely assumptions are (1) that there is a lacuna after it (Munro); and (2) that the missing line(s) reaffirmed the plurality of causes (Bailey). It would be characteristic of L. to round off the section with a summarizing statement.

705–50. Causes of the moon's light and phases. (1) She may reflect the sun's light, and her phases may be due to her changing position relative to the sun. (2) Or she may shine with her own light which varies (*a*) because another moving body obscures it, or (*b*) because she has a light half and a dark half which show in turn as she revolves. (3) Or new moons may be created daily in a fixed succession of phases, just as the seasons follow each other in a regular succession.

This discussion has points in common with the brief discussion of the moon at *Ep. Pyth*. 94–5, and it echoes a debate about the moon which had been going on for centuries past. The discovery that the moon reflects the sun's light is probably due to Anaxagoras (T. Heath, *Aristarchus of Samos*, 78–9, Guthrie, i, 286, ii, 66), correcting the view that she gives out her own light held at least by Anaximander and Xenophanes (Anaximander A22 D–K). The idea that the moon has a light and a dark half was allegedly held by the third-century Chaldaean astronomer Berosus (Aëtius 2.25.12, Vitruvius 9.2.1): cf. 727–8 below. The theory of a daily re-created moon is obviously linked to the similar theory about the sun (660 ff., and cf. *Ep. Pyth*. 92).

705–14. This explanation of the moon's light and her phases is of course correct, though as an account of the phases it is ludicrous on the Epicurean assumption of the sizes of sun and moon (564–84), with a relatively enormous earth coming between them.

706–7. nobis ad speciem: 'to our gaze': cf. 569, 724.
      orbi: 'orb', not 'orbit'.

708. eum contra: 'in opposition', in astronomical terminology, contrasting with 711–12 where the moon approaches 'conjunction' with the sun.

709. The moon sees the sun go down – and is herself more conspicuous thereafter.

710. retro: probably to be taken with *condere*, as it is with *contorquet* 725, but it might stand on its own, meaning 'moving backwards'.

712. labitur: almost a technical term for the movement of heavenly bodies: cf. 718, 1216, *OLD* s.v. 2.

> **ex . . . orbem:** 'from the opposite region through the zodiac': *signorum orbis = signifer orbis* 691.

713. faciunt: 'assume', 'maintain'.

714. sub sole: i.e. between the sun and earth (629 ff.).

715-30. The moon may shine with her own light, and show her phases (716, 722) in two possible ways.

715. est . . . quare . . . possit: 'there is (an explanation) whereby she can'.

717 ff. Epicurus and some earlier thinkers seem to refer to the theory of another moving body which occludes the moon's light: see Bailey on *Ep. Pyth.* 94.

718. officiens: the verb is often used of obstructing light or view: cf. 776, 4.372, *OLD* s.v. 2.

724. oculosque patentis: the phrase need not be otiose if it suggests 'wide-eyed' wonder at an impressive sight; but at 3.655 it simply indicates the physical appearance of life.

725. Cf. 710.

726. glomeraminis atque pilai: 'its round mass'.

727-8. See 705-50 n. The reference must be to Berosus in particular, whose writings introduced much Babylonian astronomy to the Greek world. The *astrologi* are presumably those referred to at 713-14.

> **refutans . . . tendit:** 'refuting the science of the astronomers, tries to prove in opposition to it'.

729-30. Both views could be true, both equally acceptable. Again L. stresses tolerance of alternative explanations: cf. 526-33.

731-6. A new moon may be created daily.

732. formarum . . . figuris: 'fixed phases in fixed shapes': for the chiastic pattern with *certo certis* cf. 1439.

733. privos: 274 n.

> **aborisci:** 'fade', 'pass away': an inchoative form of *aboriri* which is found nowhere else.

734. illius . . . in parte locoque: 'to take over its function and place'.

735. vincere: 'prove': 99 n.

736. possint: Lachmann's supplement, comparing 750 (the word is omitted by OQ), but *videas* Q *corr.* C 131 might be right (cf. 669).

737-47. This famous tableau of the seasons is simply an illustration of the fixity of natural successions, but it develops into a poetic display piece of great power and pictorial beauty. The description might derive from a painting of the subject which L. had seen, though Lessing strenuously denied that L. needed the assistance of art here

(*Laokoon*, Chap. 7); and there has been much discussion whether 737–40 in turn indirectly influenced Botticelli's *Primavera*, through Politian's poem *La Giostra*, which was influenced by L. See G. D. Hadzsits, *Lucretius and his Influence* (New York, 1935), 264–6; and, sounding a note of caution, E. Wind, *Pagan Mysteries in the Renaissance* (Harmondsworth, 1967), 127 n. 47. Horace may have had our passage in mind in his own picture of the seasons at *C.* 4.7.9–12; cf. too Virg. *G.* 2.516–22.

737–40. With the usual punctuation of these involved lines the order of the procession is Zephyrus, Flora, Cupid (*Veneris praenuntius*), *ver*, and Venus. It is also possible to take *Zephyri* as nom. pl. with *gradiuntur* understood, punctuating after *propter*, so that Zephyrs follow Cupid, Spring, and Venus, and Flora precedes them all (*quibus*), preparing the way (C. L. Howard, *CPhil* 56 (1961), 156–7).

737–8. Spring is the time of life-giving love: see the poem's invocation to Venus, 1.10 ff.

 Veneris praenuntius . . . pennatus: Eros/Cupid is portrayed as a child in classical and later art, and conventionally has wings: Eur. *Hipp.* 1274–5, *Anth. Pal.* 5.212 (Meleager), Virg. *A.* 1.663, below 1075.

 propter: 31 n.

739. **Flora:** an old Italian goddess of flowers or the flowering season. She was loved by Zephyrus (note his presence in the procession), and her festival, the Floralia, was held on 28 April. See Ovid *F.* 5.183 ff. (with Bömer's notes) and, generally, K. Latte, *Römische Religionsgeschichte*, 73–4.

 quibus: *ver, Venus, V. p.*, with this punctuation.

739–40. **praespargens . . . opplet:** 'fills the whole path with gorgeous colours and scents which she sprinkles in front of them.' *praespargens* is ἅπαξ λεγόμενον, and for *cuncta viai* see 35 n.

741. **inde loci:** 443 n.

742. **etesia flabra aquilonum:** 'the Etesian gusts of the north winds': the Etesians (Gk. ἐτήσιος 'annual') of the Mediterranean were a prevailing north wind in high summer. Seneca has an account of them at *NQ* 5.10–11. (The phrase is repeated at 6.730.)

743. **Euhius Euan:** εὔιος εὐάν: a cult title of Bacchus/Dionysus, derived from the cry of his devotees: cf. Eur. *Ba.* 566, *Tro.* 326. He here represents the autumn vintage.

744. **tempestates:** 'seasons': contrast 1083.

745. **Volturnus,** a south-east wind, and *auster*, a south wind, together bring thunderstorms. For the compound epithet *altitonans* ('thundering on high') cf. *altivolans* 433.

746–7. It is hard to decide about the punctuation of these lines and the reading *algor*. With this punctuation *bruma* and *hiemps* are virtually synonymous, and teeth-chattering cold attends the latter. If we punctuate and read 'reddit, hiemps sequitur . . . algu', *bruma* can be taken strictly as 'the shortest day' (winter solstice), followed by *hiemps*, 'mid-winter', chattering his teeth with cold.

748, 749, 750. certo tempore: 667 n.

751-770. Eclipses of sun and moon. (1) The sun's light may be cut off (*a*) by the passage of some unseen body as well as by the moon; or (*b*) because he passes through regions of air which temporarily quench his fires. (2) The moon may be obscured (*a*) by the passage of some body as well as by the earth; or (*b*) because she passes through certain parts of the sky which make her light grow dim.

In contrast with the explanations offered for previous phenomena we have here causes based on sense-perception as well as on analogy or speculation. L. seems to assume that we can see that the moon is one cause of a solar eclipse (*cur luna queat* . . . 753), and that the earth is one cause of a lunar eclipse (*cur terra queat* . . . 762), and he then offers other possibilities. The two suggestions, bodily interposition and temporary extinction, are also made in the brief discussion of eclipses in *Ep. Pyth.* 96; and the true cause of eclipses had been seen at least by Anaxagoras (A42 D-K) among earlier thinkers.

751. defectus, latebras: L. elegantly varies his vocabulary: we find *defectus* used of an eclipse in other writers (e.g. Virg. *G.* 2.478), but not apparently *latebra*.

754. a terris . . . ei: 'push her head on high in front of him in a line from the earth': the following verse clarifies this.

> **ei:** the sun: 284 n.

756-7. We can as soon imagine another similarly obstructive body even if we cannot see it.

758-61. For the temporary quenching of the sun's fires cf. 651-3.

759. recreareque: L. is fairly sparing in attaching *-que* to a short *e*, but he did not avoid this as pointedly as the Augustan writers: cf. 1021 and Kenney on 3.163.

761. faciunt: for the construction see 662 n.

> **interstingui:** 'to be temporarily quenched'.

763-4. oppressum . . . tenere: '(the earth) being herself above the sun to keep him suppressed'. When the moon appears to be eclipsed the sun must be below the earth, and the three are then in line. The moon thus 'glides through the clear-cut conical shadow', which spreads upwards from the earth as the earth intercepts the sun's light. (The cone of shadow would of course spread out from the earth on the Epicurean assumption of a tiny sun relative to the earth. In reality, with a huge sun relative to the earth the conical shadow diminishes to its apex beyond the earth. Cf. 705-14 n.)

> **menstrua:** 'in her monthly course' — but not, of course, suggesting that lunar eclipses are monthly.

765. Cf. 756.

765-6. succurrere . . . vel supra . . . perlabier: *vel* does not introduce a real disjunction. The other body must 'pass beneath' the moon relative to the earth for us to see an eclipse; or (another way of putting it) 'glide above' the sun, which as before (763) is below us at the time. *succurrere* is extremely rare in this literal sense.

767. Cf. 287.

768. fulget: the normal classical second conjugation form: cf. 1095 n.

769-70. This idea corresponds to 758-61; cf. also 731 ff.

770. per: for the postponement cf. 31 n.

771. Excluded as an obvious dittography of 764.

772-1457. In the third main section of the book L. discusses the origins of life on earth (772-924), the living conditions of primitive man (925-1010), and the origins and growth of civilization (1011-1457).

772-82. An introduction which both summarizes the content of the last main section and introduces the first topic of the next one.

773. resolvi: 'I have unfolded, explained', like *exsolvere* 2.381.

774. Cf. 76 and n.   **varios:** as discussed above 614-17, 637-42.

776. offecto: 718 n.

    obire: used of heavenly bodies setting at 4.433, Cic. *Arat.* 465, *Rep.* 6.22: here of eclipses.

777. quasi conivent: 'they seem to wink': L. keeps up this vivid metaphor with *aperto lumine* and *convisunt.*

780 redeo: i.e. resuming from 508 after the intervening astronomical section.

781-2. quid . . . crerint: '(to tell you) what they first decided to bring forth . . . '. Or with Giussani and Müller punctuate after *novitatem*, not after *arva*: 'I return to the world's youth and what the soft fields . . . '. For another use of the simple *cernere = decernere* see 393 n.

    in luminis oras: 224 n. This passage may have suggested Virg. *G.* 2.47 'se tollunt in luminis oras'.

    incertis: a standard epithet of winds, but here it may also suggest the precariousness of the earliest life on earth: cf. Virg. *A.* 11.560 'dubiis committitur auris' of a hazardous spear-cast.

783-836. The creation of plants and animals (783-92) and the motherhood of Earth (793-836).

    This is a carefully constructed section, though its train of thought has not always been clearly seen. See an important discussion by D. A. West in *CQ* 14 (1964), 99-102, who rejects the difficulties earlier editors found in the passage and clarifies the sequence of L.'s narration: plants 783-5; trees 786-7; these two groups repeated and animals added 788-92; the motherhood of Earth emphasized 793-825; the present decline of her fertility 826-36.

    The origins of life on earth were much discussed in antiquity, and behind L.'s arguments we can detect several scientific theories of earlier philosophers, whether adopted or rejected by him: plants as the first life on earth 783 ff. (Empedocles); animals generated from warm moist earth 797 ff., 805 ff. (Anaximander, Anaxagoras, Democritus); wombs in the earth 808 ff. (Epicurus, Diodorus); nourishment by earth-milk 812-13 (Archelaus, Epicurus); rejected theories of the Stoics 793, and of Anaximander 794. (See notes on these lines.) The belief in the earth as mother of all living things is of immemorial antiquity and was rationalized by early thinkers, and the obvious analogy between the generative earth and a human mother was widely applied: for details see W. K. C. Guthrie, *In the Beginning*, Chaps. 1 and 2, *History of Greek Philosophy*, ii, 207, 343. The important point here is that L. is squarely in line with the Epicureans, who adopted this notion of the earth as mother and nourisher of living things, and he stresses it repeatedly: 795-6, 821-2, 1402, 1411, 1427.

783 ff. Some earlier thinkers taught that vegetation preceded animal life in creation: Empedocles (A70 D-K) πρῶτα τὰ δένδρα τῶν ζῴων ἐκ γῆς ἀναφῦναι ... ; Euripides fr. 484N (from his *Melanippe* and quoted by Diodorus Siculus, 1.7.7., to illustrate his discipleship of Anaxagoras): (after the separation of heaven and earth) τίκτουσι πάντα κἀνέδωκαν εἰς φάος / δένδρη πετηνὰ θῆρας οὕς θ'ἅλμη τρέφει / γένος τε θνητῶν.

783-5. A carefully visualized picture of verdure covering the landscape. There should probably be no punctuation after *omnis* (as in the OCT), giving a smoother link between the lines.

787. immissis ... habenis: a vivid metaphor suggesting the trees' race to out-top one another: it caught Virgil's eye (*G.* 2.363-4 'dum se laetus ad auras / palmes agit laxis per purum immissus habenis').

788 ff. L. uses an analogy to explain the primacy of plant life though he does not fully spell out its terms. Just as birds and animals first sprout feathers and bristles (before developing other characteristics), so Earth put forth her simpler creatures before the more complex organisms of animal life. The analogy may have been suggested by Empedocles' close comparison of hair, leaves, and bird-feathers (B82 D-K).

789. A resounding chiastic line. *pennipotentum* is perhaps a Lucretian formation that occurs also at 2.878 and nowhere else.

790. virgulta: 'saplings', 'young trees'.

791. inde loci: 443 n.   **mortalia saecla:** i.e. animals.

793-4. L. begins his declaration of the motherhood of Earth by rejecting two opposing theories held by the Stoics and by Anaximander. The same two theories are dismissed in slightly different terms at 2.1153-5: 'haud, ut opinor, enim mortalia saecla superne / aurea de caelo demisit funis in arva / nec mare nec fluctus plangentes saxa crearunt.' Here *de caelo cecidisse* is partly a jeering overstatement of the Stoic theory of the πνεῦμα, *anima* (a compound of fire and air), which fills the cosmos and also forms the soul of animals and the texture of plants (see H. von Arnim, *Stoicorum Veterum Fragmenta*, ii, 716), and partly a hit at particular stories, e.g. that the Nemean lion fell from the moon (Epimenides, B2 D-K). 794 alludes to the theory held by Anaximander (A30 D-K), and no doubt by others, that the first animals were born in water and subsequently migrated to dry land.

    salsis . . . lacunis: the same bombastic periphrasis for 'the sea' occurs at 3.1031, and the phrase *Neptunias lacunas* is given in *Ad Herennium* 4.15 to illustrate a bombastic style.

795 ff. Of the traditional four cosmogonic elements air, fire, and water have been eliminated in the last two lines, leaving earth. But L. also adds three positive arguments: (1) Earth still generates creatures, so *a fortiori* she could have produced larger ones when she was young (797–800). (2) Just as even now cicadas emerge spontaneously from their chrysalises, so (by analogy) the first animals were winged creatures hatched out of eggs, conditions in the ground being suitable (801–6). (3) The conditions of primeval birth and nurture prove Earth's right to the name of mother: wombs were attached to her from which the young emerged in due time, to be suckled by her like a human mother and given their essential physical needs (807–20).

795. Cf. 2.998 'quapropter merito maternum nomen adepta est', below 821–2.

797–8. In Book 2 L. repeatedly illustrates the thesis that insensate matter can produce organisms with sensation by the example of earthworms emerging from putrefying mud and other rotting matter (2.871–3, 898–9, 928–9; cf. 3.719 ff.). The idea of spontaneous generation from mud was current among many earlier philosophers — Anaximander (A11 D-K), Anaxagoras (A42 D-K), Democritus (A139 D-K) — and seriously discussed by Aristotle, *HA* 539a22 ff., *GA* 762a10 ff. See further Ernout–Robin on 2.871.

800. adulta: 'reaching their full growth' in the greater energy and fertility of the young earth and air.

801. genus . . . volucres: a stock phrase recurring at 1078.

    alituum: L. introduced and used exclusively this form of the gen. pl. of *ales* which later poets also adopted for metrical reasons: also at 1039, 1078.

802. exclusae: 'hatched', a common sense of *excludere* (*OLD*, s.v. 5b).

803. folliculos: 'chrysalises'. The same phenomenon is used to illustrate atomic 'films' at 4.58, 'cum teretes ponunt tunicas aestate cicadae'.

804. victum vitamque: a crisp, alliterative tautology, recurring at 1080, 1105.

805–6. tum tibi . . . primum: 'then, you see, for the first time', like *tum . . . primum* 790. These two lines explain that conditions were right at that time for the earth to produce animals, *mortalia saecla*, and they are best taken as a recapitulation of 790–1 (West, op. cit., 101).

807. hoc: 'therefore'.

808 ff. The young of the earth grew in wombs attached to her by roots, and when in their natural development they burst the wombs she nourished them with a milk-like juice. The origins of these strange ideas can be traced back to the fifth-century philosopher Archelaus (A1 and A4 D-K: earth-milk) and to Epicurus (Usener 333: wombs rooted to earth and earth-milk), and such wombs are described by Diodorus Siculus in his account of the origin of animal life (1.7.3–4). But L. must also have read widely in the Greek biologists, many of whom drew the parallel between the alimentary functions of veins in animals and roots in plants: this may have suggested the wombs' roots here and in Epicurus. See P. H. Schrijvers's discussion of this whole section in *Mnemosyne* S. IV 27 (1974), 245–61.

808. apti: from *apiscor*: 'holding', 'clinging to' the earth.

809. tempore maturo: 'when their time came', 'in due time'. This phrase and the general sense guarantee Marullus's *aetas* for *aestas* OQ.

810. petessens: 'trying to reach' the open air, as they struggled out of the ooze.

811. foramina terrae: 'pores in the earth': cf. 457, 6.592.

815. impetus . . . alimenti: 'flow of her nourishment'.

816. pueris: 'her children', picking up *infantum* 810 and continuing the comparison with a human mother.

818–20. But (this was not surprising for) the world was young and winds and temperatures were moderate: they like everything else took time to acquire full strength. So, too, Virgil on the perpetual spring of the young earth: 'ver illud erat, ver magnus agebat / orbis, et hibernis parcebant flatibus Euri', *G.* 2.338–9.

821–5. An emphatic re-statement summarizing the theme of 793 ff. and introduced by one of L.'s favourite assertive phrases, *quare . . . etiam*, 'so it cannot be denied that'.

823. fudit: also used of the earth producing animals below 917, Virg. *G.* 1.13 (and cf. Pliny *HN* 8.108).

824. bacchatur: 'runs wild', the word (only here in the *DRN*) suggesting unrestrained ranging over the hills.

826–36. But like an ageing woman Earth ceased to be fertile and cannot now produce as once she could. Similarly in Book 2, in the context of the inevitable disintegration of all matter, L. discusses the present exhaustion and decay of the earth (2.1150–74). The section is carefully structured (see West, op. cit., 102). The main statement of Earth's present sterility is followed by a reason introduced by *enim* (828), which is followed in turn by a further explanatory comment on it introduced by *namque* (832). Then the first reason is repeated (834–5, with close verbal echoes of 828–9), and we end with a re-statement of Earth's sterility.

826. debet: 'she is bound': the law of nature is stated and then explained.

828 ff. These lines are a lavish statement of a dominant *leitmotif* of the *DRN*: all things change as they ceaselessly come into being or pass away (cf. below 1276–80). It should thus surprise no one that Earth has weakened with age.

829. status: 'phase', 'condition'.

833. Cf. 1278. The manuscripts give us an unmetrical line and *crescit* has generally been emended to either *concrescit* (Aldine ed.) or *succrescit* (Lachmann in his commentary).

    contemptibus: 'ignominy': the plural is unusual, perhaps suggesting contempt from many quarters.

834–5. Re-emphasizing 828–9: see introductory note.

836. Bentley's emendation *tulit ut* is the neatest to give the subjunctives a construction, and with it the line has usually been translated 'so that she cannot bear what she bore, but she can bear what she did not bear before'. But there is a strong case (see West, op. cit., 102) for taking the relative clauses as subject, not object: 'so that what bore (i.e. Earth) cannot, and what did not bear before (i.e. individual species) can'. This interpretation both avoids a contradiction with 826–7 (Earth no longer gives birth), and allows L. an oblique reference to the earlier view that after Earth ceased to bear, the species of living things reproduced themselves (Archelaus A4 D–K, Diod. Sic. 1.7.6; and cf. Plato, *Politicus* 271a–c, 272a, 274a).

837–924. This section describes early attempts by the earth to produce creatures which did not survive because of bodily defects or because they could not propagate their species (837–54). Animals which survived have done so because they can protect themselves or are protected by man (855–77). Hybrids like the Centaurs and the Chimaera have never existed because there are fixed natural laws governing the distinctive homogeneous growth of all things (878–924).

837–54. Behind the thought of this passage lies L.'s own discussion of the haphazard nature of the original assembling of atoms in the creation of the world (5.419–31; cf. 1.1021–28): it was a question of 'omnia pertemptare' (425), and so too the earth made many experimental mistakes before producing viable species.(These mistakes are carefully distinguished from the special class of monstrosity, the hybrids of mixed species, which never existed at all, 878 ff.) We must note too that Empedocles seems to have believed in a series of stages in the development of living creatures, though his theory imagined far more grotesque monsters in the experimental stage than we find in L. See A72, B57, B61 D–K, and discussions in Kirk–Raven, *Presocratic Philosophers*, 336 ff., Guthrie, ii, 200 ff. Guthrie also discusses cautiously (op. cit., 203 ff.) the rather tenuous parallels between Empedocles' views and Darwinian evolutionary theory: the same caution should be observed in linking L.'s speculations with modern thinking — though he does come close to the 'survival of the fittest' theory at 855 ff.

837. There is an obvious balance with 855, though the *tum* of 855 refers to a later phase in the evolution of species.

portenta: 'abnormal creatures', monstrosities'.

839. The line as printed represents emendations by Munro and Lachmann, incorporating earlier corrections. Its uncouthness (repeated *utr* and false verse-endings felt in the third and fourth feet) to some extent arises from the difficulty of expressing a grotesque idea, though Wakefield perhaps went too far in saying 'res monstrosas versu monstroso vividius effingere poeta, ut videtur, voluit.'

androgynum: 'man-woman' (Gk. ἀνδρόγυνος, e.g. Plato, *Symp.* 189e ἀνδρόγυνον . . . ἐξ ἀμφοτέρων κοινὸν τοῦ τε ἄρρενος καὶ θήλεος): the form occurs also in Cic. *Div.* 1.98, Livy 27.11.5, Pliny *HN* 7.15 and 34, but we should probably retain *androgynem* of OQ. (See Ernout's and Bailey's notes.)

interutrasque: 472 n.

840. **partim:** virtually a pronoun 'some', as often (1083, 1143, 1310).

841. **vultu:** unusual in the restricted sense 'eyes', though the shift in meaning is natural enough, 'face-expression-eyes', and the sense 'look, expression' can be seen in phrases like 6.1184 'furiosus vultus et acer', Hor. *C.* 1.2.39-40 'acer . . . vultus in hostem'. See Ernout–Meillet s.v. *voltus*, and note the similar range of meaning in ὄψις.

842. 'bound fast by all their limbs sticking to their body', and thus immobilized as shown in the next two lines. *adhaesus* is confined to L., who has a strong preference for such fourth-declension abstract nouns (see Bailey, i, 135).

844. **foret:** Lambinus's conjecture for *volet* OQ, now generally accepted: cf. 4.830-1 'manusque datas . . . / ut facere ad vitam possemus quae foret usus'. With *foret, quod* is probably nominative, in line with L.'s archaic use of the nom. with *opus est*.

846. **absterruit:** 'withheld', 'denied': an unusual meaning, but cf. 4.1064, 1234.

847. **cupitum a. t. florem:** the same phrase at 3.770.

849. **rebus:** 'for (created) things, creatures'.

deber(e): the only hypermetric line in the *DRN*, eliding with the next line. There is no certain instance of this phenomenon in Greek hexameters (see West on Hes. *Theog.* 884), but Latin examples are found in Lucilius (547M), Catullus (64.298), and very occasionally in later poets: only Virgil used the device at all freely (about twenty times).

850. **ut . . . possint:** consecutive, of course, not final (which would admit the teleological principle: see Robin's note here).

prōpagando: in 856 *prŏpagando:* L. varies the scansion of this word as of several others: see 1163-4 n.

procudere: 'forge' (so below 856): this vivid metaphor appears also at 2.1115 (fire) and 3.1081 (pleasure). With our example we may perhaps compare Aesch. *Suppl.* 282-3 Κύπριος χαρακτήρ τ'ἐν γυναικείοις τύποις / εἰκὼς πέπληκται τεκτόνων πρὸς ἀρσένων — if the lines are genuine: see Johansen–Whittle ad loc.

851-4. 'First there must be food; then a way by which the life-giving seeds throughout the frame can flow out from the slackened body; and that the female should be able to mate with males (and) have the means by which they may both exchange mutual delight': i.e. the essentials for procreation are (1) food (2) the male organ (3) the female organs, to allow the possibility of intercourse and the means of mutual sexual delight.

The interpretation of this passage is disputed, esp. 853-4. This reading of it assumes that the words *genitalia . . . remissis* apply to the male only, and that *feminaque ut . . .* is parallel to the clauses in 851-2, with an asyndeton between *coniungi* and *habere*. (See the discussion by C. W. Chilton in *CQ* 30 (1980), 378-80; and Bailey for the conventional interpretation, whereby the clause *feminaque ut . . .* depends on what follows it.)

852. remissis: of coital enervation; the same idea at 4.1114 'membra voluptatis dum vi labefacta liquescunt'.

854. L. stresses the mutual delights of sexual intercourse at 4.1192-1207.

qui: instrumental, 'the means by which' = *qua* 852: see 233 n.

855-77. We come now to a stage in nature's trial-and-error sequence when some creatures were formed with the potentiality for successful existence (*animantum* 855 in contrast with the *portenta* of 837 ff.), but could not survive external dangers. Such survival has only been possible if they could protect themselves or win man's protection. We must of course still assume that it was only by haphazard experiment that nature eventually produced a viable species (whether it actually survived or not), and once such a success was achieved the species remained fixed 'foedere naturae certo' 924. There is no suggestion of the modern evolutionary concept of development and improvement within a species, despite a superficial resemblance to the doctrine of the 'survival of the fittest'. (See Robin's note on 855-77.) (In this section L.'s effort to make his point clearly and forcibly leads to some rather pedestrian lines: e.g. 870, and *genus id* 877 following *genus id* 859 and *eorum genus* 873-4.)

855. tum: 837 n.

saecla: 'breeds', 'races': a characteristic meaning of the word in L. (and confined entirely to him). Cf. γενεά, which also means both 'race' or 'kind', and 'generation'. L. highlights his argument with some careful alliteration in successive lines: *m* in 855 (as in 852-4), *p* in 856, *v* in 857.

856. procudere: 850 n.

857. vesci: 72 n.

858. denique: 'at any rate', 'at least'.

859. ex ineunte aevo: 'from its earliest existence' (cf. 537). Note the repetition of *tut-* sounds in 859, 861, 863.

861. manent: 'survive'.

862-3. In a passage on inherited characteristics in animals at 3.741-3 lions, foxes, and stags are similarly listed to illustrate ferocity, cunning, and swiftness in flight. For the same animals as stock examples see also Arist. *HA* 488b15 ff., Sen. *de ira* 2.16. (Note chiastic phrases in consecutive lines here: *genus acre . . . saevaque saecla / vulpis dolus . . . fuga cervos.*)

864. An elaborate and densely written description of the qualities of a good watchdog: a light sleeper, loyal, and intelligent (*corda*). As Merrill notes L. is fond of dogs: cf. 4.998 'catulorum blanda propago', 6.1222 'fida canum vis', and the sympathetic picture of dog behaviour below 1063-72.

    levisomna: a Lucretian coinage, occurring only here.

865. veterino: 'of beasts of burden': an old, technical farming word, derived by ancient grammarians from *veho*, but perhaps from *vetus*, i.e. animals too old for any but draught service (Ernout-Meillet, s.v.). 865 and 890 are the only poetic citations of the word in *OLD*.

866. Cf. 2.661-2 'lanigerae pecudes . . . / buceriaeque greges . . . ', 6.1237 'lanigeras tamquam pecudes et bucera saecla' (and an apparent imitation by Ovid, *M.* 6.395 'lanigerosque greges armentaque bucera pavit').

    bucera: lit. 'ox-horned': a Grecism (βούκερως) virtually confined to L.

867. Memmi: apart from perfunctory addresses here and 1282 Memmius has disappeared from the book since 164: see Introduction, x and G. B. Townend, *CQ* 28 (1978), 280.

869. pabula: acc. object of *secuta sunt.*

870. utilitatis . . . causa: 'as a reward because of their usefulness': *causa* is strictly unnecessary.

871. quis: dat. pl. (picked up by *haec* 875): L.'s only use of the shortened form.

    horum: i.e. self-subsistence or usefulness to man, amplified in the following *nec . . . nec . . .*

873-4. quare . . . : 'for which we would allow their race to feed under our protection and be safe'.

875. aliis . . . iacebant: 'lay exposed as prey and profit to others': *iacere* sometimes suggests helpless or degrading prostration, as at 175, 1.62-3 'foede cum vita iaceret / in terris oppressa gravi sub religione' (see *OLD* s.v. 3 a). *praedae, lucro* are datives of the predicate.

876. fatalibus . . . vinclis: 'chains of fate': the natural handicaps that precluded their survival.

878–924. The argument now turns to the impossibility that monstrosities should ever have existed composed of different species, like Centaurs, Scylla, or the Chimaera. (In 837–54 L. was concerned with monstrosities within the *same* species, doomed to early extinction.) This strongly rationalist passage is no doubt aimed in part at doctrines such as Empedocles' idea of the 'ox-man' phase of creation (βουγενῆ ἀνδρόπρῳρα, B61 D–K: see 837–54 n.); but in two other important passages of the poem L. is at pains to deny the possibility of such hybrids. At 2.700–717 he argues that the combinations of disparate atoms needed to form them are impossible; and at 4.732–48 he accounts for belief in Centaurs and the like by suggesting that *simulacra* from different animals coalesce in the air before they are perceived by the mind: hence people suppose they are actually seeing these creatures. In our passage the arguments stress the biological impossibility of the different parts of such an animal coexisting because of different growth-rates, incompatible foods, and diverse pleasures and habits. But behind these physical arguments we also recognize the crusader against superstitious belief in monsters, just as he had poured scorn on the mythologists' accounts of Hercules' monstrous opponents at 22 ff. above. It may be coincidental that Centaurs, Scyllas, and the Chimaera also appear at the entrance to Virgil's Hell, as they are not traditionally underworld monsters (*A.* 6.286, 288, with Austin's notes), but they are obvious examples for L. of grotesque and non-existent horrors.

878–80. nec . . . esse queunt . . . compacta: 'creatures composed of . . . cannot exist': the subject is contained in *compacta*.

> **bino:** 'twofold'.

880–1. potestas . . . : 'so that their strength from either kind of creature (and) their powers could be sufficiently matched (to make existence in one body possible)'. 881 is corrupt and there is no general agreement on a solution, though it is fairly clear that the sense of it is the point which is developed in 883 ff. Bailey's Oxford text (he changed his mind in his later edition) follows Giussani: it has the merit of sticking reasonably close to the tradition, though the asyndeton is awkward. Other suggestions centre on reading *partis* for *parvis* of OQ ('creatures born from this kind and that'), apparently first noted by Havercamp in his Variae Lectiones, and adopted by Lachmann, Bailey (edition), and Martin.

> **potissit:** = *possit*, an archaic form like *potesse* (*posse*) at 1.665, 2.225, 1010, 3.319; and *potestur* (*potest*) at 3.1010.

882 = 4.44. **hinc:** 'from the following'.

883 ff. The growth-rates of horse and man are vastly different.

885. quaeret: 'will generally seek', 'will tend to seek'. For this kind of 'gnomic' future see K–S i, 143.

886. senecta: the adj. occurs again at 896 and 3.772 but is hardly found after L.

888. tum demum: 'only then', 'not till then'. *iuventas* occurs here first in Latin.

889. occipit: Marullus's almost certain correction of *officit* OQ, though Wakefield stoutly defended the tradition and Martin resurrected it.

890-1. ne . . . credas: '(I say this) so you do not believe'. For a similar turn of phrase see the sequence at 2.410 ff. 'ne tu forte putes . . . neu . . . putes . . . neve . . . constituas . . . '.

   confieri . . . neque esse: 'be formed and (continue to) exist': cf. the combination 'constare neque esse' 1.479. *neque* by a common idiom stands for the strictly logical *et* or *aut*, as it does in disjunctions after negative verbs like *nolo, nego* (K–S ii, 39).

892-3. semimarinis: 'half of the sea', i.e. half sea-monster: the word occurs only here.

   Scyllas: 'creatures like Scylla'. This description of Scylla is the conventional one in Latin poetry: see Cat. 60.2, Virg. *E*. 6.74-5, *A*. 3.424-8, Ovid *Am*. 3.12.21-2, Sen. *Med*. 350-2 (whose 'rabidos utero succincta canes' recalls L. here). In Homer (*Od*. 12.85 ff.) she is a slightly more homogeneous monster who has six heads and barks like a dog.

   cetera de genere horum: a variant of the very common formula *cetera de genere hoc* suiting the line-ending (also at 1449, 2.104).

895. Cf. 820.

897-8. moribus unis / conveniunt: 'agree in matching habits'. The plural *unis* is unusual, and when it occurs can sometimes be explained by metrical convenience or use with a noun which has no singular. Elsewhere at 2.919, 3.616; and Cicero has the same phrase: '(Lacedaemonii) unis moribus . . . vivunt', *Flac*. 63.

   eadem: these might include physical conditions generally, though the following illustration suggests the reference is mainly to food.

899-900. At 4.633-41 L. explains that different foods suit different creatures: e.g. 'nobis veratrum est acre venenum, / at capris adipes et coturnicibus auget' (640-1). So too at 6.970-2 the she-goat is said to enjoy the very bitter wild olive, and the indifference of goats to bitter or poisonous plants was noted by other writers: Pliny *HN* 10.197 'venenis capreae . . . pinguescunt', Diog. Laert. 9.80.

   barbigeras: i.e. goats: one of L.'s favourite formations in *-ger*, again at 6.970 and apparently only found in the *DRN* (cf. 970 n.).

901-6. The fire-breathing Chimaera can never have existed as fire scorches lions and all other animals. The argument changes ground here, as we might have expected to learn that the three parts of the Chimaera could not cohere for the same reasons of disparity which precluded Centaurs. Instead L. fastens on the single impossibility of fire within living tissue, and so disposes of this grotesque creature of legend.

902-3. tam . . . quam . . . exstet: 'as surely as every kind whatsoever in the world that is formed of flesh and blood'.

visceris: Servius on Virg. *A.* 6.253 defines *viscera* as 'quicquid inter ossa et cutem est.'

904. ună: agreeing with *Chimaera*.

905-6. A near translation of Hom. *Il.* 6.181-2 πρόσθε λέων, ὄπιθεν δὲ δράκων, μέσση δὲ χίμαιρα, / δεινὸν ἀποπνείουσα πυρὸς μένος αἰθομένοιο. This famous creature was named from its middle section (χίμαιρα = she-goat: hence 'media *ipsa*'), and slain by Bellerophon.

909-10. Appealing just to the earth's newness is an empty (*inani*) argument for grotesque creations at that time.

910. effutiat: 'babble' other equally nonsensical theories, exemplified in 911-15. But L.'s illustrations here combine the real with the unreal, as he is presumably thinking of 'golden' rivers like the Tagus and the Pactolus, which really carried gold dust, along with the mythical Gardens of the Hesperides and giants like Atlas. However, these were not linked in legend with the first youth of the world, and we should assume only an associative reference to them here as the sort of fancy these theorists might indulge.

913-15. The existence of giants is here ridiculed, yet shortly we are told that primitive man was larger and more powerful than now (925 ff.), and the earth when young and fresh did produce huge wild beasts (2.1152).

913. impete: 'extent', 'stretch': 200 n., 505 n.

914. Cf. 1.199-201 'homines tantos natura parare / non potuit, pedibus qui pontum per vada possent / transire', because she had limited material for making things. For the phrase *pedum nisus* (i.e. stepping with an effort) cf. *pedum vestigia* 3.4, 389 and *pinnarum nisus inanis* 6.834.

916-24. A summary re-statement of the impossibility of mixed species in the early days of creation (*primum*) based on the fact that to-day (*nunc quoque*) we see that nature keeps all species firmly distinct. The argument depends of course on the assumption that nature's methods have always been fixed and unchanging.

918. nil . . . est signi: 'is no proof': the partitive gen. *signi* is similarly used with other neuter pronouns (*hoc, id*).

921. Earth's productive powers are now restricted to vegetation — but the same law applies.

922. complexa: passive in sense (as at 2.154), like the perfect participles of many deponents.

924. The whole argument in a nutshell: cf. 2.720-1 'tota natura dissimiles sunt / inter se genitae res quaeque.'

925-87. The state of primitive man — a harsh beast-like existence, without skills or communal life, and harassed by terror of wild animals.

L. now turns to an account of the original state of man and in doing so lines himself up with an anthropological view which derives from fifth-century Greek rationalism. There had been a widely held poetic and religious belief that the earliest period of man's life on earth was one of ease and innocence, where hardship was unknown and the earth without need of cultivation supplied all that man needed for food and shelter. This phase of life was conventionally labelled the Golden Age, and was thought to be followed by other ages showing a successive degeneration and corruption of human life. The earliest account of this 'golden' age or race of men is in Hesiod, *Op*. 109 ff., and it had a wide circulation among later Greek and Roman writers. An interesting variant on the myth is found in Empedocles (B128 D–K), who described this early ideal existence as the Age of Love, dominant over Strife: see Guthrie, ii, 248–9.

In the fifth century, however, there is plenty of evidence that evolutionary theories arose which saw the earliest history of man not as a fall from a state of primeval purity but as a slow progress from disorganized and brutish ignorance to civilization. Living originally like animals, without proper dwellings or any sense of community, and perishing from cold, bad food, and their natural enemies, men only gradually learned the need for communal living, cultivation of the soil, and articulate speech. This technical advance of mankind was attributed to various causes: in Aeschylus, *Pr*. 442 ff., Prometheus claims the credit for teaching men; the Hippocratic treatise *On Ancient Medicine* 3 and 7 (fifth/fourth century BC: text and translation in W. H. S. Jones, *Philosophy and Medicine in Ancient Greece*, Baltimore, 1946) gives necessity as the stimulus; the tragic poet Moschion (fr. 6N: perhaps third century BC) suggests time itself, operating through Prometheus, necessity, or experience; Euripides' Theseus in *Supplices* 201 ff. refers vaguely to a beneficent god who brought order out of primitive brutishness. Critias (fr. 1N, from his *Sisyphus*) similarly speaks of the primeval state of man as disorderly and beastly. Rationalizing philosophy too was similarly changing the course of Greek ideas on anthropology, as we can see most clearly in the great sophist Protagoras, whose theories we can assume are given in detail in Plato's dialogue, *Protagoras* 320c ff. Here we find a rationalist account, with mythic adornments, of the rise of human civilization from primitive origins, based on technical skill and the gift of reason. Much later Diodorus Siculus (1.8), probably writing a little after Lucretius in the first century BC, tells a rather similar story of man's emergence from a beast-like existence: he is probably dipping into the pool of ideas which had become current in the fifth century.

To some extent we can only guess at the beliefs of the Epicureans about primitive man. Epicurus himself has not left us his thoughts on anthropology, but it is very likely that Democritus shared the evolutionary view of civilization, to judge from what we otherwise know of his thinking (see Guthrie, ii, 473 ff.): he might even have discussed it with his older contemporary Protagoras – they both came from Abdera. Epicurus probably followed Democritus, though both would have rejected the idea of any divine assistance in the progress of mankind. As for Lucretius, whatever his immediate source he had a long and firmly established rationalist tradition behind him, and his own account of early man is in accord with his secular and materialist beliefs. Even so, traces of the 'Golden Age' theme, or at least phraseology, survive in the occasional references to the earth producing food *sponte sua* 937–8 (cf. 2.1157–9) – but see note on 937–8.

On all this see in general Seneca, *Ep.* 90 (with Blankert's commentary) – the main extant continuous discussion from antiquity; W. K. C. Guthrie, *In the Beginning*, Chaps. 4, 5, and 6, *History of Greek Philosophy*, iii, 60 ff.; A. O. Lovejoy and G. Boas, *Primitivism and Related Ideas in Antiquity*, Chap. 8; L. Edelstein, *The Idea of Progress in Classical Antiquity*, 160–5; P. Boyancé, *Lucrèce et l'Épicurisme*, Chap. 8; E. E. Sikes, *Lucretius, Poet and Philosopher*, Chap. 8; E. R. Dodds, *The Ancient Concept of Progress*, Chap. 1; L. Robin, 'Sur la conception épicurienne du progrès', *Revue de Métaphysique et de Morale* 23 (1916), 697–719 (arguing that the Epicureans did not see the progress of man from a primitive state as a betterment of his moral condition).

925. at: Lachmann's suggestion for *et* OQ is preferable on logical as well as stylistic grounds. Though not strongly adversative it moves on to a new point: we must reject the idea of freaks (including giants 913–15), 'yet' men were hardier.

illud: i.e. 'that ancient', as the context makes clear.

926. quod: relative and object of the causal subj. *creasset*: 'seeing that the hard earth had created it'. The harsh alliteration of *d* and assonance of *u* in the line reflect the stolid earth and stolid men.

927. maioribus . . . ossibus: Belief in an earlier race of greater stature occurs in various parts of the ancient world: cf. the legends of the discovery of the larger-than-life bones of Orestes and of Theseus (Hdt. 1.68, Plut. *Theseus* 36). Frazer on Pausanias 1.35.7 and 8.29.1 suggests that this idea might have arisen by the discovery of the bones of prehistoric animals. But perhaps L. is simply picturing primitive man as a hulking bestial creature: cf. the word θηριώδης used by both Diodorus (of early man's life) and the Hippocratic *On Ancient Medicine* (see introductory note).

928. fundatum: 'based firmly on'. **aptum:** 'fitted with'. Both words are used similarly in a description of body-structure at 4.827 ff. 'ideo fastigia posse / surarum ac feminum pedibus fundata plicari, / bracchia tum porro validis ex apta lacertis . . . '.

929. caperetur: 'suffer, be afflicted': a common meaning of *capere*; see 1.941 'deceptaque non capiatur' and *OLD* s.v. 13a and 21.

930. novitate cibi: 'strange', 'unfamiliar food'.

931. lustra: 'revolutions': *lustrum* has the special meaning of the time taken by the sun's apparent revolution, as at Manilius 3.580, Sen. *Ag.* 42.

932. volgivago: 'roving', 'unsettled': a Lucretian formation, apparently recurring only at 4.1071 (of Venus!).

933. L. clearly savoured his epic-style phrase for the ploughman as he repeated it at 6.1253. In 'Golden Age' descriptions early man does not plough because he has no need to (e.g. Virg. *G.* 1.125): here because he does not know how.

934. scibat: Editors since Munro have noted the prevalence of such archaic fourth-conjugation imperfects in the latter part of this book (949, 953, 959, 996, 1003, 1324). They are metrically more tractable than *-iebat* forms, and as Duff points out the narrative character of this section accounts for the cluster in Book 5.

molirier: used of 'working' the ground also by Virg. *G.* 1.494 'agricola incurvo terram molitus aratro' (where the phraseology suggests a recollection of 933-4 here); Columella 2.16.1; Livy 40.29.3.

935. Virtually repeated at 1366.

937-8. These lines look like a hint at the Golden Age, especially the words *sponte sua* and *donum*, as at 2.1157-9 where the earth 'nitidas fruges vinetaque laeta / sponte sua primum mortalibus ipsa creavit, / ipsa dedit dulces fetus et pabula laeta'. But there L. was pointing a contrast in his argument that the earth has decayed and lost the potency she had in early times to produce huge creatures and luxuriant vegetation. The same theme recurs earlier in our book (esp. 799-800, 826-36), and lies behind the present passage: it was the 'novitas florida mundi' 943 which caused the earth to produce 'sponte sua' 937, and even arbute-berries 'plurima tum tellus etiam maiora ferebat' 942. The earth was not responding to the simplicity and moral purity of a 'golden' race of men: she was just younger and stronger.

939 ff. Acorns and arbute-berries are linked again at 965 among primitive man's wooing gifts, and acorns especially were commonly said to be part of his staple diet: below 1416, Virg. *G.* 1.148, Ovid *M.* 1.106 (both Virgil and Ovid also link acorns and arbutes), Tib. 2.1.38, Juv. 6.10 (sardonically of the cave-dwelling wife 'horridior glandem ructante marito') – and not only by the poets: see also Pliny *HN* 16.1 '(arbores) glandiferas, quae primae victum mortalium aluerunt'.

curabant corpora: generally of looking after one's physical well-being, and here especially by food and shelter: similarly 2.30-1 'sub ramis arboris altae / . . . corpora curant.'

plerumque: the word is frequent in L. but rare in other poets: see Axelson, *Unpoetische Wörter*, 106. For its emphatic late position in the sentence and beginning a line see 1128 and Hor. *C.* 1.34.7 (with Nisbet-Hubbard's note).

942. plurima . . . etiam maiora: see n. on 937–8.

943. florida: adds a pretty pictorial touch to the phrase *novitas mundi* (which we have met before at 780, 818) – and in contrast to *pabula dura*.

944. pabula dura: *dura* is in strong contrast to the stock phrase *pabula laeta* (1.14, 257; 2.317, 364, 596, 875, 1159), and gives point to the almost formulaic *miseris mortalibus*. There is some conflict here with the 'nitidas fruges vinetaque laeta' produced by the young earth at 2.1157, but L. is making a different point there (937–8 n.), and the food here is at least *ampla*, though it was rough and presumably uncooked as they had no fires (953).

945–52. Men drank from rivers and springs like beasts to-day, and they knew where to find running water.

945. sedare . . . vocabant: for the rare infinitive after *vocare* cf. Plaut. *Truc.* 547; Hor. *C.* 2.18.38–40.

946. decursus aquai: 263 n.

947. claru' citat late: The sound of the mountain torrent attracts thirsty animals from far and wide. This is Forbiger's correction of *claricitatiate* OQ (adopting *late* from Simeon Bosius's *claricitat late*), and it remains the neatest and most convincing – adopted by Munro, Duff, Giussani, Merrill, Bailey (in his OCT but not his later edition), Müller. For discussions of Bosius's conjecture, followed essentially by Lachmann and seriously considered by many, see the notes of Bailey and Munro. For *clarus citat*, 'loudly summons', editors quote the somewhat similar usage at Virg. *A.* 7.141–2 'pater omnipotens ter caelo clarus ab alto / intonuit' (though *clarus* there might mean 'cloudless').

    saecla ferarum: (also 967, 982) 'races, tribes of wild beasts': 855 n.

948 ff. denique . . . nympharum: 'moreover they dwelt in the woodland haunts of the nymphs, known to them in their wanderings.' The dative *vagis* referring to the subject of *tenebant* is slightly awkward but is preferable to altering it to *vagi* (Lachmann) and thus isolating *nota*.

    templa: 'haunts' (not of course 'temples', though with *nympharum* it is hard not to be conscious of this sense), as at 1188 'in caeloque deum sedes et templa locarunt': see 103 n. The nymphs are conventional in poetic landscape descriptions from Homer onwards, being especially associated with caves (cf. *saxa* 950–1): Homer *Od.* 12.318, 13.104; Theocr. 7.136–7; Virg. *A.* 1.167–8 'intus aquae dulces vivoque sedilia saxo, / nympharum domus'. See G. Williams, *Tradition and Originality in Roman Poetry*, 641–2. The poet in L. takes charge in these lines with a charmingly lush picture of running water and mossy rocks. This is achieved by the remarkably dense cluster of 'wet', 'flowing', 'dripping' words, which with the literary devices of alliteration (*l*s and *r*s in 950, *s*s in 951, *p*s in 952) and epanalepsis

(repetition of *umida saxa*) create for its own sake a highly sophisticated poetic description.

949. **quibus e**: the preposition is postponed for metrical convenience
(cf. 31 n.), and the phrase itself is almost formulaic: 3.375, 839,
858.

    umori' fluenta . . . : 'flowing streams of water washed the dripping
rocks with abundant flood – yes, the dripping rocks – and trickled
over the green moss.'

950-1. **umida saxa / umida saxa**: The device of repeating a word or words
from the end of one line at the beginning of the next goes back to
Homer, and it was a notable Alexandrian mannerism taken over by
Catullus and Lucretius and handed on to their Latin successors. For
Catullus see Fordyce's edition, pp. 255, 275; for Virgil see Austin
on *A*. 2.406 and 6.164. L.'s characteristic pattern is to repeat a
word from the previous fifth foot in the following first foot, e.g.
2.955-6 'vincere saepe / vincere', 3.12-3 'aurea dicta / aurea', but
sometimes he repeats the last word of a line, e.g. 5.298-9 'instant /
instant'. The combined double repetition *umida saxa* here impresses
us with the everlastingly dripping stones, and is unique in the *DRN*;
but it can be paralleled in Cic. *Arat. Progn.* 220-1 (in *Div*. 1.14)
'vocibus instat / vocibus instat', and examples are common in Ovid.
(There is a more complex repetition at 5.1189-90.) Austin quotes a
famous English example in *Lycidas* 37-8, 'But O the heavy change,
now thou art gone, / Now thou art gone and never must return!' –
one of the many devices which Milton owed to classical poetry.

952. **scatere atque erumpere**: 598 n. The construction involves a slight
anacolouthon, as the verbs are governed by *scibant* but not *quibus
e*: *partim* shows that these waters on the plain are different from
those in the rocky caves just described.

953-61. They lacked fire (953), clothing (954-7), sense of community,
moral code, laws (958-61). Similarly Diodorus (1.8: see introductory
note) remarks that primitive men ἐπιπόνως διάγειν, γυμνοὺς μὲν
ἐσθῆτος ὄντας, οἰκήσεως δὲ καὶ πυρὸς ἀήθεις, τροφῆς δ᾽ ἡμέρου
παντελῶς ἀνεννοήτους.

953. **tractare**: 'to work things with fire' probably includes cooking food:
it is mentioned as an innovation following the introduction of fire at
1102-3.

954. **spoliis**: elsewhere in the *DRN* only at 4.62, also in the rather rare
sense of an animal's skin. *et* is explanatory: 'to use hides *by* clothing
their bodies in the skins of wild animals'.

955. For these standard items of the landscape see 41, 992.

956. **squalida**: 'filthy', 'unkempt'.

957. Note the *v*- alliteration here and at 964.

959. **moribus / legibus**: traditional, unwritten codes of behaviour / formal,
written laws. With this statement and 961 cf. Hobbes's famous

chapter 'Of the Natural Condition of Mankind': ' . . . the time where-in men live without other security than what their own strength, and their own invention shall furnish them withal . . . The notions of right and wrong, justice and injustice have there no place. Where there is no common power, there is no law . . . ' (*Leviathan*, Part I, Chap. 13).

960. quod . . . praedae: together, 'whatever prize', 'any prize'.

961. valere: 'thrive', 'flourish', or perhaps closely with *vivere*, 'live by his own strength'.   **doctus:** by instinct, experience, or necessity.

962-5. Women were won by mutual passion, force, or bribery.

963. conciliabat: the verb has a special sense of winning a woman as wife or mistress: e.g. Plautus *Mil*. 801; Cat. 68.130 (see *OLD* s.v. 1.b).

965. For a similar picture of primitive lovers' gifts see Prop. 3.13.27 ff. L. is mildly satirizing the conventions of pastoral wooing (e.g. Theocr. 3.10, Virg. *E*. 3.64 ff.).

966-9. They were strong and swift enough to hunt most wild animals.

968[975]: Naugerius's transposition of the line is the most persuasive: see apparatus and Bailey's note for other suggestions.

    magno pondere clavae: 'a club of great weight': the periphrasis is like those with *vis* discussed at 28 n.

969. vitabant: the subject is probably the huntsmen, who had to avoid the fiercer animals (cf. 984 ff.), rather than the animals.

970-87. At night they slept on the ground, fearing not darkness but prowling beasts.

970. saetigeris: another of L.'s favourite compounds in *-ger* or *-fer*: see *spumigeri* 985, and the same phrase at 6.974 'saetigeris subus acre venenumst'. Merrill on 3.11 has a list of such compounds, many of which L. seems to have invented.

    sūbus here, *sŭbus* at 6.974, 977: the variation in quantity is quite acceptable (see Ernout's note here and Ernout–Meillet, s.v.), and there is no need for the various suggested devices to ensure *ŭ* here.

    silvestria: 'woodland-dwelling', 'rough'. The word is used also by Horace of primitive men, 'silvestres homines', *Ars* 391.

972. circum: adverb.

973-81. Editors since Wakefield have quoted Manil. 1.69-70 'tum velut amissis maerens, tum laeta renatis/sideribus', and Stat. *Theb*. 4.282-4 'hi lucis stupuisse vices noctisque feruntur / nubila et occiduum longe Titana secuti / desperasse diem', and suggested that L. is deliberately attacking a theory that primitive men feared that each day's setting sun would not return. Whether such a theory, strictly formulated, was current is unknown, but L. certainly goes to some length to stress that early man had an empirical common-sense faith (based on πρόληψις?) in recurring phenomena, and was not afraid that each day's light would be the last he would see. What he did realistically fear was being attacked in his sleep by wild animals (982 ff.).

975–6. respectabant . . . dum: 'waited for': 375 n.
   rosea face: cf. 610 'rosea sol . . . lampade'.
979. non erat . . . mirarier: 'there was nothing to make them ever capable
   of surprise' – not one of L.'s happier lines: the construction is flat
   and awkward, in which *mirarier* and *diffidere* must be taken as nouns
   subject to *fieri posset*. (The simpler and common form of the periphrasis is *est ut* + subjunctive, as at 126–7.)
980. diffidere ne: this is the only quoted example of *ne* with *diffidere*
   before Tertullian (see *TLL* s.v.): it usually takes infin. or acc. and infin.,
   as at 1157, but *ne* is quite logical with a verb virtually meaning 'fear'.
985. spumigeri: 970 n.
986. intempesta: already an epithet of *nox* in Ennius (*Ann.* 102 and
   167V) and conventional in later prose and poetry. It is explained by
   Varro (*LL* 6.7, and cf. 7.72) as the time between dusk and dawn
   when (according to the grammarian Aelius Stilo) 'tempus agendi est
   nullum'. Perhaps night is simply 'timeless' when it is too dark for
   any impression of passing time: if so, 'dead of night' would give the
   right suggestion of an inert and unseen world. Theocritus has the
   phrase νυκτὸς ἀωρί (11.40, 24.38), which may be comparable.
987. hospitibus: 'visitors', 'guests', with an obvious touch of irony – and
   all they had to give up was their couch of leaves: cf. 972.
988–1010. An ironic coda to this section: early men did not die in much
   greater numbers from their natural enemies than modern men from
   their self-induced perils of warfare and seafaring. The sardonic tone
   here can be compared with 3.59–86, one of L.'s few clear references
   to contemporary society, in which he bitterly attacks the avarice,
   cruelty, and ambition to be seen in public life.
988. mortalia saecla: 'mankind', as at 1169, 1238; contrast 791, 805
   ('animals').
991. haustus: 'torn', 'ripped' (so as to 'drain off' blood): for this sense
   of *haurire* see 1324, Virg. *A.* 10.314 (where Servius glosses *haurit* by
   ferit), Ovid *M.* 9.412. The usage might be military (see *TLL* s.v.
   2573.61 ff.), and probably extended to the cognate noun *haustus*,
   as at 1069 (D. A. West, *CQ* 15 (1965), 271–80).
992. 41 n.
993. vivo sepeliri . . . busto: The beast of prey as a tomb of its victim
   has been a famous and long-lived conceit in European literature, at
   least from Aeschylus to Shakespeare: for characteristic examples
   note Aesch. *Septem* 1020–1 πετηνῶν τόνδ' ὑπ' οἰωνῶν . . . ταφέντ'
   ἀτίμως, Soph. *El.* 1487–8, Gorgias B5a D–K γῦπες ἔμψυχοι τάφοι,
   Ennius *Ann.* 138–9V 'crudeli . . . sepulchro' (a vulture), Ovid *Her.*
   10.123–4, Spenser *Faerie Queene* ii.8.16 'be entombed in the raven
   or the kight', Shakesp. *Macbeth* iii.4.72 'Our monuments shall be
   the maws of kites.' Here the pointed *viva/vivo* and the alliteration
   underline the grim irony of the idea.

994. adeso: 'mangled'.

996. They prayed for death in agony from the wounds they could not treat. Orcus (elsewhere at 1.115, 6.762) is sometimes the ruler of the underworld, sometimes the underworld itself (see *RE* 18.1.908 ff.): all three Lucretian references are ambiguous.

997. vermina: 'griping pains': the word seems not to occur elsewhere in classical Latin.

> **privarant:** The pluperf. indic. with *donec* seems to be unparalleled (*TLL* s.v. 1995.11), though the pluperf. subj. is occasionally found (e.g. Livy 21.28.11): hence many editors have adopted Creech's *privarunt*. But we might explain the pluperfect in relation to the following line: they had died before they could get help or learn to cure their wounds.

998. expertis opis: 'helpless' 'without assistance': the same phrase is used at 6.1242 of victims of the plague dying abandoned.

> **vellent:** 'needed', 'required' to heal them.

999. sub signis . . . ducta: i.e. on active service, ready for battle.

1000. una . . . exitio: cf. 95 n.

1000 ff. The hazards of navigation and the temerity of the first men who risked their lives on the sea are a commonplace in classical poetry, especially as a symptom of the end of the Golden Age: Aratus *Phaen.* 110-11, Virg. *G.* 1.136 ff., Ovid *M.* 1.94 ff., Sen. *Med.* 301 ff. However, in our passage the contrast is not between sea dangers and an idyllic earlier existence but between the deaths which modern men invite and those which primitive men could not avoid.

1001. lidebant: 'dashed'. The simple verb occurs only here and may be a back formation from the compound *allido* (Ernout ad loc., *OLD* s.v.), which is used in this sense.

1002. hic: If we accept this correction by Lachmann of *nec* OQ it must mean 'in these circumstances', as in 432. But Lambinus's *sed* is safer: the unintelligible *nec* may have come in from 1004.

> **temere incassum frustra:** A notable string of synonyms, also found at 2.1060: it is used here to make a serious point very forcibly.

1004-5. Cf. 2.559 'subdola cum ridet placidi pellacia ponti' – one of L.'s memorable alliterative expressions, and especially so from the great rarity of the noun *pellacia*. The force of the couplet is further increased by the 'figura etymologica' *pellacia . . . pellicere* and the cluster of words involving the meaning 'treacherous'. For a similar emphatic combination of alliteration and 'figura etymologica' see 3.144, 188.

> **ridentibus:** 1395 n.

1006. improba navigii ratio: 'the presumptuous art of navigation'. But the line has been emended or (perhaps rightly) deleted as an interpolation by many editors because (1) it is flat and abrupt in the context, (2) the required meaning of *navigii* ('navigation' not 'ship') seems to be unparalleled and the form of the genitive suspect. (In Republican Latin nouns in -*ius* and -*ium* always have genitive in -*i*.) See the discussions by Ernout and Bailey.

1008. mersat: 'overwhelms': a strong word (significantly following close on the perils of the sea), also used metaphorically by Catullus, 'accipe, quis merser fortunae fluctibus' (68.13) and Horace (*Ep.* 1.1.16).

1010. vergebant: 'used to pour': for this sense of *vergere* see Ovid *M.* 4.506-7 'vergit furiale venenum / pectus in amborum', Stat. *Theb.* 6.211 'spumantesque mero paterae verguntur.' The tradition gives us a defective line and the OCT prints the early Juntine correction — still one of the best of the very many suggestions. Any proposed solution must take account of the whole drift of the section and the immediately preceding 1007-8, which compel us to assume that in this final couplet L. works up to a biting contrast between the ignorant carelessness of the past and the sinister cunning of the present. In spite of the textual uncertainty it looks like a climax of which Juvenal himself might have been proud. (Besides the standard editions see more recent discussions by M. F. Smith, *CR* 16 (1966), 264, M. L. Clarke, *CR* 20 (1970), 10.)

1011-1457. The last and longest section of the third main division of the book treats of the origins and growth of human civilization. After a brief preliminary paragraph (1011-27) L. deals selectively and at varying length with major achievements and discoveries — language, lawgiving, religion, metalwork, agriculture, music — which have been landmarks in mankind's progress from primitive barbarism.

The earlier part at least of this section is not logically structured, and if we follow the manuscript tradition the introduction of topics is somewhat random and inconsequent: e.g. fire is assumed at 1011 ff. but its origin is not discussed until 1091 ff., and 1105 ff. would follow more naturally on 1011-27 (cities after the start of community life). It is possible that there has been some dislocation in the text, and editors have proposed varying degrees of surgery to produce more topical coherence. But it seems best to keep the manuscript order of subjects here: as elsewhere L. probably wrote rapidly as ideas seized his imagination, and reverted later to topics he had mentioned previously — and if he had lived to revise the poem he might well have tidied up this part of the book himself. (See further Bailey, iii, 1490-1, Kenney, *DRN 3*, p. 13.)

An interesting attempt has been made to analyse 1011-1457 into two phases of man's cultural development, corresponding to the two phases briefly suggested by Epicurus in *Ep. Hdt.* 75-6. On this analysis 1011-1104 deal with the stage when men were taught ὑπο αὐτῶν τῶν πραγμάτων, and 1105-1457 with the stage when they began to use λογισμός. This scheme may be found helpful, though it does not resolve all the difficulties mentioned above. (See

K. Barwick in *Philol.* 95 (1943), 193–229; B. Manuwald, *Der Aufbau der lukrezischen Kulturentstehungslehre* (Mainz/Wiesbaden, 1980).)

1011–27. A summary introduction, surveying the first rudimentary physical comforts of shelter and warmth, the formalized cohabiting of men and women, and the beginning of community life – all these being marked improvements on the bestial and haphazard existence described in 925 ff.

1011. inde: 'next', marking an important phase of improvement.

1012–13. Unless we drastically alter *cognita sunt*, a line must have fallen out which clarified *unum* and provided a subject for *cognita sunt*. Something like Munro's 'hospitium ac lecti socialia iura duobus' must be the general sense. *videre* presumably refers to the fathers who, in stable family units, could now know their own children.

1015–18. Warmth and love-making sapped their physical toughness and family life made their tempers less harsh.

1015. ignis: L. returns in more detail to the crucial discovery of fire at 1091 ff.

      alsia: 'shivering' (*algeo*): an unparalleled adjectival form, though Cicero twice has a neuter comparative *alsius* from **alsus*.

1016. caeli sub tegmine: L. liked this phrase and used it also at 1.988, 2.663: as Merrill notes (on 1.988) this may be one of his borrowings from Cicero's translation of Aratus' *Phaenomena*, where the phrase is found, e.g. 47, 233. Cf. 1437.

1017. Venus . . . viris: cf. 4.1121 (through sexual passion) 'absumunt viris pereuntque labore'.

1019–20. The rise of a community spirit and social co-operation was based on the principle that people should not harm each other. This theory of the primitive structure of society is in line with the Epicurean doctrine of justice as a compact between men to avoid mutual hurt. The key texts here are K.Δ. 31, 32, 33, 36, and L.'s *nec laedere nec violari* is a clear echo of Epicurus' τὸ μὴ βλάπτειν μηδὲ βλάπτεσθαι. The reference to friendship here may also derive from Epicurus' well-known emphasis on friendship (*Sent. Vat.* 52, Cic. *Fin.* 2.82), though the vivid details about pity and protection for women and children seem to be L.'s own. At any rate, his account is very different in emphasis from the most famous discussion in classical literature of this concept of the nature of society. In Plato's *Republic*, ii. 358–9, Glaucon similarly derives justice from a compact neither to do nor to suffer wrong, but he puts forward a theory that it is accepted merely as a social convenience, because men find they cannot both enjoy the advantages of doing wrong and escape the disadvantages of suffering it. (See further Robin's valuable note on 1019–23, and below 1136–60 n.)

1020. finitimi: noun, 'neighbours', as at 4.581.

      inter se: with *amicitiem iungere*.

1021. commendarunt: i.e. to each other for protection.

    muliebre saeclum: 'womankind': 988 n.

1022. balbe: 'inarticulately': early moral concepts were hard to express coherently in the primitive state of language. The run of the sentence suggests that the subject of *significarent* is still *finitimi*, though some editors take it to be the women and children themselves.

1024–7. A realistic note: of course there was not complete harmony, but most men kept their promises and this mutual help secured human survival.

1025. bona magnaque pars: an unusual tautology (*bona pars* itself regularly means 'a considerable *or* the greater part'), for which editors quote Ter. *Eun.* 123, Val. Max. 2.9.7.

    caste: 'honourably', 'uprightly'.

1028–90. The origin of language.

    The origin of language was much discussed by ancient thinkers, though tantalizingly few texts have come down to us. The most extensive discussion is in Plato's *Cratylus* in which the two main current theories are fully canvassed. These were (1) that language and names for things arose naturally (φύσει) in primitive societies; (2) they arose by deliberate invention and arbitrary imposition (θέσει) of words upon objects. The φύσις theory seems to have assumed a sort of natural affinity between word and thing described which expresses itself in primitive utterance; and the θέσις doctrine at least recognized the importance of expressing such a natural relationship in the invented word: it is stressed that the all-wise lawgiver, νομοθέτης in the *Cratylus* (see esp. 388e ff.) who prescribes names for things must bear this affinity in mind. The θέσις view of language also appears in Protagoras' account of the development of human society: ἔπειτα φωνὴν καὶ ὀνόματα ταχὺ διηρθρώσατο τῇ τέχνῃ (Plato, *Protagoras* 322a5–6: see introd. note to 925–87). Turning to the Atomists we find that, according to Proclus in his commentary on the *Cratylus*, Democritus too believed that names were arbitrarily imposed (θέσει, see Democritus B26 D–K): for a discussion of Democritus' views see Guthrie, ii, 474–6. In a careful and important discussion of the origin of language Epicurus combines the two theories (*Ep. Hdt.* 75–6). At first men uttered natural sounds which spontaneously expressed their feelings and reactions to the world around them, and names were not deliberately imposed (τὰ ὀνόματα ἐξ ἀρχῆς μὴ θέσει γενέσθαι). Later in individual communities names were arbitrarily chosen to clarify meanings and aid communication (ὕστερον δὲ κοινῶς καθ' ἕκαστα ἔθνη τὰ ἴδια τεθῆναι). Lastly Epicurus seems to suggest that new names for new and unfamiliar objects arose both naturally and by convention or analogy (see Bailey's notes on the whole passage). Diodorus (1.8.3–4) in his account of primitive society already referred to (note on 925–87) gives a similar picture: man's originally inarticulate and meaningless sounds gradually gave way to conventionally agreed expressions to describe things (πρὸς ἀλλήλους τιθέντας σύμβολα).

L.'s account of the rise of language is a firm statement of the φύσις theory and a sardonic rejection of the idea that words are conventionally attached to things — at least in the sense that there ever was an all-wise being who could arbitrarily allot names. He thus rejects explicitly the form of the θέσις theory which appears in the *Cratylus*, and by implication (for he says nothing about it) the version found in Epicurus and Diodorus where names are devised by corporate agreement among men. His attack on the notional namegiver has an interesting parallel in another important Epicurean thinker, Diogenes of Oenoanda. In a surviving text (fr. 10, col. II. 11-col. IV Chilton), in language as strong as L.'s, Diogenes pours scorn on the utterly ridiculous idea that one single man could give names to things. (For a discussion of this passage see Chilton, *AJP* 83 (1962), 159–67.) Bailey may be right (iii, 1488) in thinking that later Epicureans were not interested in the second and third stages of Epicurus' analysis of word-origin: in any case it is not very important to decide (a point he and other editors discuss at length) whether Lucretius, Diogenes, and perhaps Epicurus himself were attacking the particular statement of the name-giver theory which appears in the *Cratylus* or some other authority. The important point is that the ludicrous impracticality of the theory of a single νομοθέτης became widely recognized, but this did not discount the idea that primitive men came to agree on conventional labels for things, a phase of language development which it seemed reasonable to distinguish from earlier spontaneous and reactive cries. It is not clear why L. chose to ignore this version of the θέσις theory — though it is just possible that *utilitas* 1029 is an oblique reference to it (see Giussani, *Studi Lucreziani*, 283). He would surely not have denied that at some stage men agreed on names for things, but he clearly wants to stress the physiological side of human utterance (1028, 1057, 1090). Hence the comparison with babies' gestures and the prolonged analogy with animal sounds, 1063–86: here are physical processes at work which are of interest to the materialist philosopher.

The origins of human speech do not much interest modern students of linguistics, and 'evolutionary' theories of language in particular are regarded with suspicion. See, for example, J. C. Marshall, 'The biology of communication in men and animals' in J. Lyons (ed.), *New Horizons in Linguistics* (Harmondsworth, 1970), 229–41, who attacks evolutionary arguments based on comparisons between human language and methods of communication among animals.

1028–40. It was nature which caused early man to utter speech sounds, a primitive reaction like the gestures of babies and the spontaneous attempts of young animals to use their scarcely developed bodies.

1028–9. varios linguae sonitus: these must be the originally spontaneous and incoherent sounds, scarcely yet words, which the 'convenience' (*utilitas*) of having recognized labels for things forced men to formalize into 'names'. *utilitas expressit* is the nearest L. gets to the θέσις theory (see introd. note), but he does not develop the idea, and *utilitas* is hardly more than an instinctive feeling for the practical need to communicate. Horace expresses a similar idea in a passage probably influenced by ours: 'donec verba quibus voces sensusque notarent / nominaque invenere' (*Sat*. 1.3.103–4).

subigere with the infin. also at 3.1076–7, 6.736–7.

1030. videtur: a strict passive, 'is seen', as at 1073, 1189.

1031. infantia: 'inability to speak', which 'causes them to point at . . . '. The literal sense is extremely rare (see *TLL* vii 1.1350), though the phrase 'infantia linguae' recurs in Claudian, *Carm. Min*. 30.103 in the sense 'childish tongue'. Herodotus (2.2) records an experiment of the Egyptian king Psammetichus with two children: he excluded them from human speech from birth to see what word they first uttered of their own accord — an amateur exploration of the φύσις theory.

1033. 'for each one feels to what purpose he can use his own powers'.

vis: an old form of *vires* found also at 2.586, 3.265. *quoad* is Lambinus's suggestion for *quod* OQ, accepted by many editors. The word is rare in poetry and regularly monosyllabic when it occurs, as below 1213, 1433, Hor. *Sat*. 2.3.91: see Axelson, *Unpoetische Wörter*, 22.

abuti: 'make full use of' (at 2.656 'misuse' — the only other occurrence in the *DRN*). As in early Latin it is here transitive with the accusative.

1034–5. For his analogy L. adapts a proverbial thought: Anacreontea 24.1–2 φύσις κέρατα ταύροις, / ὁπλὰς δ' ἔδωκεν ἵπποις . . . , Hor. *Sat*. 2.1.52 'dente lupus, cornu taurus petit', [Ovid] *Halieutica* 2–3 'vitulus sic namque minatur, / qui nondum gerit in tenera iam cornua fronte' (which may imitate L.), Cic. *ND* 2.127.

nata: 'budding'.

frontibus: the plural is used probably because L. is thinking of the two horns growing on opposite sides of the forehead; but in any case Latin has a tendency to use the plural even of singular features of the body, e.g. *cervices, fauces* (Löfstedt, *Syntactica* 1.30–1).

inurget: 'pushes': the compound is found elsewhere only at Apul. *Met*. 8.10.

1036. scymni: σκύμνοι: the Greek word is used as *variatio* with *catuli*, or perhaps, as Ernout suggests, because of the origins of these animals in Greek-speaking Egypt and Asia Minor (just as the words *panthera* and *leo* are Greek in origin). However, L. is fond of using Greek words whether or not he had a Latin equivalent to hand (Bailey, i, 138-9). The panther and lion appear together also at 4.1016.

1039. alituum: 801 n.

genus: in the context this seems to refer specifically to the young (*OLD* s.v. 2).

1040. tremulum: 'unsteady'.

auxiliatum: one of L.'s many fourth-declension coinages: 303 n.

1041-61. L. attacks the view that one man could have invented names and words and taught them to others in four arguments: (1) Why should one man only have this power? (1043-5) (2) Without already hearing words used around him he would not have the necessary *notities*, general concept, of language. (1046-9) (3) He alone could not have compelled all the others to learn, and they would not have endured his unintelligible sounds. (1050-5) (4) It is quite reasonable that men as a race should express their feelings in varying sounds just as animals of all kinds do. (1056-61)

1041. aliquem: 'some one man' (the singular is to be stressed), the ὀνοματουργός of the *Cratylus* (389a): it is this version of the θέσις theory that L. is attacking, though we cannot be sure if he had the *Cratylus* itself in mind (see introductory note).

1043. desiperest: 165 n.

1044. varios sonitus linguae: the same phrase 1028.

emittere: from the earliest writers *emittere* was used of speech: see *OLD* s.v. 6.d.

1046-9. Without first hearing words from others how could he have the model or pattern to form his own *notities* (πρόληψις) or concept of language, or the power of knowing what to do? The *notities* argument was used at 181-6 to prove that the gods could not have created the world as they had no *exemplum* to follow (see notes there). The *potestas* (1048) is the enabling power derived from the mental images which are an essential preliminary to action: see 4.877 ff. where L. explains that it is only after the mind receives *simulacra* of movement that a chain-reaction is set up in the body which enables us to move. For *utilitatis* see 1029 n: *notitiam utilitatis* occurs also at 4.854.

scirēt: the syllable is lengthened by a combination of the metrical ictus falling on it and a recollection of the originally long quantity of the vowel. The only other similar example is at 2.27, but see 396 n.

1050-55. The physical impossibility of one man's persuading all the others to learn.

1051. poterat: 'could': the regular idiomatic imperf. indic. for subjunctive: cf. 18 n. (a somewhat different idiom).

1052. surdis: 'uncomprehending (of the outlandish new sounds)', further explained in 1053-5.

1054-5. amplius . . . obtundere: 'din into their ears for long'. *obtundere* is common in this sense: see *OLD* s.v. 1.c and 2.

1056-61. The argument from the analogy with animals which obviously utter different sounds expressing different feelings. L. marks a climactic argument with a display of poetic effects: a notable alliteration of *v* in 1057, 1058, 1060, and a complex pattern of *c* and *um* sounds in 1059. See also the sound effects in the passage on the dogs below, 1063 ff.

1058. sensu: 'feeling, 'perception'.

notaret: there is no need to alter to *notavit* (Frerichs, Brieger, on the ground that L. regularly has the indic. after *mirum si*, e.g. 193, 749, 799, 1238). The construction is virtually equivalent to the subjunctive with *mirabile cur* or *quare* (2.310, 4.258), or we may say it is influenced by *vigeret.*

1059. mutae: 'dumb' in the sense of 'inarticulate', as at 1088 and exactly as we say 'dumb animals': *mutus* is commonly thus applied to animals, though L. uses it more literally of fish at 2.342 and 1082.

1060. ciere: 'utter', often but not invariably used of anguished, emotional utterance: Cat. 64.131, Virg. *A.* 3.344, Val. Fl. 3.156. For a similar thought (and slightly different use of *ciere*) see Apul. *Florida* 17 'voces animalium . . . quas infesta rabies vel propitia voluptas ciant'.

1061. gliscunt: 'increase, grow strong': an old, possibly agricultural word (see Kenney on 3.480), which L. uses elsewhere of passionate love, 1.474, 4.1069, and of the violent symptoms of drunkenness, 3.480. Pacuvius has the same phrase 'gliscit gaudium' (fr. 294R).

1062-86. L. illustrates his analogy by the different sounds made by dogs (1063-72), horses (1073-7), and birds (1078-86).

The passage on the dogs is remarkable for the matching of the sound of the lines to the different moods of the animals. The preliminary, threatening signs of 1063-4 are heard in the menacing *m um* and *d* sounds, which give way to the open echoing vowel sounds of the barking in 1066. Then come the smooth *l*s of 1067 where the dogs are affectionately licking their pups, followed by the mock-threatening *s* sounds of 1068-9; and finally the slow, echoing vowels of 1071 where the dogs are howling in an empty house. This is one of L.'s most sustained onomatopoeic passages.

1063-4. 'when the large flabby lips of Molossian hounds first begin to open and snarl in anger, baring their hard teeth': a notable accumulation of epithets (*irritata, magna, mollia*) for which see 13 n. Molossian dogs (originally from Epirus in north-west Greece) were one of the most famous breeds of hunting and sheep dog in the ancient world, and are often referred to in literature, e.g. Arist. *HA* 608a26 ff., Aristoph. *Thesm.* 416, Grattius *Cyn.* 181, Nemesianus *Cyn.* 107, Virg. *G.* 3.405, Hor. *Epode* 6.5, *Sat.* 2.6.114.

ricta: properly 'open mouth' and hence 'lips'. For the neuter form of *rictus* cf. Cic. *Verr.* 4.94 and see 205 n. Note the pointed contrast *mollia/duros.*

1065. restricta: Lachmann's correction of the manuscripts' *stricta* or *districta* is supported by Plautus *Capt.* 486 'si non arriderent, dentes ut restringerent', Apul. *Apol.* 6 'restrictis forte si labellis riseris', and is generally accepted, together with Pontanus's *minantur.*

1066. et cum: 'than when'. L. several times has *et cum* after *alius* instead of the more usual *ac/atque*, perhaps to avoid *ac* followed by another *c* (see Munro on 1.280). See below 1071, 1082, 1.281, and cf. 'neu simili . . . et cum' 2.414–6 and the variation 'nec minus . . . et ille' 3.1092–3. For the comparative use of *et* see also *TLL* V.2.894.4–29.

1068–9. iactant: 'toss': Naugerius's conjecture for *lactant* OQ is probably right (it is used at 4.992 of dogs jerking their legs in sleep). *lactant* is unlikely to be right in either of the senses (as some editors argue) 'attack' or 'wheedle', but a more persuasive case for retaining it in the sense 'suckle' has been argued by D. A. West, *CQ* 15 (1965), 278–9, though the verb is not attested as transitive until the Vulgate.

petentes: 'playfully nipping' (with *morsu*), though the strongly attested *potentes* OQL could be right in a concessive sense: 'though powerful in bite they restrain their teeth and gently pretend to nip them.'

haustus: probably feigned 'nips' or 'lunges' at them, rather than swallowings (the usual interpretation): see 991 n.

1070. 'fondle them with growls of a far different kind.' *gannitu* and *adulant* have here their primary application to the behaviour of dogs: see citations in *OLD* s.vv.

1071. baubantur: 'howl', 'bay', an obviously onomatopoeic word (cf. Greek βαΰζειν). The only other cited example of its use apart from glossators (Suet. fr. 161, p. 250Re) shows that it too was used especially of dogs.

1072. This vivid description rounds off a well-observed account of varied dog behaviour, which Giussani compares as an example of L.'s eye for the animal world with the picture of a cow searching for her lost calf, 2.352–66. See also 864 n.

1073. hinnitus hinnit (1077): Again onomatopoeic. Bailey points out the paucity of words L. had for horse sounds compared with dogs.

1074. iuvencus: 'young': very rare as an adjective, but cf. Pliny *HN* 10.146 (of hens).

1075. pinnigeri: For winged Cupid/Amor see 738 n. His usual weapon is his bow and arrow, but here he is pictured appropriately as riding the stallion and spurring it to sexual excitement. L. may also be influenced by phrases like Eur. *Hipp.* 38–9 κἀκπεπληγμένη / κέντροις ἔρωτος (quoted by Wakefield), Plato *Rep.* 573a7 πόθου κέντρον.

1076. 'and snorts with flaring nostrils for the battle'. *arma* is here the 'battle' of mating, like *proelia* in Virgil's discussion of stallions,

G.3.98 'si quando ad proelia ventum est'. Earlier in the same passage Virgil imitates our line: 'collectumque fremens volvit sub naribus ignem' (3.85).

1077. et cum: Parallel to *ubi* 1074.

sic alias: *sic* like οὕτως sometimes idiomatically qualifies another adverb and can express various nuances. Here it may mean 'as it happens at other times' (εἰ τύχοι), or it may be deictic, 'as you see at other times'. See Nisbet-Hubbard on Hor. *C*. 2.11.14 'sic temere'.

concussis: 'shaking' with some fear.

1078. genus . . . volucres: A formulaic phrase: see 801.

1079-80. ossifragae: Usually translated 'ospreys', but more probably lammergeyers or bearded vultures: see D'Arcy Thompson, *A Glossary of Greek Birds* s.vv. ὀστοκατάκτης and φήνη. If this is correct only the *mergi*, 'cormorants' or 'gulls', are water birds and the descriptive words *marinis . . . petentes* refer specifically to them.

marinis fluctibus: A slightly awkward local ablative close to *in salso*: take both phrases together as a hendiadys, 'among the salt sea-waves' (Latham). *salso* is an unusual substantival use without *aequore*, like the jocular English 'on the briny'.

1082. praedaeque repugnant: 'and their prey fights back'. Avancius's correction *praedae* should be taken as nom. plur., not dat. sing. ('they fight against their prey'). Editors quote Petronius 109.6 'alius hamis blandientibus convellebat praedam repugnantem', and for the plural *praedae* cf. Manil. 5.434, Juv. 11.101. (The passage is discussed by C. L. Howard in *CPhil* 56 (1961), 157-8.)

1083. partim: 'some': 840 n.

tempestatibus: 'the weather', the plural suggesting its changes and varying moods. Cf. 744 where *tempestates* means 'seasons'.

1084. raucisonos: a rare epithet, used of the blaring of horns at 2.619 and Cat. 64.263.

1084-6. Crows and ravens were widely famous for both longevity and weather prophecy. For their proverbial long life see Hesiod fr. 304 M-W, Aristoph. *Av*. 609, Cic. *Tusc*. 3.69, Ovid *M*. 7.274, Sen. *Ben*. 2.29.1; as weather prophets, Virg. *G*. 1.388-9, 410 ff., Lucan 5.555-6, Pliny *HN* 18.362-3. Both characteristics are linked with typical Horatian economy at Hor. *C*. 3.17.12-3 'aquae nisi fallit augur / annosa cornix'.

1087-90. The argument from analogy with animals is rounded off with a recapitulation of the statement in 1056-61.

1088. tamen: Not misplaced in this clause (Duff) but idiomatically with *cum*: 'while yet they are dumb', 'dumb though they nevertheless are'. The collocation is common in the *DRN*, e.g. above 16, 479, 518.

1089. aequum: 'reasonable'.

1091-1104. The origin and use of fire. Men first experienced it through lightning (implying thereby it was not a gift of the gods), or the sparks

caused by tree branches rubbing together in the wind, and they then
learned to cook by it. We are told that Democritus wrote a (now
lost) treatise on the origins of fire (Diog. Laert. 9.47): L. may have
read and used it, but on the other hand he had only to look around
at the natural world for the phenomena he describes here.

1091. tacitus . . . requiras: 'ask yourself', 'wonder'.

1092. Lightning is discussed at length at 6.160–218: one of its causes is
said to be 'seeds of fire' struck out by the collision of clouds.

1094. incita: 'kindled': Marullus's correction of *insita* OQ, accepted
hesitantly by Bailey. But *insita* ('implanted', 'grafted') is rightly
retained by many editors and supported by 1.901 'lignis . . . insitus
ignis'.

1095. fulgĕre: the older third-conjugation form, as at 6.165 (but *fulgēre*,
6.213, and see 768 n.): one of many examples of fluctuating conjugations at the time that L. was writing. Seneca discusses the point,
giving *fulgere* as an example, at *NQ* 2.56.

1096 ff. A more practicable illustration to early man of how to create
his own fire. The phenomenon of fire caused by tree branches rubbing
together is described at 1.897 ff.: it must have occurred frequently
in dry, well-wooded terrain and is mentioned in a wide variety of
authors (Thuc. 2.77.4, Manil. 1.857, *Aetna* 365).

1096–7. L.'s word-order here exemplifies the scene he is describing. The
juxtaposition of the words *arboris arbor* suggests the physical closeness of the two trees, and the unusually wide separation of *ramosa
. . . arbor* enclosing *ramos . . . arboris* pictures their interlocking
branches.

   aestuat: 'sways', 'is tossed about'.

1097–8, extritus: quite literally 'forced out by rubbing', but unusual in
this sense, though the word was used of threshing grain (Varro *RR*
1.52, Pliny *HN* 18.298). The alliteration *ex ex, v v* and the asyndeton
with *emicat* suggest the force and suddenness of the combustion.

1100. mutua: an adverbial acc. used several times by L. (2.76, 3.801,
4.301, 6.1084).

1102–4. Observing that the sun's warmth made crops ripen (*mitescere*:
for this sense see *OLD* s.v. 1) and so edible, man used his new mastery
of fire to cook his food. Editors quote Ovid *M.* 15.78–9 'herbae . . .
quae mitescere flamma / mollirique queant.'

   inde: 1011 n.

1105–35. The further development of early society, the emergence of
kings, and the acquisition of property. This last theme leads L.
(1117 ff.) to discuss the demoralizing effects of wealth and vain
ambition in contrast with the Epicurean ideal of contented quietism.

   We resume here the story of man's social progress as it was left at
1027 (see introductory note to 1011–1457). This phase sees the rise
of outstandingly gifted individuals as leaders of society, and here L.

may be influenced by the historical theories of his elder contemporary Posidonius. Seneca in his *Epistle* 90 to Lucilius is our best witness for Posidonius' view that philosophers were the rulers and lawgivers among early men and the inventors of civilizing arts and crafts. L.'s discussion is of course too summary to reveal how far he might have accepted the details of this theory, but that he drew upon it is very likely. (For this aspect of Posidonius' thought see K. Reinhardt in *RE* s.v. 805-8.)

This section is also notable for including one of L.'s fairly rare ethical polemics: for others see the more extended homilies at 2.1-61 and 3.830-1094. The stupidity of seeking wealth and power, and the wisdom of being content with supplying only natural needs were among Epicurus' most oft-repeated lessons, and L. echoes him closely here. K.Δ. 15 is typical: ὁ τῆς φύσεως πλοῦτος καὶ ὥρισται καὶ εὐπόριστός ἐστιν · ὁ δὲ τῶν κενῶν δοξῶν εἰς ἄπειρον ἐκπίπτει; but see also K.Δ. 7, *Sent. Vat.* 25, *Ep. Men.* 130, Usener 135, 469, 548-60. After L. the λάθε βιώσας ideal was invoked by a wide range of Latin poets: Hor. *Ep.* 1.17.10 'nec vixit male qui natus moriens-que fefellit', Ovid *Tr.* 3.4.25 'bene qui latuit bene vixit', Sen. *Thy.* 391-403.

1105. hi: Naugerius's correction of *in* OQ gives a rather too emphatic antecedent to *qui* 1107, and Bockemüller's *hinc* should perhaps be read.

1106. et igni: fire is strongly particularized after *rebus*, presumably to stress again its primary role in early man's advance, but the allusion comes in very abruptly here.

1107. corde: 'intelligence', 'mind', as at 864, 882, 1456.

1109. reges: clearly the same highly gifted men now given formal supremacy over their socities. But the tenure of such power was precarious, so they had citadels for their own 'protection and refuge'.

1111-2. pro facie . . . et viribus: the same phrase is used of visions of the gods at 1174, and the ideas are repeated in different words just below at 1114 and 1116. Early men were naïvely impressed by physical beauty and strength: editors quote Pomponius Mela on the Ethiopians: 'mos est cui potissimum pareant specie ac viribus legere' (3.86).

1114. res.: 'wealth', i.e. personal possessions distinct from the allotted land and animals of 1110.

aurumque repertum: the phrase − and the thought − may have suggested Horace's 'aurum irrepertum et sic melius situm' (*C.*3.3.49).

1117. vera ratione: 23 n.

1118-19. This is close to the thought of *Sent. Vat.* 25 (ἡ πενία μετρου-μένη τῷ τῆς φύσεως τέλει μέγας ἐστὶ πλοῦτος · πλοῦτος δὲ μὴ ὁριζόμενος μεγάλη ἐστὶ πενία 'poverty if measured by the natural purpose of life is great wealth, but unlimited wealth is great poverty'), and earlier Democritus too had stressed the relativity of riches and poverty (B 283, 284 D-K).

1120 ff. The Epicurean argument against seeking public life and power appears also at 2.11–3 and 3.59–64, 995–1002 (where the legend of Sisyphus is said to be an allegory of the man cursed with political ambition).

1124. iter . . . viai: for similar pleonastic phrases cf. 714 'cursusque viam', 2.626 'iter . . . viarum'.

1125–6. fulmen / invidia: lightning and envy are each proverbially said to attack elevated places and people (see Otto, *Sprichwörter* s.v. *fulmen*), and they are explicitly linked as here by Livy 8.31.7 and Ovid *Rem.* 369–70.

1126. Tartara: L. is speaking allegorically as he does at 3.1023 'hic Acherusia fit stultorum denique vita', since Hell does not literally exist for men (3.966 'nec quisquam in barathrum nec Tartara deditur atra').

1127–8 [1131–2]. Munro's transposition of these lines is virtually guaranteed by the successive repetition of the initial *invidia* in 1126–7, which would have caused their original displacement. For the thought cf. 6.459–60.

1127. vaporant: 'blaze', 'burn': the rare intransitive use is found also at Sen. *NQ* 2.30.4, Pliny *HN* 31.5.

1128. plerumque: emphatic as at 940.

1130. regere imperio res: these words may have inspired one of Virgil's most famous lines, *A.* 6.851 'tu regere imperio populos, Romane, memento'.

1131. sanguine sudent: cf. 6.1147–8 'sudabant . . . fauces . . . sanguine': the phrase survives first in Ennius, *Scen.* 181 V.

1132. angustum: i.e. 'crowded'.

1133–4. The moral blindness of power-hungry men arises from listening to others instead of following their own perceptions (*sensibus ipsis*), which are for the Epicurean the only reliable standard for judging the true in the physical world and the good in the sphere of conduct: see 1.699–700, 4.478–521, *Ep. Hdt.* 38 κατὰ τὰς αἰσθήσεις δεῖ πάντα τηρεῖν, *Ep. Men.* 129 ὡς κανόνι τῷ πάθει πᾶν ἀγαθὸν κρίνοντες.

1135. est: 'succeeds', 'avails'. *mox* 'in the future'. *est . . . erit . . . fuit* is a stereotyped and sometimes parodied sequence: see Kroll on Cat. 21.2 f.

1136–60. The overthrow of the kings, followed by a spell of anarchy and then the establishment of constitutions based on law and run by magistrates. Since then the fear of punishment by the laws has prevented evildoers from enjoying peace of mind.

L.'s purpose here is to show how laws in place of men have become all-powerful in the regulation of societies, and his model for such a constitutional development in some ways resembles that of Rome. But his account is historically selective, and he was of course aware of the continued existence of kings in his own day in (e.g.) North

Africa and the East. The discussion of the fear of punishment again reflects the Epicurean doctrine that justice is not a moral absolute but a compact, sanctioned by law, by which men undertake not to harm one another because they would risk being harmed or punished in return. (See 1019-20 and n.) This punishment, or the fear of it, would ruin their peace of mind on which alone happiness depends. (See K.Δ. 5, 17, 31-36, *Sent. Vat.* 7, Usener 532, Rist, *Epicurus, an Introduction*, 123-4.)

1136. ergo: Because of the *invidia* mentioned at 1125-6, from which point L. now picks up his argument.

1138. summi: 'the supreme', 'the foremost' head, i.e. the king's head (not 'the top of' the head).

> **cruentum:** predicative and closely linked with the following words: 'when bloodstained and trampled by the mob'.

1139. lugebat: either 'bewailed (the loss of) its high honour' or 'bewailed its high honour (as the cause of its downfall)' (Giussani).

1140. conculcatur: both literally and metaphorically, like καταπατεῖν.

1141. A notoriously ambiguous line. Probably it means 'thus things came to the utmost dregs of disorder' rather than 'thus rule passed to the lowest dregs of the mob', as the sense 'anarchy' is more strongly supported by 1142 than 'mob rule' by 1139. But *non liquet.*

1142. summatum: 303 n.

> **c(um) ac:** elision of *cum* (conjunction) is fairly common, though elision of *cum* (preposition) is found only once (at 3.159) in epic poetry from Cicero to Silius (Soubiran, 404-5).

1143. partim: 'some': 840 n.

1145. colere: the infinitive with *defessus* is an archaic construction found in Plautus, Terence, and Ennius *Ann.* 153 V.

1146. ex inimicitiis languebat: 'was faint from its feuds'.

1148-50. A surviving fragment of Democritus makes a similar point (B 245 D-K).

1150. est . . . pertaesum: emphatic *per-*: 'was thoroughly sick of'.

> **vi colere aevum:** cf. 1145: the repetition probably jars more on us than it did on ancient readers (1179 n.).

1151. praemia vitae: 'the (unjustly won) prizes of life'.

1153. A piece of widely attested, proverbial folk-wisdom: cf. Hesiod *Op.* 265-6 οἷ τ' αὐτῷ κακὰ τεύχει ἀνὴρ ἄλλῳ κακὰ τεύχων, / ἡ δὲ κακὴ βουλὴ τῷ βουλεύσαντι κακίστη (with parallels cited by West ad loc.), and the Latin proverb *malum consilium consultori pessimum est* (Otto, *Sprichwörter* s.v. *consilium*). It is worth noting that the conventionally moralizing tone of this whole passage is also reflected in the everyday idiomatic phrases *divum genus humanumque* 1156, *id fore clam* 1157.

1156-7. Similarly the Epicurean Torquatus in Cic. *Fin.* 1.50: 'quamvis occulte fecerit, numquam tamen id confidet fore semper occultum.'

1158-60. Cf. 4.1018-9 – men often betray themselves by talking in their sleep.

1159. protraxe: = *protraxisse*: such consonant-stem contractions are unusual but are found also at 1.233 *consumpse*, 3.650 *abstraxe*.

1160. Marullus's emendation of the defective line in OQ: 'et celata in medium et peccata dedisse'. Palaeographically better perhaps is 'et celata alte in medium et peccata dedisse' (M. F. Smith's revised Loeb edition).

1161-1240. The origin of religion.

L. turns to the origin of man's belief in the gods and gives us the most extensive discussion in the poem of the nature of religious belief and its original causes. Since one of his prime concerns is to dispel fear of the gods we expect to hear much more about them, but apart from a brief discussion of their abode earlier in this book (146-55) we have only the fairly brief references at 1.44-9 (= 2.646-51), 3.18-24, 6.68-78. This is clear evidence for the unfinished state of the *DRN*: see Introduction, xiv–xv, 155 n. At any rate it is natural for him to discuss the topic in the course of his account of the origins of civilized life.

The history of earlier speculation on the origin of belief in the gods is not very easy to trace, but certain lines of approach can be detected. The fifth century seems to have been fertile in ideas. We hear of the theories of the sophist Prodicus, who is credited with the belief that the gods were in origin simply primitive man's deification of beneficial natural objects like the sun, moon, rivers, and bread. He may also have propounded (though the evidence for this is less clear) a theory of a later stage in which the gods were the deified human discoverers of things that benefited mankind, like foods, shelter, and the practical arts. Critias, the poet, politician, and associate of Socrates, produced an early variant of the 'opium of the people' theory: he asserted that the gods were an astute political invention, designed by rulers to provide a supernatural sanction for the good behaviour of their subjects. In the account credited to Protagoras of the development of early man (see note on 925-87) religious worship began as a primitive and instinctive urge deriving from man's share in the divine nature (θεία μοῖρα: see Plato, *Prot.* 322a). The Atomists followed different lines. Democritus is credited with two apparently independent theories: first, that belief in gods derived from terrifying natural phenomena, which men attributed to divine beings; secondly, men are visited by larger-than-life images which they interpret as derived from gods. These two theories tally with L.'s account. (For valuable discussion of all these fifth-century thinkers and the evidence for their theories see Guthrie, ii, 478-83, iii, 238-44, *In the Beginning*, 88-9.)

For Epicurus the existence of the gods was a datum of our

experience: θεοὶ μὲν γὰρ εἰσίν · ἐναργὴς γὰρ αὐτῶν ἐστιν ἡ γνῶσις
(*Ep. Men.* 123). From Sextus Empiricus (*Math.* 9.25 = Usener 353)
we learn of his view (like the second theory attributed to Democritus)
that men are aware of the gods through large anthropomorphic
images (εἴδωλα) which come to them in their sleep. There is little
else we can say about Epicurus' views from his own writings, but he
would certainly have rejected firmly any inference about the existence
of the gods derived from natural phenomena. A general account of
Epicurean theology is given by Velleius in Cicero's *De Natura Deorum*
(1.18 ff.); see too Bailey's discussion in his commentary, i, 66–72,
J. M. Rist, *Epicurus, an Introduction*, Chap. 8, A. J. Festugière, *Epicurus and his Gods.*

This must suffice for an outline of pre-Lucretian speculation.
Modern anthropologists and religious theorists seem to be no nearer
agreement than the fifth-century enlightenment on the origins of
primitive religious thought. For a useful discussion of the whole topic
and contemporary ideas about it see Ninian Smart, *The Religious
Experience of Mankind* (New York, 1969), Chap. 2.

L. begins with a preamble (1161–8) in which he states that it is
not difficult to explain why men came to believe in the gods and to
fear them. He then offers two causes: (1) 1169–82 splendid visions
of the gods came to men, especially in sleep, to which they attributed
sensation, everlasting life, and pre-eminent happiness; (2) 1183–93
men supposed that the orderly patterns of the heavenly bodies and
the seasons must be due to divine control, and they placed the gods'
abode in the sky. The first cause is to be accepted as orthodox
Epicurean Canonic; the second receives its derisive condemnation in
1194 ff.

1161–8. One long sentence in which we have to wait until the eighth line
for the main clause. The reason may be to keep the words *rationem
reddere* for the end, just before launching into the explanation at
1169 ff.

1161–2. quae causa . . . pervulgarit . . . compleverit . . . curarit: governed
by *rationem reddere* 1168.

ararum: for the gen. see 39–40 n.

1163–4. sollemnia: 'established', 'customary'.

sācra . . . săcra: the *a* is short by nature, but as it stands before
two consonants the syllable can be treated as long according to its
position in the line. This and similar types of variation in the scansion
of the same word, sometimes in the same line, were an affectation
of Latin poetry and derived from Greek practice. Other examples in
the *DRN* are at 3.145, 4.1222, 1259, and see 850 n. (*propagando*).
Ovid plays the same trick with *sacer*: 'sive sǎcro pavi, sedive sub
arbore sācra', *F.* 4.749. (See Munro on 4.1259, Austin on Virg. *A.*
2.663, Nisbet–Hubbard on Hor. *C.* 1.32.11, Bailey, i, 130–1.)

rebu' locisque: the sense of *rebus* is not clear and has caused much discussion. It could be abstract ('power', 'property') coupled with the concrete *locis*, or combining with it in a hendiadys: 'in great and powerful (or civilized) places'. (See Giussani's note: as he points out, a contrast seems desirable in this context with a more primitive state of society.) Alternatively the words might pick up *magnas . . . gentis . . . urbis* (1161–2): 'in great states and in great places'.

1165. unde: i.e. from the ancient *sacra*.

horror: 'shuddering awe' (Munro): 1.28–9 'divina voluptas . . . atque horror'. L. stresses that it is this fearful dread which even to-day forces men to build shrines and hold religious festivals. He may, but need not, be alluding specifically to the spread of fashionable oriental cults in Rome. No doubt they are part of his picture, but *toto orbi* suggests a wider view.

1166. suscitat: 'raises', 'builds': a rare sense of the verb (*OLD* s.v. 2 b).

1167. celebrare: 'to throng them', sc. *delubra*.

1168. non ita difficile: 'not so very difficult', 'not all that difficult'; a prosaic idiom: cf. 4.1147, Quint. *Inst.* 2.5.18 'non ita difficilis . . . quaestio', Cic. *Fam.* 10.25.3 'plura me scribere . . . non ita necesse arbitrabar'.

1169 ff. Visions of the gods appeared to men both awake and asleep. This passage is best elucidated by two other indirect witnesses to Epicurus' thinking. Sextus Empiricus (*Math.* 9.25) tells us Ἐπίκουρος δὲ ἐκ τῶν κατὰ τοὺς ὕπνους φαντασιῶν οἴεται τοὺς ἀνθρώπους ἔννοιαν ἐσπακέναι θεοῦ · μεγάλων γὰρ εἰδώλων, φησί, καὶ ἀνθρωπομόρφων κατὰ τοὺς ὕπνους προσπιπτόντων ὑπέλαβον καὶ ταῖς ἀληθείαις ὑπάρχειν τινὰς τοιούτους θεοὺς ἀνθρωπομόρφους. 'Epicurus believes that men derived the conception of god from visions in their sleep: "for", he says, "when large images of human shape confronted them during sleep they supposed that some such gods in human shape really existed."' In Cicero's *De Natura Deorum* the Epicurean apologist Velleius explains: 'nam a natura habemus omnes omnium gentium speciem nullam aliam nisi humanam deorum; quae enim forma alia occurrit umquam aut vigilanti cuiquam aut dormienti?' (1.46); 'Epicurus . . . docet eam esse vim et naturam deorum ut primum non sensu sed mente cernantur, nec soliditate quadam nec ad numerum . . . sed imaginibus similitudine et transitione perceptis . . .' (1.49). L. himself refers again briefly to the idea at 6.76–7: 'de corpore quae sancto simulacra feruntur / in mentes hominum divinae nuntia formae'. This form in which the visions of gods appear to men is only a special case of the way in which we perceive physical objects, i.e. by fine atomic films (εἴδωλα, *simulacra*) which are thrown off from their surfaces and travel to us to be apprehended by our sense organs. This is all explained in detail in Book 4 (4.26 ff.

and *passim*): the difference with the gods is that their *simulacra* are so rarefied and fine that they cannot be perceived by the senses but only by the mind. Cf. above 148–9 'tenvis enim natura deum longe-que remota / sensibus ab nostris animi vix mente videtur.'

1169–71. The word-order is intricately involved, as though to suggest the complete absorption of the divine image by the human mind.

    iam tum: i.e. in primitive times.

    mirando . . . auctu: 'of marvellous physical stature'. *auctu* suggests their 'increased size' compared with men.

1174. pro: 'befitting', 'in keeping with': cf. 1111.

1175–6. aeternamque . . . vitam: cf. Cic. *ND* 1.49 '(Epicurus docet) in eas imagines mentem intentam infixamque nostram intellegentiam capere quae sit et beata natura et aeterna.'

    semper . . . : 'their appearance was perpetually renewed and their shape remained (the same)': this seems to mean that the *simulacra* from the gods were unceasing and showed no signs of the changes and ageing to which mortal creatures are subject. *suppeditare* is often used of keeping up a succession or supply, e.g. of light or water: above 283, 293, 298, 386.

    facies: 'appearance' as revealed by the stream of *simulacra*.

1177. et tamen omnino: 'yet also above all'.

1179. putabant: the repetition has no stylistic point, but many ancient poets of otherwise high literary sophistication, e.g. Virgil, were less sensitive to repetition than we are: see Austin on Virg. *A.* 2.505 and the discussions he refers to.

1180. vexaret: the subjunctive of the reported thought in men's minds.

1183 ff. False inferences about the gods from observing the heavens and the seasons.

1183. caeli rationes: 'the orderly workings of the sky' i.e. of the heavenly bodies: cf. 196.

1186–7. perfugium . . . tradere et facere: 'their refuge was to consign everything to the gods and to suppose'. *perfugium* suggests a desperate explanation of what was incomprehensible to them, the only way of escape from blank bewilderment.

    nutu: the 'nod' of the gods' authority was a poetic commonplace: Hom. *Il.* 1.528 ἦ καὶ κυανέῃσιν ἐπ' ὀφρύσι νεῦσε Κρονίων, Virg. *A.* 7.592 'saevae nutu Iunonis eunt res', 9.106.

1188. sedes et templa: 'abodes and haunts': *templa* as at 948, and see 103 n. At 146 ff. L. argues that the gods cannot exist in any part of the *mundus*.

1189 ff. This section ends with a list of the natural phenomena whose awesomeness persuaded early man that some divine power lay behind them. The theme is resumed below, 1204 ff., and it is clear that in both our passage and 1204–10 L. is thinking primarily of the phe-nomena of night: note the repetition *nox . . . nox . . . noctis . . .*

noctivagae. It is a common human experience that to look up at a
clear starlit sky fills us with awe, and we can feel an atavistic fear at
the thunder, lightning, and winds of a violent storm. L. has a scornful
pity for early man for ascribing these awesome phenomena to the
gods (1194 ff.), but he admits that it is difficult to avoid an anxious
doubt when faced by unknown powers we cannot understand
(1204–40).

There are difficulties arising from the apparently illogical sequence
of items in this catalogue of natural phenomena. (1) *nox luna / luna
nox* is an odd epanalepsis, seeing that these are not the main phenomena which persuaded men of the existence of the gods. (2) *dies*
looks out of place in 1190 in a list of night phenomena. (3) *sol* is
not mentioned until 1192. (It is worth pointing out that *dies* is not
a synonym of *sol*: L. was probably aware that primitive man had
not yet identified daylight with sunlight. See M. L. West on Hes. *Th.*
124.) Various attempts have been made to adjust the text (Lambinus
proposed *sol* for *nox* in 1189; for *luna* in 1190 Diels proposed *inde*
and Bockemüller *alma*); but we should probably leave the passage as
it stands and persuade ourselves that L. is painting an impressionist,
not a logical, picture. (For a defence on these lines see West, 126–8.)

1189–90. nox luna / luna nox: for the repetition see 950-1 n.

severa: 'stern' or 'solemn' stars, as they seemed to men: cf. 4.460
'severa silentia noctis'.

1191. Meteors and comets. For the compound *noctivagae* cf. *vulgivago*
932.

1192. Almost the same list as at 675.

fulmina: at 6.219–422 L. gives a detailed scientific account of
thunderbolts to show that they have no supernatural origin.

1193. Two sound-effects of thunder (cf. 1221, 6.410) – and a notable
alliteration.

minarum: a sort of defining genitive, equivalent to an adjective:
'threatening rumbles'.

1194–1240. This superstitious reaction only created misery for themselves and subsequent generations, and no true piety resulted. Yet
doubt and fear do afflict our uncertain minds when faced with the
terrors of thunder, storms, and earthquakes.

1194. o: the interjection is used very sparingly by L. (only here in this
book), and consequently carries much emotional emphasis. Editors
quote Empedocles in similar vein: ὢ πόποι, ὢ δειλὸν θνητῶν γένος,
ὢ δυσάνολβον, τοίων ἔκ τ᾽ ἐρίδων ἔκ τε στονάχων ἐγένεσθε (B124
D–K).

1195. iras: expressed, as they thought, in thunder, storms, etc. But the
true Epicurean knows that the divine nature is untouched by anger:
'nec bene promeritis capitur neque tangitur ira' 2.651; 'non quo
violari summa deum vis / possit, ut ex ira poenas petere imbibat
acris' 2.71–2; K.Δ.1.

1196-7. The sorrow and the harm continue for generation after generation. For *vulnera* cf. 3.63, where avarice and ambition are called 'vulnera vitae'.

1198-1203. These lines, which refer of course to traditional and contemporary Roman religious ritual, have been thought to fit rather awkwardly into their context (see Bailey and Giussani). The sequence of thought, expressed rather elliptically, seems to be that early man's wrong inferences about the gods found expression eventually in such pointless acts of ritual as veiling the head, prostration, and blood-sacrifice. Giussani might be right in treating the lines as a later addition not yet harmonized with their context, in which case we can take them as parenthetic, with *nam* 1204 following 1197 (or 1193). More simply *nam* follows 1203 with the sense '(true piety is to regard all things with a tranquil mind) for when we gaze at celestial phenomena it is very hard not to be smitten with dread . . . '.

L. is criticizing what he sees as the ostentatious (note *videri*) and ridiculous ritual actions of Roman religion, and his reference to the 'tranquil mind' is a hint at the *topos* developed by later moralizing writers on the difference between pure and selfish prayers: see Hor. *Ep.* 1.16.57 ff., Persius 2, Juv. 10, Lucian *Icaromenippus* 25, Maximus of Tyre *Diss.* 11. It should be noted that L. may here be arguing rather beyond his Epicurean brief: Epicurus himself practised and recommended customary religious observance (Usener 387).

1198. velatum: The Romans prayed with their heads covered, the Greeks bareheaded: Virg. *A.* 3.405 'purpureo velare comas adopertus amictu' (Helenus instructs Aeneas in ritual, and goes on to explain that the reason is to prevent seeing any ill-omened sight), Ovid *F.* 3.363 '(Numa) caput niveo velatus amictu' (see Bömer's note).

1199. vertier ad lapidem: *vertier* refers to the ritual flanking approach of the worshipper in which he kept the altar or statue concerned on his right: Plaut. *Curc.* 69-70 'quo me vortam nescio . . . si deos salutas, dextrovorsum censeo', Val. Fl. 8.244-6 'precari / incipiunt . . . et dextrum pariter vertuntur in orbem', Suet. *Vit.* 2 'capite velato circumvertensque se, deinde procumbens', Plut. *Camillus* 5.

lapidem: Stones were cult-objects in the ancient world and are referred to in literature over a very wide period. They were usually either at a crossroads (a place also associated with Hecate) or at land boundaries, where they both literally marked a division of property and symbolized the divinity Terminus. For crossroads stones see Theophrastus 16.5 (the superstitious man worships) τῶν λιπαρῶν λίθων τῶν ἐν ταῖς τριόδοις, Tib. 1.1.11-2 'nam veneror, seu stipes habet desertus in agris / seu vetus in trivio florida serta lapis.' For boundary stones see Ovid *F.* 2.641-2 (an account of the cult of the Boundary God) 'Termine, sive lapis sive es defossus in agro / stipes, ab antiquis tu quoque numen habes', Prop. 1.4.24 'sacer . . . lapis',

Apul. *Apol*. 56 'in finibus . . . lapidem unctum'. Munro gives other references, and see also R. G. Ussher's note on Theophr. l.c. for an interesting account of stone-worship in antiquity.

1200. pandere palmas: The ancients prayed with the hands held open, palm upwards to the sky: Aesch. *Pr*. 1004–5 λιπαρήσω . . . ὑπτιάσμασιν χερῶν, Virg. *A*. 3.263–4 'passis de litore palmis / numina magna vocat', 9.16, Hor. *C*. 3.23.1.

The alliteration underlines the scornful description of the pointless rigmarole of ritual prayer.

1202. votis nectere vota: 'to link vows with vows', i.e. to pray endlessly: cf. *Prop*. 3.5.12 'armis nectimus arma'.

1203. pacata: 'at peace', without superstitious fears. (But there is no need to accept this Juntine correction of *placata* OQ, as do most modern editors: see M. F. Smith in *CR* 16 (1966), 265–6.) This is the ideal of ἀταραξία, and it is only in this state of tranquility ('placido cum pectore' 6.75) that men can receive the images of the gods into their minds. Epicurus himself taught τὸ μὴ φοβεῖσθαι θεὸν ἀλλὰ παύσασθαι ταραττομένους (Usener 384).

1204. nam: See note on 1198–1203.

1205. templa: 'regions': 103 n.

super . . . fixum: Probably the meaning is 'the ether above studded with gleaming stars', though *super* might be a preposition and the sense 'the ether set firm above the gleaming stars'. As Bailey notes, L.'s view of the spatial relation of stars and *aether* is not clearly enough expressed elsewhere to help us, but Ennius fr. 159V 'caelum prospexit stellis fulgentibus aptum' (imitated by L. at 6.357) may support the first meaning. Ovid *M*. 2.204 'altoque sub aethere fixis . . . stellis' (quoted by Munro) is not decisive either way. *fixum* in the sense of *aptum* is certainly hard to parallel, but cf. Manil. 5.202 'valida venabula cuspide fixa' ('tipped with').

1206. venit in mentem . . . viarum: This construction, on the analogy of *memini* and *reminiscor* with the genitive, is found elsewhere in Republican Latin, e.g. Ter. *Phorm*. 154, Cic. *de Or*. 2.249, *Fin*. 5.2.: see K–S i, 472.

1207–8. 'then against our hearts already afflicted by other woes this anxiety too begins to rouse and lift its head': a vivid, impressionistic image which has bothered literal-minded editors. See Bailey's sensible note: he rightly discounts attempts to alter the text or distort the meaning. Superstition (*religio*) similarly shows her head at 1.64: 'caput a caeli regionibus ostendebat.'

1209. nobis: 'we are up against', 'we have to deal with': for the dative see 260 n.

1211. rationis egestas: 'the lack of a reasoned explanation' afforded by the Epicurean system (*ratio*). At 4.502 *rationis egentem* is used of one who cannot explain illusory shapes.

1212. genitalis origo: cf. 176, 324.

1213. quoad: 1033 n: here relative in sense after *finis*, 'until which'.

1214. solliciti: Bentley's conjecture for *et taciti* OQ. *taciti motus* could be a second subject of *possint*, but it would leave *laborem* awkwardly undefined and interrupt the concord *moenia . . . donata* (1215). *et* may have intruded from 1213, and the phrase *sollicito motu* occurs at 1.343, 6.1038.

1215. salute: 'existence'.

1216. 'gliding on through the everlasting course of time'. The line is repeated from 1.1004.

　　labentia: as usual of heavenly bodies (712 n.), though the *moenia mundi* do not 'glide' in quite the same sense as sun or stars: see the account of their formation and structure at 452 ff.

1217. Repeated from 379. This repetition of consecutive lines from elsewhere in the poem has caused the awkward repetition of *aevi*.

1219. contrahitur: 'shrink' with fear: cf. Cic. *Tusc.* 4.14 'animos demittunt et contrahunt rationi non obtemperantes', Sen. *Clem.* 2.5.5. 'maeror contundit mentes, abicit, contrahit.'

　　correpunt: 'creep', as in English of the tingle of horror in one's limbs (though this sense is hard to parallel); or 'crawl', 'cower' away from the terror.

1220-1. Cf. 6.287–8 'inde tremor terras graviter pertemptat et altum / murmura percurrunt caelum': the earth is both scorched and shaken by the impact of the thunderbolt. This seems a more pointed meaning of *torrida* than just 'parched' from lack of rain.

1222. populi gentesque: 'communities and nations': a conventional pair (the second group subsumes the first), e.g. Virg. *A*. 6.706, 7.236/8. On such expressions for 'peoples' see F. Cramer, *Archiv für lat. Lex.* vi, 341 ff. Note that *superbi* and *superbe* 1224 are not just stock epithets: the proud too are helpless with terror.

1223. corripiunt membra: 'huddle up their bodies', 'shrink in their limbs': cf. 6.1161 'corripere adsidue nervos et membra coactans' (of the spasmodic contractions caused by the plague).

1225. poenarum . . . solvendi tempus: The construction is most simply explained as a conflation of the two more usual idioms *poenas solvendi* and *poenarum solvendarum*. It is fairly common in the comedians and Cicero, but this is the only example in the *DRN*. See also 43–4 n.

　　adactum: 'forced upon them': Pontanus's correction of *adauctum* OQ, supported by a similar corruption at 1330.

1227. induperatorem: An archaic form (also at 4.967) which L. uses for metrical convenience, like *indupedita* 876: cf. 102 n. It is found several times in Ennius (frs. 83, 326, 347V) and revived later by Juvenal (4.29, 10.138).

　　verrit: of wind again: 266 n.

1228. elephantis: The Romans first met the elephant when they were defeated by Pyrrhus and his war-elephants at Heraclea in Lucania in 280 BC: Pliny *HN* 8.16. (Bailey suggests that L.'s general crossing the sea with troops and elephants may derive from Pyrrhus' invasion.) Subsequently Regulus was defeated by the Carthaginians under Xanthippus also by the aid of elephants in 255 BC, but the Romans learnt in time to cope with them in war. See below 1302, 1339. (This historical association and the use of *induperatorem* suggest that L. may have had an Ennian passage in mind.)

1229. A deeply Roman line. 'The peace of the gods' was an immemorial phrase of Roman religious ritual, the prayer invoking in a wide sense divine blessing and approval for the worshipper: Plaut. *Amph.* 1127 'ut Iovis supremi . . . pacem expetam', Virg. *A.* 3.370 '(Helenus) exorat pacem divum', Livy 3.7.8 'pacemque exposcere deum'. See R. Heinze, *Virgils Epische Technik*, 127, n.2. Again, *adire* is a technical term for approaching a holy place for prayer, e.g. 6.75 'nec delubra deum . . . adibis', Virg. *A.* 4.56–7 'delubra adeunt pacemque per aras / exquirunt', *OLD* s.v. 9. Here by an unusual brachylogy the verb governs the requested favour (= *adit ut pacem petat*), for which the only quoted parallel seems to be Apul. *Met.* 6.3 'adire cuiuscumque dei veniam'. The solemnity of the line is maintained by the old form *quaesit*. Surviving forms of this verb apart from *quaeso* are rare and archaic, and even *quaeso* to Quintilian was 'satis vetus' (*Inst.* 8.3.25).

1230. paces: 'times of peace', 'peaceful lulls' in the winds. The plural is uncommon but cf. Hor. *Ep.* 2.1.102 'hoc paces habuere bonae ventique secundi' (perhaps based on this line), *Ep.* 1.3.8.

   animas: 'breezes': 236 n.

1231–2. violento turbine . . . correptus: We have had *violento turbine* at 217, 368, and cf. 6.395 'turbine caelesti . . . correptus', Virg. *A.* 1.45 'turbine corripuit'.

   saepe: a common compression for *ut saepe fit*: so too 3.912–3 'ubi discubuere tenentque / pocula saepe homines', 4.34–5 'in somnis cum saepe figuras / contuimur', Virg. *A.* 1.148, 8.353.

   vada leti: Munro suggests a fusion here of literal and metaphorical senses. For *vada* used of dangerous shallows cf. Cic. *Cael.* 51 'emersisse iam e vadis . . . videtur esse oratio mea', Ovid *Ars* 1.437 'cera vadum temptet'.

1233. vis abdita quaedam: 'some secret power'. For the *vis* of nature see 77 n.: it is the controlling force of the atomic *mundus*, which men do not understand when they misdirect their prayers to the gods, but which is the real power that grinds down human hopes and achievements.

1234. Another Roman touch, with the rods and axes of the lictors symbolizing political power: cf. 3.996 'petere a populo fascis saevasque securis'. Virg. *A*. 6.819 'saevasque securis' shows that *saevas* is a stock epithet, but see Kenney's note on 3.996 for a possible reference to the proscriptions. On the origin of the *fasces* see Ogilvie on Livy 2.1.7-2.2.

1236. vacillat: 'reels' in an earthquake: the same verb is used of the earth moving and of buildings tottering in an earthquake, 6.554, 575, in a passage in which L. discusses the causes of earthquakes (6.535-607).

1237. dubiaeque minantur: 'totter as they threaten to fall': cf. 6.572 'minitatur terra ruinas', again of an earthquake; Sen. *NQ* 6.1.2 'Herculanensis oppidi pars ruit dubieque stant etiam quae relicta sunt' (of an earthquake probably in AD 62).

1238. quid mirum: sc. *est*, like *neque/nec mirum* at 2.87, 338, 6.130: L. fairly often omits *est* with a gerund or neuter adjective (Bailey, i, 103).

1239. relinquunt: 'admit', 'allow', a sense of *relinquere* rather affected by L.: 1.515, 658, 703, 743, 3.40; (so too Hor. *Sat.* 1.1.52 'dum ex parvo nobis tantumdem haurire relinquas'). This probably reflects a similar philosophical usage of ἀπολείπειν (*LSJ* s.v. 14) and καταλείπειν (*LSJ* s.v. IIIb) which L. found in his sources.

1241-80. The discovery and use of metals (copper, gold, iron, silver, lead). L. has already discussed the discovery of fire, 1091-1104, and now after dealing with the rise of rulers and cities, and with the origin of religion, he returns to the development of technology. This section is a vividly written piece of imaginative speculation, apparently based on traditional ideas, but L. for all his lack of evidence for primitive metallurgy may not be far from the truth. At any rate his account of the accidental nature of the discovery of metals is comparable with modern expert opinion: ' . . . most metals lay entirely outside man's conceptual environment until some chance event revealed their hidden presence and methods of smelting ores were discovered . . . Copper and gold, found in the native state in Stone Age times, were the malleable foundation of modern metallurgy' (C. Singer, E. J. Holmyard, A. R. Hall (edd.) *A History of Technology* I (Oxford, 1954), 65-6). In his account of the sequence of metals too L. is of course right in putting the discovery of iron late (1286-7), but his statement that copper was originally more highly valued than gold (because usefulness produced value, 1273-4) is historically suspect. It seems to be uncertain whether the use of copper preceded that of gold, and L. himself must have known that gold was highly valued in the Bronze Age (Singer etc., op. cit., 579; E. J. Kenney, *G & R* 19 (1972), 19). The purpose of this comment is rather to set up the rhetorical climax which follows, in which L. moralizes on the mutability of fashion (1276-80) — just the sort of moralizing coda we have had at 1007-10, 1129-35, and 1151-60.

1241. aes: 'copper' here and 1257; probably 'bronze' (an alloy mainly of copper and tin) from 1270 onwards, where the tools and weapons referred to would have been made of the tougher alloy.

1244 ff. L. in his usual way offers alternative explanations of the conflagration which caused man accidentally to discover melted metals: cf. the alternatives offered for the discovery of fire itself, 1091 ff. The same theory was canvassed by Posidonius (cf. introductory note to 1105–35): Seneca pointedly dissents from his view that 'sapientes fuisse qui ferri metalla et aeris invenerint, cum incendio silvarum adusta tellus in summo venas iacentis liquefacta fudisset' (*Ep.* 90.12). For what it is worth Athenaeus too (6.233d) reports that the heat of forest fires caused the Alps to ooze silver.

1246. formidinis ergo: 'to create fear': *ergo = causā* is an archaic preposition sometimes adding solemnity or dignity (e.g. 3.78 'statuarum et nominis ergo', Virg. *A.* 6.670), here perhaps a flavour of antiquity.

1248. pandere: 'to clear' of trees.

1250–1. An explanatory parenthesis: huntsmen lit fires to start game before dogs were used.

1252 ff. A vividly composed passage as L. pictures a dramatic moment in man's history. We hear the sound of the raging forest fire in the *s*-alliteration of 1253, and there is a further sustained and interwoven alliteration of *c* and *t* in the successive pictures of 1254–61, leading up to the crucial mental break-through of 1262 ff.

1252. quidquid id est: 'be that as it may': cf. 577.

1255–7. Cf. Sen. *Ep.* 90. 12, quoted above.

1258–9. The surprise and pleasure (*capti*) of those who first saw the gleaming ingots is underlined by the cluster of colour-words: *claro . . . splendere colore, nitido . . . levique lepore.*

1261. lacunarum . . . vestigia cuique: 'the outlines of the hollows where each had been'. The *lacunae* are the *loca concava* of 1255–6.

1262. penetrabat eos: 'it got through to them': a startling and original use of the word to which there is no real parallel (see *OLD* s.v. 5). It expresses the effect of this new idea hitting them forcefully, and may reflect the Epicurean theory that the *animus* is corporeal and perceptions do physically penetrate the mind. (So G. Townend *ap.* Dudley, 114 n. 35; E. J. Kenney, *G & R* 19 (1972), 18.)

1265. mucronum . . . fastigia: 'pointed tips'.

procudendo: the spondaic verse-ending perhaps imitates the hammer-blows on the forged metal.

1266. parent, possint: The present tenses are not in strict sequence after *penetrabat*, but like many similar examples (especially in earlier Latin) can be explained either as 'vivid' for the imperfect or as indicating a continuing aim or consequence: see K–S ii, 192, and Bailey, i, 100–1 for a general discussion of L.'s 'irregularities' in sequence of tenses.

1266–7. caedere . . . dolare . . . radere: successive stages of carpentry: 'cut', 'rough-hew', 'plane'.

1268. A triumphantly climactic line in L.'s manner, as the threefold repetition stresses man's mastery over his materials. Nor is it irrelevant that the ability to drill a hole opened up enormous areas of primitive technology.

1269. haec: the weapons and tools of 1266.

1271. potestas: (cf. 1242) sc. of silver and gold, which proved too soft for tough use.

1273 ff. See introd. note.

nam: affirmative: 'yes, 'indeed', 'certainly'.

1276. One aspect of the universal law of change stated at 828 ff.

tempora rerum: 'fashions': lit. 'the seasons of things'.

1279. repertum: 'when found'.

1281-1349. Excursus on the technology of warfare: the use of metals for weapons and of animals in fighting tactics.

In a partly transitional passage (1281–96) L. rounds off his account of metals by showing how iron replaced bronze as a tougher and more efficient metal for tools and weapons. This leads to a discussion of the use in turn of horses, chariots, and elephants in battle (1297–1307), and of the disastrous experiments to make similar use of bulls, boars, and lions (1308–49).

1281-2. The reference to Memmius, though casual (867 n.), marks the discovery of iron as a climax in early technology. This view is endorsed by modern scholarship: 'Iron ores are widely distributed and readily available; iron tools were cheaper and more efficient than those made of bronze . . . Thus iron was the democratic metal, and it greatly reinforced man's equipment for dealing with the forces of nature . . . For the technology of tools, the advent of iron was an event of the greatest importance' (Singer etc., op. cit., 592–3, 618).

1283-6. A similar point is made in different contexts at 966-8 above and 4.843-5 'at contra conferre manu certamina pugnae / et lacerare artus foedareque membra cruore / ante fuit multo quam lucida tela volarent'; and by Horace, discussing the role of experience among the earliest creatures: 'unguibus et pugnis, dein fustibus, atque ita porro / pugnabant armis quae post fabricaverat usus' (*Sat.* 1.3.101-2).

1288. facilis: 'easily worked', 'malleable'.

1289-90. belli . . . fluctus: 1434-5 n.

1291-2. Those armed with the new bronze weapons were invincible. The neuter *omnia* seems intended to depersonalize into a faceless mass their helplessly unarmed opponents.

1296. 'and the contests of (now) doubtful battle were equalized', because both sides in due course had iron weapons: cf. 1281-2 n.

creper: 'doubtful', 'uncertain' is an archaic word (Pacuvius, Accius, Lucilius), occurring only here in the *DRN*. It may be linked etymologically with *crepusculum.*

1297-9. L. is wrong: chariots preceded cavalry in warfare and were not

replaced by horsemen in Greece and Italy until after *c*.700 BC
(somewhat earlier in the Middle East). See J. K. Anderson, *Ancient
Greek Horsemanship* (Berkeley, 1961), 7, 10–11. Presumably L.
thought that in principle a man on horseback must have been a
more primitive development than a man in a chariot drawn by horses.

    moderarier: sc. *sinistrā.*

    vigere: 'lay about him', 'fight' with his free right hand.

1301. falciferos . . . currus: L. mentions scythed chariots also at 3.642,
though they were an oriental invention and never used by Greek or
Roman armies. Xenophon mentions them (*An.* 1.8.10), and Livy
(37.41) records their use by Antiochus III during the battle of
Magnesia in 190 BC.

1302. boves lucas: elephants were 'Lucanian cows' because the Romans
first saw them in Lucania in Pyrrhus' army: see 1228 n. They mark
a climax as the most fearsome war-machine employed in ancient
armies.

    turrito corpore: i.e. bearing a howdah from which the soldiers
fought. Milton perhaps remembered this line at *P.R.* 3.329 'Elephants
endorst with Towers'.

1303. anguimanus: a picturesque Lucretian invention, used similarly at
2.537 (and exhibiting a unique fourth-declension adjectival ending).
The elephant's trunk is called a 'hand' also by Cicero (*ND* 2.123)
and Pliny (*HN* 8.29).

    Poeni: 1228 n.

1305-7. Another typical moralizing summary of the developments in
battle techniques just described.

    alid: an archaic form of *aliud* used several times by L. and always
in this phrase.

    augmen: 681 n.

1308-49. Men also tried using bulls, boars, and lions in battle, but this
was disastrous as they turned round and wreaked murderous havoc
on their own side.

    This is probably the most notorious passage in the whole poem.
It has baffled generations of commentators, who have been disturbed
both by the extent of the macabre and gory detail L. gives us and by
our ignorance of the tradition which he is clearly following. Without
sharing the extreme reactions of Bailey and others (see his introductory note to 1308-49) we must face the real and crucial problems
of this section.

    1. The passage is not integrated properly into its context. We
have had a satisfactory Lucretian climax at 1307 and could move
without a hitch on to 1350, but L. suddenly seems to start in again
with more wild animals after the elephants, introducing these experiments with the vague *temptarunt*. As there is no reason to doubt the
authenticity of the lines – the style is manifestly Lucretian at his

vigorous best – it is plausible to see the passage as a later composition never properly integrated into its context. (See Kenney cited below for the speculation that it was inspired by Pompey's celebratory games in September 55 BC – if L. was still alive then.)

2. The source of the tradition we do not know, though there is some evidence for the use of animals other than elephants in warfare, e.g. oxen (Livy 22.16–7), dogs (Aelian *VH* 14.46, Pliny *HN* 8.143), camels (Hdt. 1.80). On the other hand, to account for the gruesome details it is a plausible suggestion that L. was thinking of the horrors of the popular wild-beast shows, *venationes*, with which he would have been all too familiar (cf. Aymard and McKay cited below).

3. The biggest difficulty has been the interpretation of 1341–9: again see Bailey's note for the history of attempts to make sense of the lines. Though their logical development is not obvious, it is at least clear that L. is reflecting on the tradition he has just reported and trying to explain why men tried such self-destructive tactics. So a possible sequence of thought is: 1341–3 he says that if the tradition is true he can hardly believe that they could not foresee disaster; 1344–6 he offers a desperately unlikely solution that it happened in some other world than this; 1347–9 he rejects this solution and affirms that it did happen here, but it was only utter despair that drove men to the horrors of these suicidal tactics. It is hard to decide whether the reference to other worlds in 1344–6 invokes Epicurean ἰσονομία, as some think: in any case, if the suggested interpretation is right, L. is saying that you cannot avoid the difficulty by an explanation of that sort.

For all its difficulties and its gruesome details this section is a powerful piece of virtuoso writing. Note the frequent use of assonance and alliteration (1309, 1315, 1321, 1325, 1327, 1333, 1334, 1342); the relentless pile-up of nouns in asyndeton in 1336; the hammer-blow effect of the repeated imperfect tenses from 1314 ff.; the emphatic 'run-over' words followed by a metrical pause (*undique* 1319, *cornibus* 1325).

Among many discussions of the passage see J. Aymard, *Essai sur les chasses romaines* (Paris, 1951), 107–8; E. L. B. Meurig Davies, *Mnemosyne* ser. 4, 2 (1949), 74–5; E. J. Kenney, *G & R* 19 (1972), 19–24 (on whom much of the above interpretation is based); K. L. McKay, *AJP* 85 (1964), 124–35; R. B. Onians, *CR* 44 (1930), 169–70; P. H. Schrijvers, *Horror ac divina voluptas. Etudes sur la poétique et la poésie de Lucrèce* (Amsterdam, 1970), 296–305.

1308. temptarunt: the subject is vague and detached from its context: see introductory note.

    moenere: 'service'.

1310. partim: 'some': 840 n.

1311. A stylish line, with the synonymous *doctoribus* and *magistris* ('trainers') arranged chiastically around their adjectives.

1313. permixta caede calentes: the same phrase occurs at 3.643 of scythed chariots in battle: in both passages the literal and figurative senses of *calentes* ('reeking', 'inflamed') are scarcely to be distinguished.

1315. Repeated from 2.632, with *undique* for *numine*. There *cristas* referred to the headgear of the Curetes; here it means the lions' manes.

1318–22. L. highlights the lionesses perhaps because the savagery of the female wild animal was often noticed, especially in defence of her young.

1319. adversum . . . petebant: 'leapt straight at the faces of those who opposed them': *adversum* goes with *venientibus*.

1321. deplexae: 'grasping down', 'gripping to pull down' seems to be the meaning of this compound, found only here. The accumulation of the two *de-* verbs and the phrase *dabant in terram* vividly picture the relentless lionesses bearing down all before them in their onslaught.

1324. hauribant: 'ripped wide open': 991 n.

1325. ruebant: 'churned up': for this sense cf. 6.726 'cum mare permotum ventis ruit intus harenam'.

1327 and 1328 are an obvious doublet and 1328 is usually excluded: it could be either a gloss on *infracta* or an alternative version by L. himself. Virgil imitates at *A*. 10.731 'tundit humum exspirans infractaque tela cruentat'.

1330. transversa . . . exibant: 'by swerving aside tried to avoid the savage thrusts of the tusk'. *adactus* is Marullus's correction of the MSS, though the word does not occur until late Latin.

1332. ab nervis succisa: 'hamstrung', lit. 'cut at the tendons': for this quite common sense of *succidere* see *OLD* s.v. 1 b.

1333–8. They thought the beasts had been sufficiently tamed at home for controlled fighting, but in the heat and terror of battle their natural wildness re-asserted itself.

1334. siquos: sc. *apros* strictly speaking, but the other wild beasts are probably included.

1339. boves lucae: 1302 n.

mactae: 'wounded': *mactus* in this sense is very rare and of uncertain derivation, perhaps connected with the common frequentative form *mactare* (*mactatus*). See Walde–Hofmann, *Lat. Etym. Wört.* s.v. *mactus.*

1340. suis: an important point in the comparison: even the more trusted elephant not only panics but damages its own allies.

1341–9. On the special problems of these lines see introductory note.

1341. adducor: 'am brought to believe', 'am convinced': see *OLD* s.v. 7.

[1343] [1342] Lachmann's transposition is not essential but it certainly smooths the construction.

[1343] **commune:** 'on both sides'.

1344. in omni: '(somewhere) in the universe': *omne* as at 527.

1345. = 528.

1347-9. The only possible solution. In these elliptical lines *sed* both rejects the tentative suggestion in 1344-6 and stresses that only despair could have driven men to such tactics in war.

1350-60. The art of weaving, which was practised by men before women.

There is a link here with the section on metals in the reference to iron for building looms (1351), but the theme was a likely one any-way for an Epicurean writer if we may judge from a fragment of Diogenes of Oenoanda (fr. 10 col. I.. 4 ff. Chilton), which gives an account of the development of primitive clothing up to the invention of the loom.

L. is envisaging the vertical wooden loom, which was the only one known to the Greeks and Romans. The horizontal loom did not appear, at least in Europe, until about the thirteenth century: see Singer etc. (edd.) *A History of Technology* II (Oxford, 1956), 211-12. The basic principles and techniques of weaving have not changed, but the meaning of some of L.'s terms (*insilia, scapi*) remains uncertain. For a discussion of the passage see F. G. Moore, *CR* 4 (1890), 450-1.

1350. nexilis: 'plaited (by hand)', as opposed to 'woven' (*textile*).

1351. ferro tela paratur: 'the loom is built with iron tools', which can shape the parts precisely and make them smooth (*levia* 1352). L. does not envisage earlier, cruder looms made before the use of iron was discovered.

1353. 'treadles, spindles, shuttles, and noisy leash-rods'; but the meaning of *scapi* is uncertain, and 'treadles' is a desperate stop-gap for the wholly obscure *insilia*.

1355-6. The same general claim is made by Socrates in Plato's *Republic* (455c), but he allows weaving and cooking as exceptions at which women are better.

1357. vitio vertere: 'made it a reproach', 'poured scorn on it'.

1359 and 1360 seem to be alternative lines (cf. 1327-8), and L. would probably have excluded 1359 (which is in any case a near repetition of 1272). With its double alliteration 1360 effectively marks the end of this short section.

1361-78. Agriculture: observation of natural propagation taught men to sow, graft, and plant slips, and so they gradually learnt to grow crops.

This short paragraph is one of the most attractive in the book, and offers a strong contrast of tone with 1297-1349. With carefully descriptive art L. evokes the sympathetic enjoyment men took in learning to cultivate the land and the visual delight the success of their efforts gave — and still gives — them. The poet seems to share this enjoyment in his choice of evocative vocabulary: *libitumst, dulcis agelli* (an affectionate diminutive), *indulgendo blandeque colendo, laeta, lepore, dulcibus, felicibus.*

1361–2. Nature (not the gods) is again the efficient cause and creator (cf. 831, 1028), and she provides a model to men here as she does not to the gods at 186. The phrase *rerum natura creatrix* occurs also at 1.629, 2.1117.

    specimen: 'pattern', 'model': men thus learnt the three normal ways of propagating plants, sowing (*satio*), grafting (*insitio = stirpis committere ramis* 1365) and planting slips (*nova defodere virgulta* 1366).

1364. pullorum: 'seedlings'.

1366. The echo of 935 recalls that this technique was unknown to the earliest men.

1368. terra: 'in the ground': local abl., like *collibus, campis* 1373.

1369. indulgendo blandeque colendo: 'with gentle care and kindly tillage'.

1370–1. 'they forced the woods to retreat up the mountains' by progressively clearing the ground for cultivation.

1373–4. olearum . . . : 'the clear line of a grey-green belt of olives might run between', perhaps to form a boundary. *caerula* is the standard colour-word for the olive (Ovid *Ars* 2.518, Manil. 5.260), like γλαυκή in Greek (Soph. *OC* 701, Eur. *Tro*. 801–2, *IT* 1101). For the effect of the tmesis *inter . . . currere* see 287 n.

1376–8. L. now visualizes the delightful patchwork effect of contemporary Italian farm fields, and *distincta* picks up *distinguens* in the comparison.

    omnia: 'all the ground', 'the whole place'.

    quae . . . circum: 'which men beautify by planting sweet orchards here and there, surrounding them with fertile vine-plantations'. *arbustis* probably has its common meaning of support-trees for vines.

1379–1435. The origin of music: reflections on progress and moral decadence.

    L. now gives a brief account of man's first efforts to sing and play music, which were derived from hearing the natural sounds respectively of bird-song and the wind blowing through reeds (1379–87). This is followed by a description of the simple pleasure and relaxation men derived from music and dancing, with a special word for its consoling power to those who cannot sleep (1390–1411). This delight in music-making leads to wider moralizing reflections on how men take pleasure in a novelty only until it is superseded by something better, with examples taken from primitive food, bedding, and clothing (1412–29). The passage ends with reflections on the futility of struggling anxiously for more possessions and an allusion to the Epicurean doctrine of the limits of pleasure (1430–35).

    We do not know what views Epicurus may have had on the origin of music, but we are told by Philodemus that Democritus thought

music a fairly recent development in man's history because it arose
not from necessity but out of an existing abundance (μουσικήν φησι
νεωτέραν εἶναι καὶ τὴν αἰτίαν ἀποδίδωσι λέγων μὴ ἀποκρῖναι
τἀναγκαῖον ἀλλὰ ἐκ τοῦ περιεῦντος ἤδη γενέσθαι: B144 D–K).
According to Plutarch he also believed that men learnt arts and crafts
from animals, e.g. weaving from the spider, housebuilding from the
swallow, and singing from birds (*De Sollertia Animalium* 974a =
B154 D–K). If Aulus Gellius is to be trusted (4.13) Democritus also
believed in the healing powers of pipe-playing for those suffering
from snakebite and many other disorders (see Guthrie, ii, 470 n. 2).

This section is not tightly structured, as L. first plays with ideas
about primitive music; then enjoys portraying a scene of alfresco
pastoral merrymaking, alludes briefly to contemporary Roman
watchmen, and finally (with a rather loose logical connection)
moves on to Epicurean moralizing. The writing too is occasionally
loose or ambiguous (1388–9, 1399–1400, 1414) – perhaps L. was
hurrying to get to the end of a long book.

1379. See Democritus' similar theory quoted above. According to
Athenaeus (9.390a) the Peripatetic Chamaeleon (born *c*.350 BC)
also derived music originally from bird-song.

  liquidas: 'clear': used of bird-song also at 2.146 (and probably
4.548), Virg. *G*. 1.410, Ovid *Am*. 1.13.8. The word was probably
regarded as equivalent to λιγύς or λιγυρός (see Nisbet–Hubbard on
Hor. *C*. 1.24.3).

  imitarier: infinitive as noun subject of *fuit*.

1380. lēvia: 'smooth', 'harmonious', compared with their earlier unsophisticated imitations of bird-song: cf. Cic. *ND* 2.146 'vocis genera
permulta . . . leve asperum'. *levis* was a technical term of the rhe-
toricians for a smooth style, and λεῖος was similarly used, e.g. Plato
Philebus 51d ἠχὰς τῶν φθόγγων τὰς λείας καὶ λαμπράς.

1381. concelebrare: seems to mean 'do frequently' i.e. 'practise', an
extension of its usual senses. The nearest parallel quoted is Cic. *Inv*.
1.4 'videntur . . . studia . . . per otium concelebrata ab optimis
enituisse'.

1382. zephyri . . . sibila: 'the whistling of a breeze through hollow reeds',
zephyri being gen. sing. For the locution *cava calamorum* see 35 n.

1383 ff. L. envisages two stages of primitive pastoral instrument: (1) The
Pan-pipe, a series of reeds of graduated length tied together and
played by running the lips along the level ends. This is referred to
below 1407 and at 4.588 'unco saepe labro calamos percurrit hiantis'.
(2) The single reed with stops (*tibia . . . digitis pulsata* 1385) which
allowed more varied and refined effects. Hemlock stalks (*cavas . . .
cicutas*) are conventionally referred to in pastoral poetry as the
material for pipes: Virg. *E*. 2.36, 5.85, Calp. Sic. 4.20, 7.12.

1383. inflare: Cf. Virg. *E*. 5.2 'tu calamos inflare levis'.

1384. inde minutatim: cf. 710.

1385 = 4.585, the antecedent to *quas* in both passages being *dulcis querellas.*

1386. avia: 'trackless', 'untrodden': 397 n.

1387. otia dia: 'their places of relaxation in the open air' or 'the peace of the open air' (Rouse's Loeb translation) seems to be the meaning of this mysterious and evocative phrase. The word *dius* (cf. δῖος, and see Ernout-Meillet s.v.) means essentially 'bright' or 'radiant' and is used of both the brightness of the open sky and a supernatural radiance as of the gods. Cf. the two other passages in the *DRN* where it is found: 1.22 'dias in luminis oras' ('bright', 'shining'), 2.172 'dia voluptas' ('divine', 'divinely inspired'). *otia* in the physical sense 'place where one relaxes' is unusual, but cf. Stat. *Theb.* 6.110-1 'linquunt flentes dilecta locorum / otia'.

1388-9 = 1454-5 where they make much better sense and continuity. Since Lachmann they have generally been regarded as an interpolation.

1391. As Bailey suggests, there may be a reference to the Epicurean view that after the pain due to want has been removed pleasure can be not increased, but at any rate varied: Κ.Δ. 18 οὐκ ἐπαύξεται ἐν τῇ σαρκὶ ἡ ἡδονή, ἐπειδὰν ἅπαξ τὸ κατ᾽ ἔνδειαν ἀλγοῦν ἐξαιρεθῇ, ἀλλὰ μόνον ποικίλλεται. After eating we enjoy anything – here music.

1392-6. Repeated from 2.29-33 with minor alterations to fit the new context. There is more point to the repetition than just recalling an agreeable description, the familiar *locus amoenus topos*: the passage in Book 2 pictured the Epicurean ideal of life, and ours shows that primitive men in fact conformed to this ideal in his simple pleasures and lack of luxuries. (See B. Farrington in *Hermathena* 81 (1953), 59-62.) The picture of alfresco eating or resting by a stream was a *topos* of simple contentment which we find in much pastoral and other poetry, and L.'s version had some detectable influence on later writers. For a selection of passages see Hes. *Op.* 588-96 (and cf. his phrase κεκορημένον ἦτορ ἐδωδῆς with L.'s *cum satiate cibi*), Theocr. 1.21-3, Moschus 5.11-3, Hor. *C.* 1.1.21-2 'nunc viridi membra sub arbuto / stratus, nunc ad aquae lene caput sacrae', *Epode* 2.23 ff., *Ep.* 1.14.35, Virg. *E.* 8.87 'propter aquae rivum viridi procumbit in ulva', Tib. 1.1.27-8 'sed Canis aestivos ortus vitare sub umbra / arboris ad rivos praetereuntis aquae', *Culex* 68 ff. 'at pectore puro / saepe super tenero prosternit gramine corpus, / florida cum tellus, gemmantis picta per herbas . . . '.

1394. iucunde . . . habebant: 'gave themselves bodily pleasure', 'refreshed themselves physically'.

1395. tempestas: 'the weather': 1083 n.

ridebat: a long-established image, as we see from Ennius fr. 457-8 V 'tempestatesque serenae / riserunt' and the similar use of γελᾶν to express pleasure or rejoicing: Hes. *Th*. 40 γελᾷ δέ τε δώματα πατρός, *h. Dem*. 13–14 πᾶς τ᾽ οὐρανὸς εὐρὺς ὕπερθεν / γαῖά τε πᾶσ᾽ ἐγέλασσε, Theog. 8–10. Elsewhere in a similar metaphor *ridere* is used of something shining or sparkling: above 1005 (waves), 1.8 and 2.559 (the sea), 2.502 (peacocks), 3.22 (bright air), 4.1125 (luxurious slippers).

1398. agrestis . . . musa: Cf. 4.589 'silvestrem . . . musam' (in a passage already quoted in notes to 1383 ff. and 1385), Virg. *E*. 6.8 'agrestem tenui meditabor harundine musam.' In the Lucretian passages the phrase refers to primitive rustic musical efforts; in Virgil it has become a pastoral pose.

1399–1400. The construction is ambiguous, with *floribus et foliis* either in explanatory apposition to *coronis* or taken with *plexis* ('woven from flowers and leaves').

lascivia laeta monebat: 'cheerful playfulness prompted them'.

1401–2. extra numerum: 'out of time', 'unrhythmically' (cf. Cic. *Parad*. 26, Hor. *Ep*. 1.18.59): it is the opposite of *ad* or *in numerum* as at 2.631 'ludunt in numerumque exsultant', 4.788 'in numerum procedere', Virg. *G*. 4.174–5.

pellere: Even apart from rustic clodhopping (as here) ancient dancing was vigorous and unsophisticated exercise: Hom. *Od*. 8.264 πέπληγον δὲ χορὸν θεῖον ποσίν, Cat. 61.14 'pelle humum pedibus', Hor. *C*. 3.18.15–16 'gaudet invisam pepulisse fossor / ter pede terram', 1.37.1–2 'nunc pede libero / pulsanda tellus', Ovid *Ars* 1.112. See Nisbet-Hubbard on Hor. *C*. 1.4.7, and note Seneca on early Roman dancing, *Tranq. An*. 17.4 'Scipio . . . corpus movebat ad numeros, non molliter se infringens . . . sed ut antiqui illi viri solebant inter lusum ac festa tempora virilem in modum tripudiare.' L. echoes the primitive dance in a suitably pounding line.

matrem: In Epicurean biology the earth is literally mankind's mother. See above 790 ff., esp. 795–6 'merito maternum nomen adepta / terra sit, e terra quoniam sunt cuncta creata', 821–2: hence too *terrigenarum* 1411, *terrigenas* 1427.

1403. dulcesque cachinni: On the repetition of the phrase in 1397 see 1179 n.

1404. 'for all these things then were strong in freshness and wonder' (Bailey).

1405. vigilantibus: Either insomniacs or those who work at night.

solacia somno: 'consolation for their (lost) sleep': the sense is clear but the expression unusual, where the dat. *somno* = *pro somno*. There seems to be no precise parallel (hence Lambinus's *somni*), but for the dat. editors quote Livy 25.16.20 'solacium suae morti inventurum' and *Ciris* 181 'malis . . . solacia tantis'. For another elliptical expression with *solacia* see 21 and n. (But if *vigilantibus* means those whose duties keep them awake could *solacia* have the sense of *remedium*? – i.e. a cure or antidote: music helped them stay awake. *somno* would then have its normal meaning and there would be added point to Lachmann's quotation of the *vigil* in Aesch. *Ag*. 17 ὕπνου τόδ' ἀντίμολπον ἐντέμνων ἄκος (see Fraenkel's note).)

1406. ducere: 'prolong', 'draw out' the tunes (like the owl at Virg. *A*. 4.463 'longas . . . ducere voces'), distinguished from *flectere* which is a technical term, 'to modulate', 'vary the pitch' (*OLD* s.v.11).

1407. See note on 1383 ff.

1408. vigiles: Presumably city watchmen, though possibly camp sentinels. Roman *vigiles* had no official status until AD 6, when seven *cohortes vigilum* were created whose main function was to act as a fire-brigade. In L.'s time this duty seems to have been performed by public slaves under the control of the aediles and *tresviri nocturni*: see P. K. Baillie Reynolds, *The Vigiles of Imperial Rome* (Oxford, 1926), 18 ff.

haec accepta tuentur: 'keep up this tradition' of singing to pass the time or keep awake.

1409. numerum . . . genus: The meaning is presumably something like 'the (appropriate) type of rhythms' (for different songs and tunes), *numerum* being gen. pl. as in the phrase *omnium numerum* at Petr. 63.3, 68.8. (Creech paraphrases 'variis etiam numeris utuntur'.) *genus* may be technically used of metre, as Giussani suggested, but there is no need to press a too sophisticated interpretation in this context, though L. is certainly saying that modern *vigiles* have made musical advances compared with their primitive forbears. The phrase is slightly odd but not so as to warrant the many conjectures (see apparatus).

hilo: 358 n. They get no more pleasure than the primitives presumably because for both music removes the painful desire for sleep, and the pleasure is the same.

1410. capiunt dulcedini' fructum: cf. 2.971 'fructum capiant dulcedinis almae', which strongly supports Lambinus's correction of *dulcedine* OQ.

1411. terrigenarum: see n. on *matrem* 1402.

1412 ff. L. proceeds to generalize from music to other things which are most enjoyed when they are a novelty — food, bedding, and clothes.

1412-5. For a similar thought see 3.1082-4 'sed dum abest quod avemus, id exsuperare videtur / cetera; post aliud, cum contigit illud, avemus, / et sitis aequa tenet vitai semper hiantis.'

1414. probably = *posterior melior res reperta perdit illa*, 'a later improvement when discovered destroys those former things', but the construction is ambiguous.

1415. sensus: 'our feelings'. For this sense of *ad* ('with regard to') cf. Cic. *Arch*. 19 'durior ad haec studia', *OLD* s.v. 30.

1416. glandis: 939 n.

1417. frondibus aucta: 'piled up with leaves': cf. 987.

1419-22. L. enlivens his moralizing by imagining (*reor*) an incident to illustrate early man's shortsighted violence: the inventor of the first skin-garment is killed by his envious friends, who then tear it apart in their squabble to possess it themselves.

1422. convertere: Intransitive as at 4.310 'redit et convertit eodem', Cic. *Brut.* 141 'hoc vitium . . . in bonum convertebat'.

1425. nobis: 'us' of the present day in contrast with the ancients, who at least had the excuse that they fought over essentials.

1428. auro signisque ingentibus apta: 'embroidered with enormous designs in gold brocade'. Cf. Virg. *A.* 1.648 'pallam signis auroque rigentem': as Austin points out in his note the hendiadys *auro signisque* avoids the metrical problem of the oblique cases of *aureus*.

1429. plebeia: sc. *vestis* from 1427: cf. 2.36 'si in plebeia veste cubandum est'.

defendere: sc. *nos* or *frigus.*

1430. incassum frustraque: cf. 1002 n.

1431. inanibus: explained by *quia* . . .

1432-3. L. alludes here to two related doctrines of orthodox Epicureanism. (1) There are three classes of desires: natural and necessary (e.g. food, clothing), natural but not necessary (e.g. sexual desire), neither natural nor necessary (e.g. luxuries). The first should be satisfied, the second may be satisfied in moderation, the third should be abolished as unsatisfiable and therefore painful. (*Ep. Men.* 127, K.Δ. 29, Cic. *Fin.* 1.45.) (2) The limit of pleasure is reached when natural desires are satisfied and the pain due to want is removed: after that point pleasure cannot be increased, only varied. (*Ep. Men.* 130–1, K.Δ. 3 and 18, Cic. *Fin.* 1.38.) See 1391 n. and 2.20 ff. 'ergo corpoream ad naturam pauca videmus / esse opus omnino, quae demant cumque dolorem . . . ' (shortly before the passage noted on 1392–6).

omnino: 'above all' or perhaps 'in general'.

quoad: 1033 n.

1434-5. vitam . . . aestus: 'has carried human life out to the deep sea and stirred up from the depths great billows of war': i.e. men have lost their moral bearings and even go to war in their greed for possessions. A complex double metaphor with the linking image of seadanger in *altum* and *aestus*. Cf. Epicurus' 'tempest of the soul' image at *Ep. Men.* 128 (quoted 11–12 n.); also 1289–90 'belli/miscebant fluctus' and Cic. *Tusc.* 4.42 'ipsaque sibi imbecillitas indulget in altumque provehitur imprudens', *de. or.* 3.145. (The lines have been much misunderstood: there is no literal reference to navigation, and to translate *in altum* 'to a high plane (of prosperity)' (Giussani, Bailey) introduces a harsh clash of images.)

1436-9. Observation of the sun and moon taught men the regularity of the seasons. This section looks at first sight cursory and flat following the discussion of music, and this impression might support the possibility that the book originally ended at 1435 (see n. on 1440–57). But in any case L. can dismiss this topic briefly here because he has already dealt at length with the sun and moon in the astronomical section at 564 ff. (See also B. Manuwald, *Der Aufbau der lukrezischen Kulturentstehungslehre*, 13–15, who regards these lines as a reference to the prehistoric beginnings of natural philosophy.)

1436. mundi . . . templum: cf. 1204–5 'magni caelestia mundi / templa'. For the theory of the revolving *mundus* see 510 ff.

1437. lustrantes lumine: 575–6 n. This may be another example of the influence on L. of Cicero's translation of Aratus: 'aeterno lustrantes lumine mundum' 237; cf. 1016.

circum: adverb.

1439. Again a section is rounded off by a stylish line, with the repetition of *certa, certo*, and the chiasmus *certa ratione . . . ordine certo*. For sense and phrasing cf. 677–9, 732, 1183–4.

1440–57. This final section of the book is both a résumé of some of man's progress which has already been discussed and a summary catalogue of further advances. These include literature and other arts of cultivated life, which appropriately mark the climax of man's civilized achievements in the last line of the book. However, it can be argued that these last paragraphs are not as highly wrought as one might expect in a conclusion, and there are some grounds for thinking that the passage on music (1379–1435) was the original, or at least an alternative, ending. (See D. J. Furley in *Entretiens Fondation Hardt* xxiv, 1977, 22–7.) On the other hand L. does not generally compose formal or carefully structured endings to the books: only Book 1 finishes with any kind of epilogue (see Heinze on 3.1092).

1440–1: Both these developments have been alluded to before (1108, 1110), as *iam* implies.

1442. tum: picked up by *cum* 1444. L. links navigation and alliances by treaty with the first poetic narratives, presumably because they formed the typical subject-matter of early epic.

velivolis: 'sail-flying': an Ennian word (*Ann.* 388, *Scen.* 79 V), but whether it is here adjective or noun is uncertain owing to the corruption in the line.

florebat: 'was blooming': primarily pictorial, but perhaps also suggesting the bright hopes or prosperity of the sailors. Editors quote Aesch. *Ag.* 659 ἀνθοῦν πέλαγος . . . νεκροῖς, Cato *Orat.* 31 'mare velis florere videres'.

propter odores; an unsolved problem, as few believe that L.'s first sailors were hunting for spices. It is possible, as some think, that the phrase intruded from 2.417, but there is wide disagreement on the true reading it displaced. Perhaps the most convincing suggestions so far (arrived at from different approaches to the problem) are *navibus altum* (Merrill) and *propterea quod* (M. F. Smith). See the extensive discussions on the line by Housman in *J.Ph.* 25 (1897) 243–5 (= *Classical Papers* ii, 436–8), Bailey, and M. F. Smith (revised Loeb ed.).

1445. elementa: 'letters'. L. of course knew that early bards (as in Homer) sang their lays without a text, but he is concerned here with the period of the written text as a source of historical knowledge. Such information, in association with arguments from analogy, was for the Epicureans a valid means of extending our knowledge of the present world: see Philodemus, *de signis* 16.24 and 20.35 (De Lacy).

1446–7. For knowledge of what happened before written records we are dependent entirely on inferences from analogy. Our reason (*ratio*) has to indicate to us surviving traces (*vestigia*) of the past from which it reconstructs the early world. From 326–7 above it is clear that L. regarded Homer and the *Thebais* as the earliest surviving poetic records. *vestigia* has the same sense as at 3.673 'nec vestigia gestarum rerum ulla tenemus'.

1448–57. A final summary of man's achievements, with the winning at last of 'life's prizes and luxuries', the arts and style of high civilization. These advances were made gradually through a process of practical trial and error (*usus, experientia*), assisted as time passed by the refining powers of man's reason (*ratio*). Here there seems to be a cursory allusion to a basic Epicurean theory whereby men first respond as they can to the force of circumstances, and then gradually develop the use of reason to better their lot. (See *Ep. Hdt.* 75; Diog. Oen. fr. 10 col. II 8 ff. Chilton; Diod. Sic. 1.8.)

1448. agri culturas: 'methods of land cultivation' seems to be the force of the plural.

1451. daedala: 'intricately *or* artfully wrought': cf. 234 n. and 2.505, where the word is used of music.

    polire: infinitive as a noun, but there is much to be said for Bergk's correction *polita* of *polito* OQ.

1452. 'practice together with the inventiveness of an alert mind'.

1453–4. L. stresses how slow progress was with *pedetemptim* and repeated *paulatim*. The phrase *pedetemptim progredientis* has already been used at 533 of progress in knowledge.

1455. in luminis . . . oras: 224 n. *erigit* suggests raising from dark depths into the light of knowledge.

1456. So at the end of Book 1 *alid ex alio clarescet* (1115) describes the growth of understanding.

    alid: 1305 n.

    corde: 'mind', 'intelligence' as at 864, 882, 1107.

1457. cacumen: a suitably climactic word: mankind has reached a pinnacle of civilized achievement and is ready for Epicurus. This looks forward closely to the opening of Book 6, which celebrates Athens as the first home of civilized life — and of Epicurus. Men now had all they needed for material living (6.9 ff.), but it was his teaching alone which offered their minds the understanding which leads to true contentment.

INDEX RERUM ET NOMINUM

Numbers refer to line numbers as they appear in the commentary, except Roman numbers which refer to pages of the Introduction.

ablative, archaic, 233, 652–3
     descriptive, 161, 499
     instrumental, 233
     local, 1079–80, 1368
Accius, 71–2, 89–90
accusative, internal, 428
     with *fungitur*, 358
acorns, 939 ff.
adjectives, without *et*, 13–14
     see also epithets
adverbial formations, 145
adynata, 128–30
Aeschylus, 405, 925–87, 993
Aëtius, 416–508, 454, 622,
     705–50
after-life, x; *see also* Hades, Hell,
     underworld
ages of man, 925–87; *see also*
     Golden Age
agriculture, 1011–1457, 1361–78
air, 119, 273–80, 318–23, 306–23,
     416–508, 434, 513–23,
     637–42, 643–9, 652–3, 793–4,
     795 ff.; *see also aer, aether,*
     wind
Alexandrianism, 950–1
allegory, 380–415, 1120 ff., 1126
alliteration, xvi, 11–12, 49–54, 96,
     138–40, 217, 273–80, 323,
     482, 546–7, 575–6, 804, 855,
     926, 948, 957, 993, 1004–5,
     1056–61, 1097–8, 1193, 1200,
     1252 ff., 1308–49, 1357
Amafinius, 335–7
Amor, *see* Cupid
anacolouthon, 952

analogy, 348–50, 554, 564–91,
     565, 751–770, 788 ff., 795,
     1028–90, 1034–5, 1056–61,
     1062–86, 1445, 1446–7
Anaxagoras, 113, 128–30, 269–72,
     534–63, 705–50, 751–770,
     783–836, 783 ff., 797–8
Anaximander, 705–50, 783–836,
     793–4, 797–8
Anaximenes, 318–23, 534–63
animals, dangerous to man,
     218–20, 925–87, 973–81
     early types of, 837–924,
          878–924, 913–15, 937–8
     inherited characteristics in,
          862–3
     origins and creation of, 783 ff.,
          783–836, 788 ff., 793–4,
          795 ff., 808 ff.
     prehistoric, 927
     souls of, 793–4
     sounds of, 1028–90, 1056–61,
          1379–1435
     survival of, 855–77
     use of, in battle, 1281–1349,
          1308–49
     see also monsters *and under*
          names of animals
anthropology, xviii, 925–87; *see*
     also man, primitive
Apollodorus, 117
Aratus, xiii, 317–18, 1016, 1437
arbute-berries, 937–8, 939 ff.
archaisms, 102, 134, 233, 382,
     392–3, 532, 617, 652–3, 844,
     880–1, 934, 1145, 1227, 1229,

1246, 1296, 1305-7; see also
   Latin, early
Archelaus, 783-836, 808 ff., 836
Aristarchus of Samos, 113,
   509-770
Aristotle, Aristotelianism, xvii,
   110-234, 269-72, 338 ff.,
   509-770, 534-63, 797-8
arts, 324-50, 332 ff., 1105-35,
   1440-57, 1448-57
assonance, xvi, 11-12, 375, 926,
   1308-49
astronomy, astronomical phenomena, xviii, xix, 509-770,
   727-8; see also stars, planets
asyndeton, 134-43, 851-4, 880-1,
   1097-8, 1308-49
Athenaeus, 110-12, 1244 ff.,
   1379
atomic theory, atoms, xi-xii, xiv,
   xvi-xvii, xviii, 67, 70, 91-508,
   92-4, 156-94, 187-94, 194,
   235-46, 351-79, 416-508,
   420-1, 432-48, 437-9, 450,
   456, 837-54, 878-924, 1169
   ff.
Atomists, xi-xii, xiv, xvi-xvii,
   xviii, xix, 110-234, 509-770,
   534-63, 1028-90, 1161-1240;
   see also Democritus, Leucippus

babies, 222 ff., 1028-90, 1031;
   see also children
Babylonian astronomy, 727-8
Bacchus (Dionysus), 1-54, 743,
   824; see also Liber
bedding, 1412 ff.
Berosus, 705-50, 727-8
biology, Greek writers on, xix,
   808 ff., 1401-2
birds, 788 ff., 1062-86, 1079-80,
   1379-1435, 1379
birth, primeval, 795 ff.; see also
   earth, as mother; generation,
   spontaneous

boars, 1281-1349, 1308-49
body, and soul, 137, 554, 556-63
Botticelli, 737-47
brachylogy, 1229
bronze, 1241-80, 1241,
   1281-1349, 1291-2
bulls, 1281-1349, 1308-49

Callippus of Cyzicus, 509-770
Canonic, xi
Catullus, ix, x, 950-1
cavalry, 1297; see also horses
celestial phenomena, xiv, xvii;
   see also heavenly bodies
Centaurs, 837-924, 878-924,
   901-6
Ceres, 1-54, 13-14, 16-17
Chamaeleon, 1379
chance (casus), 77 ff., 162-3, 187,
   677-9
change, 253 ff., 828 ff.
chariots, 1281-1349, 1297-9,
   1301
chiasmus, 732, 789, 862-3, 1311,
   1439
children, 1019-20, 1031; see also
   babies
Chimaera, 837-924, 878-924,
   901-6, 905-6
cicadas, 795 ff.
Cicero, on Amafinius, 335-7
   on body and Animus, 137
   on Epicurus, xiii, 110-12,
      564-91
   Epicureans, and Epicureanism
      in, 8, 18, 175-6, 335-7,
      1156-7, 1161-1240, 1169
      ff., 1175-6
   on Lucretius, ix, xiv
   and scepticism, 218-20
   on size of sun, 564-91
   translation of Aratus, xiii, 108,
      317-18, 1437
circumlocutions, see periphrasis
cities, establishment of,

1011–1457; see also society,
development of
civilization, development of,
xvii–xviii, 772–1457, 925–87,
1011–1457, 1105–35, 1440–57,
1448–57, 1457
clothing, 953–61, 1412 ff.,
1432–3
clouds, 1092
coinages, Lucretian, 28, 243–4,
303, 681, 789, 964, 932, 970,
1040, 1303
colloquialisms, see idiomatic
usage
community life, 925–87, 953–61,
1011–1457, 1011–27,
1019–20, 1028–90
comparatives, idiomatic, 133
compounds, 14–15, 108, 165,
243–4, 287, 340, 745,
899–900, 970, 1189 ff.
conjugations, fluctuating, 1095
consolatio, 218–20
constellations, 687–8, 694–5; see
also stars
constitutional development,
1136–60
contractions, consonant-stem,
1159
cooking, 953, 1091–1104
copper, 1241–80, 1241
cosmology, xviii, xix, 77; see also
earth, world
crafts, 332 ff., 1105–35
creation, of plants and animals,
783–836,
of world, 77 ff., 91–508,
110–234, 162–3, 324–50,
677–9, 837–54
Critias, 925–87, 1161–1240
crows, 1084–6
Cupid (Amor, Eros), 737–8, 1075
Cybele, 110–234, 405

dancing, 1379–1435, 1401–2

Darwin, 837–54
dative, of agent, 43–4
of disadvantage, 353–4
ethnic, 260, 1209
of predicate, 875
for pro and abl., 1405
dawn, 656–79, 656, 663–5
day, daylight, 680–704, 1189 ff.
De Rerum Natura, digressions in,
xvi, 110–234
incompleteness, xiv–xv, 155,
1011–1457, 1161–1240
order of books, 55 ff.
structure, xiv
title, xii, xiii
see also Lucretius
death, x, 373, 996, 1000 ff.
Democritus, xi, 334, 534–63,
622, 629, 694–5, 783–836,
797–8, 925–87, 1028–90,
1091–1104, 1118–9, 1148–50,
1161–1240, 1379–1435, 1379
desires, Epicurean view of, 1432;
see also pleasure and pain
destruction, causes of, 351–79
Deucalion, 411–15
didactic poetry, xiii
digressions, xvi, 110–234
Diodorus Siculus, xix, 783–836,
808 ff., 836, 925–87, 927,
953–61, 1028–90
Diogenes of Apollonia, 318–23
Diogenes Laertius, xiii, 110–12,
113
Diogenes of Oenoanda, 8, 62–3,
77 ff., 509–770, 592–613,
614–49, 1028–90, 1350–60
Dionysus, see Bacchus
dogs, 864, 1062–86, 1063–4,
1071, 1072
Donatus, ix
Doxographies, 64 ff.
drilling, 1268

earth, aging and decay of, 826–36,

earth, (*cont.*)
828 ff., 836, 937-8
contraction of, 480-94,
483 ff.
as element, 91-508, 92-4,
273-80, 416-508, 795 ff.
experiments to produce
creatures, 837-54
formation of, 416-508,
449-70, 451
life on, xviii, 783-836, 925-87
mortality of, 306-23
as mother, 259, 318-23, 324-
50, 793-836, 788, 793-4,
795 ff., 808 ff., 1401-2
relation to air and heavenly
bodies, 509-770, 550 ff.,
554, 614-49, 639, 650-5,
680-704, 705-14,
751-770, 763-4, 765-6
shape of, 534-63
young of, 808 ff.
youth of, 324-50, 795 ff.,
910, 913-15, 937-8, 944
earthquake, 1236
earthworms, 797-8
eating, 1391, 1392-6; *see also* food
eclipses, lunar, 75-770, 763-4,
765-6
solar, xviii, 652-3, 751-770
ecliptic of sun, 614-49, 637-42,
680-704, 687-8, 689-91, 693
elements, 235-46, 243-4, 273-80,
276, 278, 380-415, 416-508,
432-48, 495-508, 498, 504-5,
507-8, 795 ff.; *see also* air,
earth, fire, water
elephants, 1228, 1281-1349,
1302, 1303
elision, 337, 497, 546-7, 589,
849, 1142
Empedocles, xiii, 8, 101-3,
235-46, 487, 783-836, 783 ff.,
788 ff., 837-54, 878-924,
925-87, 1194

Ennius, xiii, 1, 224, 259, 271-2,
276, 287, 1228, 1442
envy 1125-6
epanalepsis, 948 ff., 1189 ff.
epic poetry, 326-7, 396 ff., 933,
1442, 1445; *see also* Homer
Epicurus, deification of, 6, 8,
49-54
epithets applied to, 8
as εὑρετής, 8
Lucretius and, ix, x-xii, 1-54,
43-54, 49-54, 55-6, 119,
335-7, 1457
reference to in *DRN*, 2
and storm metaphor, 11-12
writings of, xii
doctrines of, Epicureanism,
summary, x-xii; on astronomy, 509-770; on biology,
1401-2; and Christianity,
47-8; on creation of world,
156-94; on day and night,
650-5, 680-704; definition
of world, 454; on early
man, 925-87, 1011-1457,
1448-57; on earth as
mother, 259, 783-836,
808 ff.; on eclipses,
751-770; ethics of, xvi, 9,
335-7; and fear, 9, 22 ff.,
49-54; on friendship,
1019-20; on frost, 205; on
justice, 1019-20, 1136-60;
on knowledge and percep-
tion, 1133-4, 1262, 1445;
on language, 1028-90;
Lucretius and, ix, x-xii,
55-6, 335-7; on moon,
94-5, 705-50, 717 ff.; on
mortality of heavenly
bodies, 80-1; on music,
1379-1435; on natural law,
677-9; on necessity and
chance, 77 ff.; opponents
of, xii, 18; on philosophic

life, 9; physics, xvi, 9,
49–54, 89–90, 335–7,
416–508; and Plato and
Aristotle, 338 ff.; on
pleasure and pain, 18,
1379–1435, 1391, 1392–6,
1432–3; on poetry, xiii; on
reason, 1448–57; quietism
of, 1105–35, 1120 ff.; on
religion and gods, 8, 49–54,
1161–1240, 1169 ff.,
1198–1203, 1203; and
salvation, xx, 1–54; and
shape of earth, 534–63;
and stars, 523–5; and
Stoics, xvii; and sun,
564–91, 592–613, 614–49,
763–4; as *vera ratio*, 23;
on wealth and poverty,
1105–35, 1118–19
Epimenides, 793–4
epistemology, *see* knowledge
epithets, accumulation of, 1063–4
  compound, 745
  transferred, 622
equator, 680–704, 693
equinoxes, 680–704, 687–8,
  689–91
Eros, *see* Cupid
erosion, 273–80, 281–305
Etesians, 742
ethics, morals, xi, xii, xvi, 335–7,
  953–61, 1022, 1105–35
Eudoxus of Cnidus, 509–770
Euripides, 259, 318–23, 405,
  783 ff., 925–87
evaporation, 273–80, 281–305
evolution, evolutionary theories,
    xix, 855–77, 925–87
  of language, 1028–90

fear, 11–12, 22 ff., 43–54, 82–90,
  113, 973–81, 136–60, 1189 ff.
feelings (πάθη), xi; *see also* desires,
  pleasure and pain

figura etymologica, 308, 392–3,
  1004–5
fire, and Chimaera, 901–6
  discovery and use of,
    1011–1457, 1015,
    1091–1104, 1096 ff.,
    1244 ff., 1252 ff.
  as element, 92–4, 119,
    281–305, 416–508, 795 ff.
  in Phaethon myth, 338 ff.,
    407 ff.
  in πνεῦμα, 793–4
  primitive man's lack of, 944,
    953–61, 953
  of sun, 680–704, 701–4,
    751–70, 758–61
films, atomic, *see* simulacra
floods, 338 ff., 380–415, 411–15
Flora, 739
food, diet, 878–924, 897–8,
  899–900, 925–87, 939 ff.,
  944, 953, 1412 ff., 1432–33;
  see also cookery, eating
formulae, stock phrases, 97,
  892–3, 944, 949, 1078; *see
  also* repetition
foxes, 862–3
friendship, xvi, 1019–20
fusion, atomic, 67, 77 ff.
future, gnomic, 885

generation, spontaneous, 797–8
genitive, adjectival, 369
  archaic, 617
  defining, 1193
  ii for *i*, 1006
  intensifying, 361–3
  partitive, 412, 443, 918
  in periphrasis, 28, 35, 968
  of refence, 97
  with words of 'fulness', 39–40,
    1161–2
  with *venit in mentem*, 1206
gerund, gerundive, 43–4, 1238
Giants, 117

giants, 910, 913–15
gifts, lovers', 965
goats, 899–900, 905–6
gods, and creation of world,
	91–508, 110–234,
	156–94, 1046–9
	and creative fusion of atoms,
		xii
	and development of civiliza-
		tion, xvii
	Epicurean theory of, x, 49–54,
		146–55, 1189 ff., 1361–2
	and fire, 1091–1104
	'nod' of, 186–7
	origins of belief in, 1161–1240
	powers of, 55–90, 80–1,
		110–234
	visions and images of, 1169 ff.,
		1175–6, 1203
	see also religion, superstition
gold, 1241–80
Golden Age, xix, 925–87, 933,
	937–8, 1000 ff.
'golden' rivers, 910
'Great Year', 643–4
Greek words, Lucretius' use of,
	866, 1036

Hades, 373; see also Hell, under-
	world
hapax legomena, 28, 340, 387,
	394, 467, 739–40
happiness, and gods, 1161–1240;
	see also pleasure and pain
heavenly bodies, 80–1, 91–508,
	509–770, 509–33, 509, 623,
	648, 1161–1240, 1183; see
	also constellations, moon,
	planets, stars, sun
hedonism, see pleasure and pain
heliocentrism, 509–770
Hell, 1126; see also Hades, under-
	world
hemlock, 1383 ff.
hendiadys, 516, 1079–80,

1163–4, 1428
Heraclides Ponticus, 509–770
Heraclitus, 564–91, 650–5
Hercules, 1–54, 22 ff., 49–54,
	878–924
Hesiod, xiii, 925–87
Hesperides, Gardens of, 910
Hipparchus, 694–5
Hippocratic treatises, 925–87,
	927
Hobbes, 959
Homer, 24–5, 146–55, 326–7,
	892–3, 905–6, 950–1, 948,
	1445, 1446–7
Horace, 24–5, 82, 117, 170–1,
	326–7, 737–47, 1028–9,
	1114
horses, 1062–86, 1073,
	1281–1349; see also cavalry
humour, in DRN, 104, 222 ff.;
	see also irony, parody, sarcasm,
	sardonic tone
hybrids, 837–924, 837–54,
	878–924
hypallage, 24–5
hypermetric line, 849

Ida, Mt., 663–5
idiomatic usage, colloquialisms,
	133, 662, 1051, 1077, 1088,
	1153, 1168, 1225
imagery, 11–12, 27, 117, 224,
	271–2, 276, 317, 329, 523–5,
	1207–8, 1395, 1434–5; see
	also metaphors, similes
images (εἴδωλα), 62–3,
	1161–1240; see also simulacra
imperfect, archaic 4th conj., 934
	effect of repeated use,
		1308–9
	indic. for subj., 1051
impersonals, 97
infinitives, after defessus, 1145
	after facere, 662
	as nouns, substantives, 156–65,

1379, 1451
after *vocare*, 1145
Ino, 656
intermundia, 146–55
Iphigeneia, xv
iron, 1241–80, 1281–1349,
    1281–2, 1296, 1350–60,
    1351
irony, 80–1, 222 ff., 312, 420–1,
    987, 988–1010, 993

Jerome, ix, xiv
justice, 1019–20, 1136–60

kings, 1105–35, 1136–60
knowledge, Epicurean theory of,
    xi, 101–3, 509–770

Lactantius, 6
lacunae, lost lines, 29–31, 257–8;
    see also text
language, origins of, 181–6,
    1011–1457, 1022, 1028–90,
    1031, 1041–61, 1046–9; *see
    also* speech
Latin, early, 13–14, 28, 195, 358;
    see also archaisms
lawgiver, 1028–90, 1105–35,
    1136–60
laws, 953–61, 959, 1136–60
    of nature, 826, 837–924
Lessing, 737–47
Leucippus, xi, 534–63
Leucothea, 656
Liber, 13–14, 16–17
lictors, 1234
life on earth, origins of, 772–1457,
    783–836
light, 281–305, of moon, 705–50
    of sun, 751–770, 763–4
lightning, 1091–1104, 1092,
    1125–6, 1189 ff.
lions, 862–3, 901–6, 1036,
    1281–1349, 1308–49, 1321
literature, origins of, 1440–57

locus amoenus topos, 1392–6
looms, 1350–60, 1351
Lucretius, on contemporary
    society, 988–1010
    on cultural history of man,
        xix–xx
    and Epicurus, Epicureanism,
        ix, x–xii, 6, 8, 1–54, 49–54,
        55–6, 119, 335–7, 1457
    life of, ix–x
    as poet and philosopher, xv–xvi
    as prophet, 110–12
    use of sources, xiii, xix,
        680–704
    see also De Rerum Natura,
        Epicurus

Macrobius, 204, 324–7
man, primitive, xvii–xviii, xix–xx,
    324–50, 772–1457, 913–15,
    925–87, 927, 939 ff., 973–81,
    1000 ff., 1011–1457, 1028–90,
    1111–2, 1189 ff., 1392–6
Matuta, 656
Memmius, x, 8, 867, 1281–2
mens, 103, 148–9; *see also animus*,
    mind
metals, 1241–80, 1244,
    1281–1349
metalwork, 1011–1457
metaphors, 11–12, 89–90, 276,
    777, 787, 850, 1231–2,
    1434–5; *see also* imagery
metre, metrical considerations,
    scansion, 7, 14–15, 28, 39–40,
    45–6, 47–8, 95, 102, 165,
    274, 284, 337, 360, 396,
    497, 504–5, 507–8, 563, 589,
    679, 801, 833, 839, 849, 850,
    897–8, 934, 949, 950–1, 970,
    1046–9, 1163–4, 1227, 1265,
    1308–49, 1428
Metrodorus of Chios, 650–5,
    652–3
milk, of earth, 808 ff.

Milton, 950–1, 1302
mind, xi, 556–63, 1169 ff.,
    1169–71, 1262; see also anima,
    animus, mens
Molossian dogs, 1063–6
monosyllabic line ending, 24–5
monsters, monstrosities, 70,
    837–54, 878–924; see also
    hybrids
moon, moonlight, xviii, 416–508,
    471–9, 509–770, 564–91, 579,
    614–49, 618–19, 623 ff.,
    635–6, 643–9, 705–50,
    705–14, 709, 715–30, 717 ff.,
    751–770, 763–4, 765–6, 1189
    ff., 1436–9
Moschion, 925–87
mud, generation from, 797–8
music, 334, 1011–1457,
    1379–1435, 1379
myth, mythologists, 380–415,
    878–924

names, naming, 1028–90, 1028–9,
    1041–61
natural science, 82–90
nature, xv, 77 ff., 107, 187, 667,
    677–9, 855–77
    laws of, 667, 677–9, 916–24,
    1361–2
navigation, 1000 ff.
necessity, 77 ff.
Nemean lion, 793–4
night, 650–5, 656–79, 680–704,
    986, 1189 ff.
Nonius, 71–2
notities, xi, 181–6, 1041–61,
    1046–9; see also πρόληψις
nouns, abstract, 303, 842
    infinitives as, 156–65, 1379,
    1451
nymphs, 948 ff.

olives, 1373–4
onomatopoeia, 375, 497,

1062–86, 1071, 1073, 1252
    ff., 1265, 1401–2
optical illusions, 623 ff.
oracles, 110–12
orbits of sun and moon, 614–49,
    618–19, 643–9, 643–4,
    680–704, 682–4
Orcus, 996
oriental cults, 1165
Ovid, 95, 396 ff., 866, 939 ff.
'ox-man' phase of creation,
    878–924

Pactolus, 910
Pacuvius, 318–23
pain, see pleasure and pain
panther, 1036
parody, 14–15, 24–5, 396 ff.
pastoral poetry, Lucretius' influ-
    ence on, 1392–6
perception, xi, 181–6, 878–924,
    1133–4, 1169 ff., 1262; see
    also knowledge
perfect, contracted, 396
    'gnomic', 150
periphrasis, circumlocution,
    14–15, 28, 35, 397, 793–4, 968
pessimism, of Lucretius, 218–20
Philodemus, xiii, 1379–1435,
    1445
Phaëthon, 380–415, 399–400,
    405, 407 ff.
Pindar, 326–7
pipes, 1383 ff.
planets, 509–770, 643–4
plants, 783–836, 788 ff., 793–4,
    808 ff., 1361–2
Plato, 113, 338 ff., 836, 925–87,
    1019–20, 1028–90, 1041,
    1355–6
pleasure and pain, xi, xii, xvi, xx,
    18, 1379–1435, 1391, 1432–3
ploughing, 933
Plutarch, 18, 113
polemics, ethical, 1105–35

Politian, 737–47
Pomponius Mela, 1111–12
Pontus (Black Sea), 507–8
Posidonius, 1105–35, 1244 ff.
prayers, praying, 1198–1203,
    1198, 1200, 1229, 1233
preconception, *see notities*
prepositions, 31
probability, argument from 345–7
Proclus, 1028–90
procreation, 851–4
Prodicus, 1161–1240
progress, 332 ff.
Prometheus, 925–87
property, 1105–35
Propontis, 507–8
Protagoras, 925–87, 1161–1240
proverbial expressions, 170–1,
    1034–5, 1153
Psammetichus, 1031
Ptolemy, 694–5
punishment, 1136–60

quietism, xvi, xvii, 1105–35
Quintilian, ix–x

races of men, *see* ages of men,
    Golden Age
rationalism, 878–924, 925–87
ravens, 1084–6
religion, 1011–1457, 1161–1240,
    1198–1203; *see also* fear,
    ritual, superstition
repetition, of ideas and themes,
    82–90, 937–8, 1111–12
    function of, xv, 416–508
    of lines, 89–90, 110–12,
        128–41, 180, 183, 187–94,
        195–9, 210–11, 266–71,
        283, 351–79, 379, 416–31,
        437–9, 935, 1216, 1217,
        1315, 1357, 1392–6
    of line-ending, 215
    of phrases, 263, 269–72, 370,
        373, 407 ff., 488, 801, 804,

847, 866, 943, 944, 998,
    1002, 1016, 1044, 1150,
    1313, 1361–2, 1403,
    1453–4
    of sounds, 660–1, 859
    of words, 273–80, 298–9,
        335–7, 444–5, 950–1,
        1179, 1268, 1439
rhythm, *see* metre
ritual, Roman, 1198–1203, 1229;
    see also prayers

sarcasm, 405
sardonic tone, 308, 380–415,
    399–400, 988–1010, 1028–90
scansion, *see* metre
Scylla, 878–924, 892–3
sea, 91–508, 92–4, 269–72,
    416–94, 483 ff., 487, 793–4,
    1000 ff., 1434–5; *see also*
    navigation
seasons, 680–704, 1161–1240,
    1436–9
Seneca, 18, 27, 269–72, 742,
    925–87, 1105–35
sensation, xiv, xvii, 509–770,
    797–8
sense-perception, xi, 101–3,
    509–770, 564–91, 565,
    751–770; *see also* knowledge,
    perception
sequence, 'irregular', 195, 211–12,
    276–8, 1266
Sextus Empiricus, 1161–1240,
    1169 ff.
sexual intercourse, 851–4, 854,
    1432–3
silver, 1241–80
similes, xv, 460–6, 476, 477–9,
    514; *see also* imagery
Sisyphus, 1120 ff.
skins, animals, 954
sky, 91–508, 92–4, 306–23,
    318–23, 416–508, 509–33,
    511–12, 623 ff., 656–79,

sky (*cont.*)
  680–704, 751–770,
  1161–1240, 1189 ff.
sleep, 1161–1240, 1169 ff.,
  1379–1435, 1405
society, contemporary and
    Lucretius, 988–1010
  development of, 1019–20,
  1105–35, 1136–60
  see also community life
soul, xiv, xvii, 59, 60, 62–3,
  65–6, 128–41, 554, 556–63,
  793–4; *see also anima, animus,
  mens*, mind
sounds, animal, 1062–86
species, animal, co-existence of,
    878–924, 916–24
  development of, 855–77
  see also animals
speech, 925–87; *see also* language
stags, 862–3
stars, 509–770, 511–12, 519 ff.,
  519, 523–5, 564–91, 614–49,
  618–19, 623 ff., 623, 639,
  643–9, 643–4, 694–5, 1205
Statius, ix
Stoics, Stoicism, xvii, 1–54, 22 ff.
  110–234, 140–3, 783–836,
  793–4
stones, as cult objects, 1199
subjunctive, causal, 926
  concessive, 122–5
  generalizing, 100–1
  in 'irregular' sequence, 195,
    211–12, 276–8, 1266
  not used in subordinate clauses
    in reported speech, 629
  after *quid mirabile si*, 1058
  of reported thought, 1180
sun, sunlight, 416–508, 432,
  471–9, 509–770, 564–91,
  592–613, 614–49, 637–42,
  650–5, 652–3, 656–79,
  665, 667, 680–704, 682–4,

  687–8, 689–91, 696–700,
  701–4, 705–50, 705–14,
  709, 751–770, 763–4, 765–6,
  973–81, 1189 ff., 1436–9
supersitition, 80–1, 110–234,
  878–924, 1207–8; *see also*
  religion, ritual
synonyms, 1002, 1311

Tagus, 910
tautology, 1025
technology, 925–87, 1241–80,
  1268, 1281–2
teleology, 156–94, 850
temperatures, of sun and earth,
  639
Tennyson, 146–55
text, xx–xxi, 29–31, 43–4, 175–6,
  201, 257–8, 266–7, 312, 359,
  385, 396, 412, 437–45, 464,
  465, 468, 485, 509–33, 549,
  570, 571, 585 ff., 590–1, 596,
  617, 679, 704, 736, 771, 808
  ff., 833, 836, 839, 844, 880–1,
  889, 925, 947, 948, 968, 997,
  1004, 1006, 1010, 1011–1457,
  1012–13, 1033, 1058, 1065,
  1068–9, 1082, 1094, 1105–35,
  1127–28, 1160, 1189 ff.,
  1203, 1207–8, 1214, 1225,
  1325, 1330, 1341, 1388–9,
  1405, 1409, 1410, 1442, 1451
Thebais, 1446–7
Theophrastus, 64 ff.
thunder, thunderbolts, 521, 550
  ff., 745, 1189 ff., 1192, 1193
time, 306
tmesis, 102, 287, 298–9, 566,
  1373–4
tools, 1241
tragedy, Lucretius and, 318–23
trees, 786–7, 787
tricolon, 444–5
Tropics, 614–49, 615–16,

637-42, 680-704, 689-91, 696

underworld, 996; *see also* Hades, Hell, Orcus
variatio, 189, 563, 751
Varro, 16-17, 134
vegetation, 783 ff., 937-8; *see also* agriculture, plants
veiling of head, 1198-1203, 1198
Velleius, 8, 1161-1240, 1169 ff.
venationes (wild beast shows), 1308-49
Venus, 8, 737-40, 737-8, 932
Vetusta Placita, 64 ff.
Virgil, on diet of primitive man, 939 ff.
    and Hell, 878-924
    hypermetric lines in, 849
    influenced by Lucretius, 8, 30, 89-90, 206-9, 375, 488, 737-47, 781-2, 787, 934, 1076, 1130, 1325
    short vowel before initial double consonant in, 47-8
    on spring of earth, 818-20
    repetition in, 950-1, 1179
    on zones, 204
Volturnus, 745

warfare, 988-1010, 1281-1349, 1297-9, 1308-49, 1432-3
water, animals born in, 793-4
    described, 602-3, 948 ff.
    as element, 92-4, 261-72, 269-72, 273-80, 281-305, 483 ff., 652-3, 795 ff.

as primitive man's drink, 945-52
wealth and poverty, 1105-35, 1118-19
weapons, 1241, 1281-1349, 1291-2
weaving, 1350-60, 1355-6
winds, 483 ff. 513-16, 637-42, 680-704, 745, 818-20, 1189 ff.
wombs in earth, 783-836, 795 ff., 808 ff.
women, 962-5, 1019-20, 1350-60, 1355-6
word order, 1096-7, 1169-71
word play, 673-4
world, atomic composition of, 91-508, 416-508
    creation and operation of, xvii, xviii, 77 ff., 91-508, 110-234, 162-3, 181-6, 235-46, 324-50, 416-508, 677-9, 837-54
    Epicurean definition of, 454
    mortality of, 65-6, 91-508, 235-415, 235-46
    parts of, 92-4, 476
    position of earth in, 451, 509-770
    see also earth

Xenophanes, 259, 269-72, 650-5, 705-50

Zephyrus, 737-40, 739
zodiac, 680-704, 689-91
zones, in heaven and earth, 204

INDEX VERBORUM

Numbers refer to line numbers as they appear in the commentary, except Roman numbers which refer to pages of the Introduction. Greek words are listed separately at the end.

aborisci, 733
abuti, 1033
adhaesus, 842
adire, 1229
aer, 434, 509–770, 534–63, 550 ff., 554
aes, 1241
aeternus, 514
aether, 434, 454, 470, 483 ff., 491, 498, 504–5, 509–770, 523–5, 648, 1205
aetherius sol, 215
aevum, 56–8
agmen, 271–2
ales, 801
alia natura, 534–63
alid (*aliud*), 1305–7
alsius, 1015
androgynus, 839
anfractus, 682–4
anguimanus, 1303
anima, 59, 110–234, 138–40, 140–3, 235–6, 556–63, 793–4
animans, 69
animi mens, 148–9
animus, 59, 103, 110–234, 134–43, 137, 138–40, 148–9, 556–63, 1262
arbusta, 1376–8
ars, 10
astra, 509–33, 509
augmina, 681
auster, 745

bacchari, 824

caelum, 434
caerulus, 1373–4
canere, 509
casus, 77 ff.
cernere (= *decernere*), 392–3, 781–2
ciere, 1060
con- words, 660–1
concelebrare, 1381
conciliare, 963
congressus, 67
coniectus, 67, 416
corpora prima, xii
corruere, 368
credo, 175–6
creper, 1296
cum, elision of, 1142; with *et*, 1066; with *tamen*, 1088
cuppedo (*cupido*), 45–6

daedalus, 234, 1451
de, 154
decidere, 193
desiperest, 156–65
diluviare, 387
dies, 95
diffidere, 980
diffusilis, 467
dius, 1387
donec, 997

effari, 104
egignere, 243–4
ei (as spondee), 284
elementa, 1445

enim, 134
ergo, 1246
ĕrunt, ērunt, ēre, 193
est, omission of, 1238
et, comparative, 1066; with *cum*,
    1066; explanatory, 954;
    omission of, 13–14
extritus, 1097–8

facere, with infinitive, 662
fas, 162–3
fasces, 1234
-fer compounds, 970
fulgere, 1095
fungitur, 358

-gen compounds, 14–15
genus, 59
-ger compounds, 899–900, 970
gliscere, 1061

haerens, 89–90
haurire, 991, 1068–9
haustra, 516
hilum, 358
horrisonus, 108

iacere, 102, 875
iam, 195
impetus, 200, 504–5
impius, 380–1
indu (in), 102
indupeditus, 1227
induperator, 1227, 1228
infantia, 1031
infractus, 230
inicere, 102
insilia, 1353
insinuare, 43–4
intempestus, 986
inter-, 287
interutrasque, 472
is, 284
iter, 652–3
iuventas, 888

letum, 373
levis, 1380
levisomnus, 864
lidere, 1001
liquidus, 1379
loci (genitive), 443
lustrum, 931
lychni, 295

machina, 96
mactus, 1339
manus, 101–3
meare, 116
meatus, 76
-men compounds, 340
mens, 103, 148–9
mergi, 1079–80
mersare, 1008
metae, 680–704
moenia mundi, 117, 119, 454,
    1216
moles, 436–7
mundus, xii, 509–770, 513–16,
    519 ff., 1233
mutus, 1059

namque, 13–14
natura, 77 ff., 187, 534–63
necessest/ necessumst/ necessust,
    343
noctivagus, 1189 ff., 1191
nodus, 680–704, 687–8
non, 306
nonne, 306
notare, 121
nothus, 575–6
notitia, 122–5
notities, xi, 181–6, 1041–61,
    1046–9

o, 1194
ollis (illis), 382
omnimodis, 190
omniparens, 259
opus est, 844

ossifragae, 1079–80
otia, 1387

pectus, 1, 103, 134–43, 138–40
pellacia, 1004–5
penetrare, 1262
pennipotens, 789
per-, emphatic, 1150; intensive, 99
pes, 271–2
plerumque, 939 ff.
potestas, 1046–9
praeditus, 199
praespargens, 739–40
primordia rerum, xii
procudere, 850, 856
propter, 31
purgare, 18
purus, 18

quaesit (*quaerere*), 1229
-que, 759
quicquid = *quicque*, 131

ratio x, xi, xvii, 23, 55–6, 64, 110–234, 335–7, 1211, 1446–7, 1448–57
rationem reddere, 197
reddere, 197
regignere, 243–4
religio, 86, 1207–8
relinquere, 1239
respectare, 375
ridere, 1395
rota, 432

saecla, 855
saepe, 1231–2
sapientia, 10
scapi, 1353
scatere, 39–40
scymni, 1036
senectus, 886
sensus, xi

severa, 35
sic, 1077
simulacra, xi, 579, 878–924, 1046–9, 1169 ff., 1175–6
solacia, 1405
spolium, 954
subigere, 211
subortus, 303
succipere, 402
succurrere, 765–6
sum, 337
Summanus, 521
summarum summa, 361–3
superantior, 394
supera (*supra*), 85

templum, 103, 948 ff., 1188
terrae, 563
texta, 92–4

unis, 897–8
utilitas, 1028–90, 1028–9, 1046–9

vegere (*vigere*), 532
vel, 765–6
velivolus, 1442
vergere, 1010
verrere, 266–7
vesci, 71–2
veterinus, 865
vigiles, 1408, 1409
vis, as ἀνάγκη, 77 ff., 1233; in periphrasis, 28; for *vires*, 1033
vitaliter, 145
vitigenus, 14–15
vultus, 841

ἄθροισμα, 67
αἴσθησις, xi
ἀνάγκη, 77 ff.
ἀταραξία, x, xii, 1203
ἄτομοι, xi–xii

εἴδωλα, xi, 1161–1240, 1169 ff.

θέσις theory of language,
1028–90, 1028–9, 1041
θηριώδης, 927

ἰσονομία, 1308–49

κανών, xi
κύκλος, 432

λάθε βιώσας, 1105–35

μετακόσμια, 146–55

ὀνοματουργός, 1041

πάθη, xi
πνεῦμα, 793–4
πρόληψις, xi, 122–5, 181–6,
973–81, 1046–9

σοφία, 10
συμφόρησις, 67
σύνδεσμος, 687–8

τύχη, 77 ff.

ὕστερον πρότερον, 5, 131

φύσις theory of language,
1028–90, 1031